E SENTIALS
of Payroll:
Management and
Accounting

Essentials Series

The Essentials Series was created for busy business advisory and corporate professionals. The books in this series were designed so that these busy professionals can quickly acquire knowledge and skills in core business areas.

Each book provides need-to-have fundamentals for those professionals who must:

- Get up to speed quickly, because they have been promoted to a new position or have broadened their responsibility scope
- Manage a new functional area
- Brush up on new developments in their area of responsibility
- Add more value to their company or clients

Other books in this series include:

For more information on any of the above titles, please visit www.wiley.com.

ESSENTIALS
of Payroll:
Management and
Accounting

Steven M. Bragg

WILEY

John Wiley and Sons, Inc.

Published by John Wiley & Sons, Inc., Hoboken, New Jersey.
Published simultaneously in Canada.

For general information on our other products and services, or technical support,
please contact our Customer Care Department within the United States at
800-762-2974, outside the United States at 317-572-3993, or fax 317-572-4002.

Wiley also publishes its books in a variety of electronic formats. Some content
that appears in print may not be available in electronic books.

For more information about Wiley products, visit our web site at *www.wiley.com*.

Library of Congress Cataloging-in-Publication Data
Bragg, Steven M.
    Essentials of payroll : management and accounting / Steven M. Bragg.
        p. cm. -- (Essentials series)
Includes index.
    ISBN 0-471-26496-2 (pbk.)
    1. Wages--Accounting. 2. Payrolls--Management. 3. Wages--Accounting--Law
and legislation--United States. I Title. II. Series.
    HG5681.W3 B72 2003
    658.3'21--dc21   2002153111

Printed in the United States of America.

10 9 8 7 6 5 4 3 2 1

To Marge, who has put up with her preoccupied son-in-law for a very long time. Marge, you definitely break the mold of the traditional mother-in-law. You are practical, sensible, and a solid rock in the midst of life's uncertainties—and don't even get me started about your vast treasure trove of cookies.

Acknowledgments

Many thanks to John DeRemigis, who always calls to ask how I am doing, and then gets to the real point of the conversation: Have I thought of any great book ideas lately?

About the Author

Steven Bragg, CPA, CMA, CIA, CPM, CPIM, has been the chief financial officer or controller of four companies, as well as a consulting manager at Ernst & Young, and an auditor at Deloitte & Touche. He received a master's degree in finance from Bentley College, an MBA from Babson College, and a bachelor's degree in Economics from the University of Maine. He has been the two-time president of the 10,000-member Colorado Mountain Club, and is an avid alpine skier, mountain biker, and rescue diver. Bragg resides in Centennial, Colorado. He has written the following books for John Wiley & Sons, Inc.: *Accounting and Finance for Your Small Business*, *Accounting Best Practices*, *Accounting Reference Desktop*, *Business Ratios and Formulas*, *Controllership*, *Cost Accounting*, *Design and Maintenance of Accounting Manuals*, *Financial Analysis*, *Just-in-Time Accounting*, *Managing Explosive Corporate Growth*, *Outsourcing*, *Sales and Operations for Your Small Business*, and *The Controller's Function*. In addition he is the author of *Advanced Accounting Systems*, published by The Institute of Internal Auditors in 1997.

Contents

Preface

This book is designed for the accountant who is setting up a payroll system, wants to improve the efficiency of an existing system, or who needs answers to the inevitable variety of compensation, tax, deduction, and record-keeping issues associated with payroll. Each chapter includes an example of how a company has addressed a specific payroll issue, as well as Tips & Techniques that offer guidance on how to handle specific payroll situations.

The book is divided into two parts. The first part addresses the overall set of policies and procedures, controls, and best practices that comprise a payroll system. The second part addresses the processing of specific transactions, encompassing compensation benefits, taxes, deductions, and other related issues. The chapters are as follows:

Chapter 1: Creating a Payroll System. This chapter covers outsourced and in-house payroll systems, emphasizing both manual and computerized systems. Flowcharts are given for each type of system and for the control points used with each one.

Chapter 2: Accumulating Time Worked. This chapter describes a variety of manual and automated methods for collecting time worked, and notes the situations in which each solution is most viable.

Chapter 3: Payroll Procedures and Controls. This chapter contains detailed policies and procedures for the primary payroll functions, which can be easily adapted to suit one's individual circumstances.

Chapter 4: Payroll Best Practices. This chapter describes a number of payroll "best practices," which are highly efficient methods for operating the payroll function. They are especially useful for any business that is striving to reduce its administrative costs in this area.

Chapter 5: Compensation. This chapter covers such key topics as the status of contractors, wage exemption and payment guidelines, temporary workers, the minimum wage, compensation computations, tips, back pay, and a variety of business expense reimbursements.

Chapter 6: Benefits. This chapter covers a number of payroll issues related to employee benefits, such as cafeteria plans, insurance, pension plans, sick pay, stock options, and workers' compensation.

Chapter 7: Payroll Taxes and Remittances. This chapter discusses the calculation of federal, Social Security, Medicare, and state income taxes, as well as taxation issues for resident aliens and citizens working abroad. It also covers the timing, reporting format, and related penalties for tax remittances.

Chapter 8: Payroll Deductions. This chapter covers the calculation and related regulations for a number of payroll deductions related to asset purchases, charitable contributions, child support, pay advances, tax levies, and other items.

Chapter 9: Payments to Employees. This chapter addresses the specific procedures for paying employees, using either cash, check, or direct deposit payments, as well as state regulations related to the frequency and timing of both regular and termination payments to employees.

Chapter 10: Unemployment Insurance. This chapter addresses the structure of the federal unemployment tax system, as well as the calculation of unemployment taxes at the state level. It also covers the completion and proper depositing of related tax forms.

For those new to the payroll function, this book is best read in sequential order from cover to cover. For those who are implementing a new payroll system, the first three chapters will be the most useful, while for those who want to improve their current systems, Chapters 3,

4, and 9 are highly recommended. For those who are searching for answers to daily payroll-related questions about compensation or benefits, Chapters 5 through 8 are the most useful. In general, this book can also be used as a refresher class for those who have been involved in payroll issues for a long time, but who have not updated their skills recently.

CHAPTER 1

Creating a Payroll System

After reading this chapter you will be able to

- Determine the differences in transaction steps between an outsourced, in-house computerized, and in-house manual payroll system

- Collect all the payroll and human resources information needed to assemble a new-employee hiring packet

- Properly assemble an employee's personnel folder and divide the information into easily accessible subsections

- Use a summary-level employee change form to centralize all employee change requests into a single document

This chapter provides an overview of how the payroll process typically functions, using either a payroll supplier, an in-house payroll process assisted by computer systems, or an in-house system in which everything is processed entirely by hand. These descriptions include flowcharts of each process and details of the controls that are most useful for each situation. The chapter also covers the types of documents used to set up a new employee in the payroll system, how to organize this information into a personnel folder, and how to process changes to employee information through the payroll system. As noted in the summary, the information in this chapter is supplemented in later chapters with more detailed descriptions of specific payroll issues.

Overview of the General Payroll Process

The next three sections describe how the payroll process flows for specific types of systems: *outsourced payroll*, *in-house computerized payroll*, and *in-house manual payroll*. This section covers, step by step, the general beginning-to-end processing of payroll, irrespective of the specific payroll system, so that you can see the general process flow. Though some of these steps will not apply to all of the processes decribed later, this overview will give you a good feel for how a payroll is completed. Here are the steps:

1. *Set up new employees.* New employees must fill out payroll-specific information as part of the hiring process, such as the W-4 form and medical insurance forms that may require payroll deductions. Copies of this information should be set aside in the payroll department in anticipation of its inclusion in the next payroll.

2. *Collect time card information.* Salaried employees require no change in wages paid for each payroll, but an employer must collect and interpret information about hours worked for nonexempt employees. This may involve having employees scan a badge through a computerized time clock, punch a card in a stamp clock, or manually fill out a time sheet (see Chapter 2, "Accumulating Time Worked").

3. *Verify time card information.* Whatever the type of data collection system used in the previous step, the payroll staff must summarize this information and verify that employees have recorded the correct amount of time. This typically involves having supervisors review the information after it has been summarized, though more advanced computerized timekeeping systems can perform most of these tasks automatically.

4. *Summarize wages due.* This generally is a straightforward process of multiplying the number of hours worked by an employee's standard wage rate. That said, it can be complicated by overtime wages, shift differentials, bonuses, or the presence of a wage change partway through the reporting period (see Chapter 5, "Compensation").

5. *Enter employee changes.* Employees may ask to have changes made to their paychecks, typically in the form of alterations to the number of tax exemptions allowed, pension deductions, or medical deductions. Much of this information must be recorded for payroll processing purposes, since it may alter the amount of taxes or other types of deductions (see Chapter 8, "Payroll Deductions").

TIPS & TECHNIQUES

Compiling time cards, determining who earned overtime hours, and gathering supervisory approval of those hours is a common last-minute rush job prior to completing the payroll. One of the major payroll bottlenecks is locating supervisors, who have other things to do than approve overtime hours. One alternative is to skip the supervisory approval and instead report back to supervisors after the fact, so they can see the hours charged on a trend line of multiple pay periods. If there are employees who continually record an excessive amount of overtime, this information becomes abundantly clear in the report. Supervisors can then use this information to work with specific repeat offenders, possibly issuing a blanket order never to work overtime. A sample of this report is shown in Exhibit 1.1, which lists overtime hours worked for the past six months for a group of employees. Note that the hours of Mr. Grammatic clearly exceed those of the other employees, making him a target for supervisory action. Also, overtime hours tend to be similar for people working in the same area; notice in the report how everyone except Mr. Grammatic works roughly the same amount of overtime in the same periods. Clearly, there is a potential overtime problem highlighted by the report that requires further investigation.

EXHIBIT 1.1

Overtime Trend Report

Name	Jan	Feb	Mar	Apr	May	Jun
Ashford, Mary	0	14.5	0	0	11.5	0
Grammatic, John	13.5	28.2	20.5	29.0	31.5	29.0
Lepsos, Harry	0	18.0	0	0	12.0	0
Morway, Alice	0	20.0	0	0	15.2	0
Zephyr, Horace	0	10.9	0	0	10.5	0

6. *Calculate applicable taxes.* The payroll staff must either use IRS-supplied tax tables to manually calculate tax withholdings or have a computerized system or a supplier determine this information. Taxes will vary not only by wage levels and tax allowances taken, but also by the amount of wages that have already been earned for the year-to-date (see Chapter 7, "Payroll Taxes and Remittances").

7. *Calculate applicable wage deductions.* There are both voluntary and involuntary deductions. Voluntary deductions include payments into pension and medical plans; involuntary ones include garnishments and union dues. These can be made in regular amounts for each paycheck, once a month, in arrears, or prospectively. The payroll staff must also track goal amounts for some deductions, such as loans or garnishments, in order to know when to stop making deductions when required totals have been reached (see Chapter 8, "Payroll Deductions").

8. *Account for separate manual payments.* Inevitably there will be cases where the payroll staff has issued manual paychecks to employees between payrolls. This may have been done to rectify an incorrect

prior paycheck; for an advance; or perhaps because of a termination. Whatever the reason, the amount of each manual check
should be included in the regular payroll, at least so that it can be
included in the formal payroll register for reporting purposes, and
sometimes to ensure that the proper amount of employer-specific
taxes are withheld to accompany the amounts deducted for the
employee.

9. *Create payroll register.* Summarize the wage and deduction information for each employee on a payroll register; this can then be
used to compile a journal entry for inclusion in the general ledger,
to prepare tax reports, and for general research purposes. This
document is always prepared automatically by payroll suppliers
or by in-house computerized systems.

10. *Verify wage and tax amounts.* Conduct a final cross-check of all
wage calculations and deductions. This can involve a comparison
to the same amounts for prior periods or a general check for both
missing information and numbers that are clearly out of line
with expectations.

11. *Print paychecks.* Print paychecks, either manually on individual
checks or, much more commonly, on a computer printer, using
a standard format that itemizes all wage calculations and deductions
on the remittance advice. Even when direct deposits are made, a
remittance advice should be printed and issued.

12. *Enter payroll information in the general ledger.* Use the information
in the payroll register to compile a journal entry that transfers the
payroll expense, all deductions, and the reduction in cash to the
general ledger.

13. *Send out direct deposit notifications.* If a company arranges with a
local bank to issue payments directly to employee accounts, a

notification of the accounts to which payments are to be sent and the amounts to be paid must be assembled, stored on tape or other media, and sent to the bank (see Chapter 9, "Payments to Employees").

14. *Deposit withheld taxes.* The employer must deposit all related payroll tax deductions and employer-matched taxes at a local bank that is authorized to handle these transactions. The IRS imposes a rigid deposit schedule and format for making deposits that must be followed in order to avoid penalties (see Chapter 7, "Payroll Taxes and Remittances").

15. *Issue paychecks.* Paychecks should, at least occasionally, be handed out directly to employees, with proof of identification required; this is a useful control point in larger companies where the payroll

 TIPS & TECHNIQUES

The control point for periodically handing out paychecks only to those who can prove their identity is not entirely useful when many employees use direct deposit, and therefore do not care if they receive an accompanying remittance advice or not. This is an especially galling problem for companies that may have many locations or that have employees who travel constantly. In both of these cases, a physical identity check is not a viable control. An alternative control is to periodically issue lists of paycheck recipients to department managers so they can see if any names on the lists are not those of current employees. But this is a weaker control, because the department managers may not take the time to verify this information. A backup control is to compare paycheck information to other information that is independently maintained for current employees, such as free life insurance that all employees sign up for when hired. A false employee name in the payroll register will not appear on a corresponding list of benefits, indicating a potential control problem.

staff may not know each employee by name and where there is, therefore, some risk of paychecks being created for people who no longer work for the company (see Chapter 9, "Payments to Employees").

16. *Issue government payroll reports.* The government requires several payroll-related reports at regular intervals, which require information on the payroll register to complete.

Overview of the Outsourced Payroll Process

Outsourcing the payroll processing function shifts a number of key payroll processing tasks to a supplier, resulting in a significant drop in the payroll department's workload, its required level of expertise in operating computer software, and in the risk that payroll taxes will not be remitted to the government in a timely manner. For these and other reasons, outsourcing payroll is an extremely popular option, especially for smaller businesses that do not have much in-house payroll expertise on hand.

The basic process flow for an outsourced payroll function is shown in Exhibit 1.2. Note that the key items in the exhibit are the tasks that are *not* shown because they have been taken over by the payroll supplier. These tasks include processing the payroll transactions, printing payroll reports and paychecks, and making tax deposits and reports to the government on behalf of the company. By outsourcing these activities, the payroll staff is required only to compile and verify incoming data about hours worked, load it into the supplier's payroll system, and verify that the results are accurate.

The process tasks noted in the exhibit can be streamlined by taking several additional steps. First, use a computerized timekeeping system that will prevent unauthorized overtime and automatically issue reports

EXHIBIT 1.2

The Outsourced Payroll Process

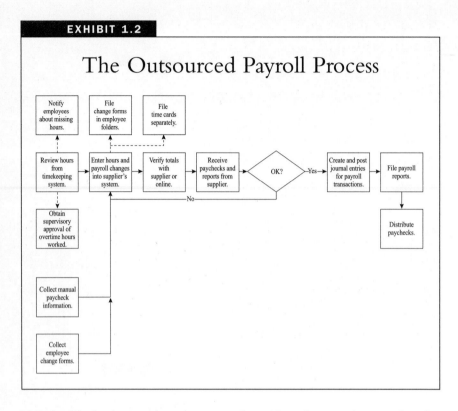

that highlight hours that were not logged in by employees, thereby eliminating two steps from the data collection part of the process. Second, some payroll suppliers sell computerized timekeeping systems that link directly into their systems, so there is no need to manually load this information into the supplier's system (or call it in to a data entry person). Third, a company can pay the supplier to create customized summary-level reports that can be used as the foundation for journal entries, which eliminates additional work. Finally, some suppliers now issue payroll reports on compact disc (CD), which nearly eliminates the filing chore. By taking advantage of these additional outsourcing features, the payroll process can become a very efficient system.

Controls over the outsourced payroll process are fewer than required for other systems, because there is no need to control the check stock or signature plates, which are handled by the supplier. Consequently, the primary controls tend to be at the beginning and end of the process. As shown in the boxes with bold lettering in Exhibit 1.3, there should be an approval process for overtime hours worked, as well as for *negative deductions*. A negative deduction is essentially a payment to an employee; if used repeatedly, even incrementally small amounts could add up to a significant pay increase for an employee. For larger companies with many employees, you should also compare the addresses on the employee paychecks to see if a "fake employee" has been added to the system, with the check being mailed to a current employee's address to be cashed by that person. You can also issue a list of the names of people receiving

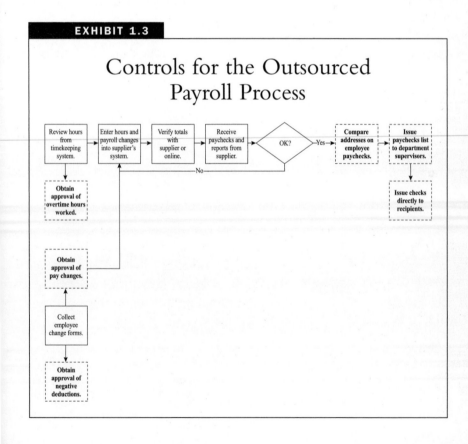

EXHIBIT 1.3

Controls for the Outsourced Payroll Process

paychecks to the department supervisors to see if any fake names or the names of departed employees crop up. Finally, you can also spot fake employees by handing out checks directly to employees *after* they show some form of identification. Not all of these controls are necessary, but you should select those that make the most sense for a company's specific circumstances.

Overview of the In-House Computerized Payroll Process

A payroll system that is just as popular as outsourcing is the in-house computerized system. Payroll software is very inexpensive, as it is now bundled with accounting software that costs just a few hundred dollars. More comprehensive systems, for use with large numbers of employees, are much more expensive, but are a cost-effective solution for large entities.

The basic process flow for an in-house computerized payroll process is shown in Exhibit 1.4. A fully automated process involves the review and verification of hours worked and other changes as entered by the employees, followed by the processing and printing of payroll reports, filing of direct deposit information and payroll taxes, and the distribution of paychecks.

The flowchart assumes a complete automation of all key payroll functions. For example, a computerized timekeeping system is assumed. This system, as described in Chapter 2, requires employees to run a badge through a time clock that can reject the scan if the employee is clocking in at the wrong time or is attempting to work during an unauthorized overtime period. By using such a system, the payroll process is considerably reduced at the front end, with the payroll staff only having to investigate missing badge scans. The process flow also assumes that employees can make their own deduction and address changes through an interface to the payroll software, so that the payroll staff only has to

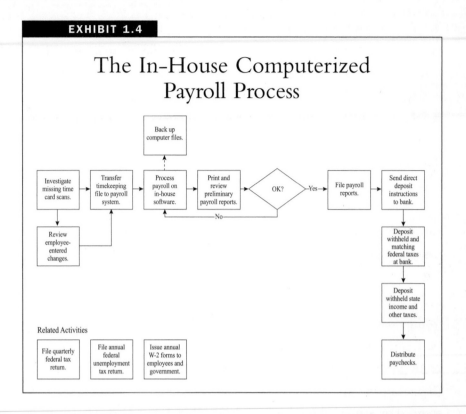

EXHIBIT 1.4

The In-House Computerized Payroll Process

review these changes. Further, the process flow assumes that the time-keeping database used by the time clock computer feeds directly into the in-house payroll software, which eliminates the keypunching of pay-roll data. If any of these automation elements are not present, then the process flowchart appears as a mix between in-house computerization and a manual system, which is shown later in Exhibit 1.6.

There are several key differences between the automated in-house system shown in Exhibit 1.4 and the outsourced solution in Exhibit 1.2. A key difference is that an in-house system requires the payroll department to file several tax returns, which would otherwise have to be filed by the payroll supplier. These include the quarterly federal tax return, the annual federal unemployment tax return, and annual W-2 forms to employees.

There may also be a variety of state reports to file. Further, an in-house system that uses direct deposit requires the payroll staff to create a database of direct deposit information and send it to the company's bank, which uses it to process direct deposits to employees; otherwise, this would have to be handled by a payroll supplier. Third, the in-house payroll database must be backed up and stored, which is normally handled by the payroll supplier. Finally, an in-house system requires the payroll staff to summarize all tax deposits, fill out remittance forms, and file payments with the federal and state governments at regular intervals. Consequently, no matter how much control a company may feel it has by using an in-house computerized system, the payroll staff will have a number of additional tasks to perform.

Controls for the in-house computerized payroll process are noted in the boxes with bold lettering in Exhibit 1.5. Due to the assumed use of a computerized timekeeping system, in the exhibit no controls are required for timekeeping activities, since the computer can spot them. (If a company does not have such a system, then review either the outsourced or manual control systems in Exhibits 1.3 or 1.7 for the controls covering this area.) In addition to those controls shown earlier for the outsourced system, new controls are also needed for check stock and signature plates, both of which should be securely locked up at all times. Be sure to note at the very end of the process flowchart the controls for reviewing uncashed checks and performing bank reconciliations. These controls are designed to spot payments made to employees who are no longer with the company and who, therefore, never received the checks (which were probably issued in error). These two controls can be added to the earlier outsourced payroll system, though some suppliers will notify a company of any uncashed checks, depending on the outsourcing arrangement.

EXHIBIT 1.5

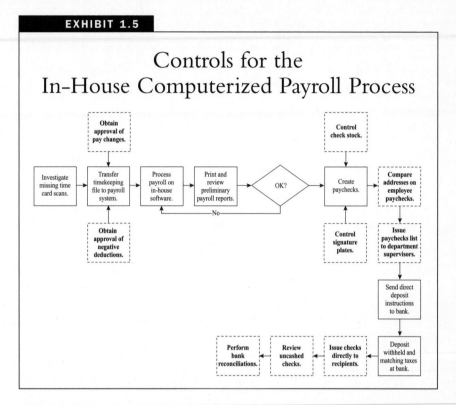

Controls for the
In-House Computerized Payroll Process

Overview of the In-House Manual Payroll Process

An increasingly rarely used payroll system is the completely manual approach that precludes all use of payroll suppliers or in-house computer systems. This type of system is most commonly found in very small organizations where the additional labor required to calculate wages and taxes is not too onerous for the small accounting staff.

The manual process requires extra labor in three key areas. First, employees are filling out time cards by hand or using a punch clock, so the payroll staff must use a calculator to add up the hours worked, verify the calculations (since this task is highly subject to errors), notify employees about missing time entries, and have supervisors approve any overtime hours worked. Second, the payroll staff must multiply hours worked by hourly pay rates to determine wages for the nonexempt

13

employees, and then use IRS-provided tax tables to determine the amount of taxes to withhold, plus the amount of matching taxes to be remitted by the company. This task is also subject to a high error rate and should be reviewed with care. Third, the payroll staff must create paychecks from the prior information and manually summarize the results in a payroll register. And because employees expect to see all deductions broken out on their paychecks, the paycheck-writing process is lengthy. In comparison to the outsourcing and in-house computer system solutions described previously, the manual payroll process is painfully slow and is at risk of so many errors that the payroll staff will find itself taking a disproportionate amount of its time to ensure that outputs from the process are correct. The manual payroll process is shown in the flowchart in Exhibit 1.6.

EXHIBIT 1.6

The In-House Manual Payroll Process

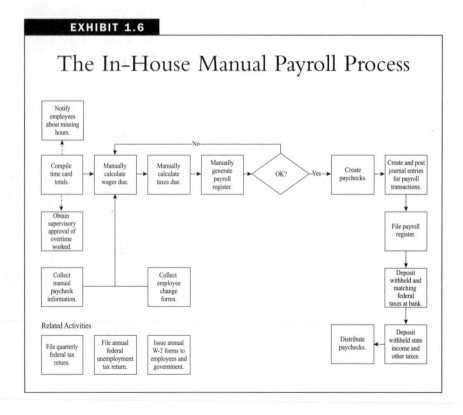

The flowchart does not mention the preparation of a direct deposit database that can be forwarded to a bank, since it is most unlikely that a company without means to calculate its payroll on a computer will be able to create the direct deposit database. Also, the three types of reports shown in the lower left corner of Exhibit 1.6 will require manual completion, which would not necessarily be the case if an in-house computerized system were used, as such systems often have the capability to produce these standard tax reports at the touch of a button.

The controls for an in-house manual payroll process are shown in Exhibit 1.7. Since there is an assumption that no automated timekeeping system is in place, two key controls are to verify total hours worked and to obtain supervisory approval of overtime hours worked. Other controls later in the process are similar to those found in the computerized

EXHIBIT 1.7

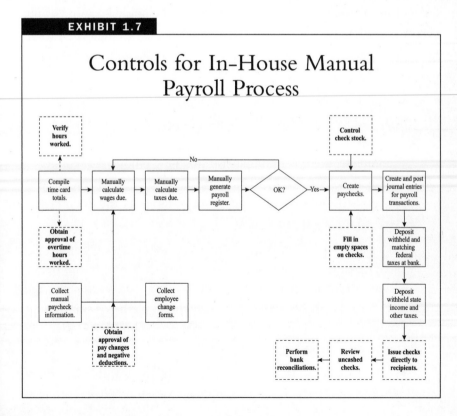

Controls for In-House Manual Payroll Process

in-house system, since some monitoring of check stock and signature plates must be maintained. However, some of the reviews for fake employees at the end of the process, such as comparing addresses on checks, can probably be discarded, since this type of process is typically used for companies so small that the payroll staff knows everyone who works for the company.

Setting Up the New Employee

When a new employee is hired, the human resources staff will go over a variety of paperwork with the person, and forward to the payroll department any items required by the payroll staff to calculate the person's wages, taxes, and other deductions. However, in a smaller firm with no human resources staff, it is common for the payroll department to perform this function, in which case the payroll staff should be aware of the variety of forms that are typically included in the new employee packet. Though some forms may be specific to an individual business, the following forms will be found in most cases:

- *Check-off sheet.* At the front of each new employee packet should be a check-off list that itemizes all documents contained in the packet. By using it to verify that a package is complete, there is minimal risk that new employees will not be issued critical information. It is also useful to include the latest form release date on this sheet, to verify the document dates contained in the packet.

- *Company go-to list.* A new employee has no idea whom to approach regarding basic daily issues, such as phone and network problems, pension plan enrollments, expense reports, and so on. This list should itemize which people he or she should approach about each type of problem; it's also a good idea to include a backup person for each item.

- *Company phone list.* For a smaller company, this list should itemize not only the work number for each employee, but also the cell phone or other number at which they can most easily be reached. It is also increasingly customary to include e-mail addresses on this list. For larger companies with lengthy phone lists, the phone list for the department to which an employee belongs may be sufficient.

- *Company seating chart.* For a smaller company, it is quite useful to issue a seating chart that lists every person in the company. As with phone lists, a larger company may have to provide a chart showing smaller subsets of the company. This chart will require a reasonable amount of maintenance, given the number of moves typically experienced in large companies.

- *Insurance enrollment forms.* Enrollment forms for a variety of insurance types can be issued to a new employee at a later date if there is a waiting period before they go into effect. That said, it is possible for some employees to "fall between the cracks" and never be issued the forms; consequently, a better approach is to issue these forms at the same time that an employee receives all other paperwork, so there is no chance of their being missed. Enrollment forms can cover medical, vision, dental, life, supplemental life, and short- and long-term disability insurance. Some insurance carriers provide a wide range of coverages in a single application, but this is the exception, so be prepared to issue a large number of documents.

- *Veterans check-off form.* Companies are required to submit the VETS-100 form to the federal government once a year, which specifies the proportion of military veterans in the corporate workforce. It is easiest to track this information by having new employees fill out a simple check-off form that itemizes whether they have been engaged in military service in the past.

- *Employee manual.* There should be a comprehensive employee manual in the new-employee packet that includes a tear-out acknowledgment of receipt. The employee signs this receipt to indicate that he or she has received and read it; the receipt goes into the employee's personnel file. This is useful in case an issue regarding employee benefits or rights arises at a later date, and an employee claims to have no knowledge of the issue, even though it is stated in the employee manual.

- *Pay period schedule.* The pay period schedule may be quite obvious for salaried personnel, since it should always fall on the same date; but employees who are paid on an hourly basis must know when a pay period ends, and this can vary in relation to the pay date. This is an especially common problem when the timekeeping system is on a weekly basis and the payroll system is on some other system, such as biweekly.

- *Form W-4.* Every employee must fill out IRS Form W-4, in which they claim a certain number of allowances and, possibly, additional tax withholdings. This information is needed in order to compute their income tax withholdings. (Chapter 7, "Payroll Taxes and Remittances" has a more in-depth discussion of this form.)

- *Form I-9.* The Immigration and Naturalization Service (INS) requires all new employees to fill out Form I-9, which is the "Employment Eligibility Verification" form. A sample copy of the form and its instruction sheet are shown in Exhibit 1.8. This form serves two purposes. First, it requires the employer to establish the identity of a new employee, which can be done with a driver's license, a variety of government identification cards, a voter's registration card, or a Native American tribal document. Second, it requires the employer to establish that a new employee is eligible to work, which can be done with a Social Security card, birth certificate, Native American tribal document, or an unexpired employment authorization document. These two requirements can be satisfied with a single document, such as a U.S. passport, certificate of U.S. citizenship or naturalization, unexpired temporary resident card, or several other documents that are specified in the exhibit.

EXHIBIT 1.8

The Employment Eligibility Verification Form

U.S. Department of Justice
Immigration and Naturalization Service

OMB No. 1115-0136

Employment Eligibility Verification

Please read instructions carefully before completing this form. The instructions must be available during completion of this form. **ANTI-DISCRIMINATION NOTICE:** It is illegal to discriminate against work eligible individuals. Employers **CANNOT** specify which document(s) they will accept from an employee. The refusal to hire an individual because of a future expiration date may also constitute illegal discrimination.

Section 1. Employee Information and Verification. To be completed and signed by employee at the time employment begins.

Print Name: Last	First		Middle Initial	Maiden Name
Address (Street Name and Number)		Apt. #	Date of Birth (month/day/year)	
City	State	Zip Code	Social Security #	

I am aware that federal law provides for imprisonment and/or fines for false statements or use of false documents in connection with the completion of this form.	I attest, under penalty of perjury, that I am (check one of the following): ☐ A citizen or national of the United States ☐ A Lawful Permanent Resident (Alien # A_____ ☐ An alien authorized to work until ___/___/___ (Alien # or Admission #) _____
Employee's Signature	Date (month/day/year)

Preparer and/or Translator Certification. *(To be completed and signed if Section 1 is prepared by a person other than the employee.) I attest, under penalty of perjury, that I have assisted in the completion of this form and that to the best of my knowledge the information is true and correct.*

Preparer's/Translator's Signature	Print Name
Address (Street Name and Number, City, State, Zip Code)	Date (month/day/year)

Section 2. Employer Review and Verification. To be completed and signed by employer. Examine one document from List A OR examine one document from List B and one from List C, as listed on the reverse of this form, and record the title, number and expiration date, if any, of the document(s)

	List A	OR	List B	AND	List C
Document title:	_____		_____		_____
Issuing authority:	_____		_____		_____
Document #:	_____		_____		_____
Expiration Date (if any):	___/___/___		___/___/___		___/___/___
Document #:	_____				
Expiration Date (if any):	___/___/___				

CERTIFICATION - I attest, under penalty of perjury, that I have examined the document(s) presented by the above-named employee, that the above-listed document(s) appear to be genuine and to relate to the employee named, that the employee began employment on *(month/day/year)* ___/___/___ and that to the best of my knowledge the employee is eligible to work in the United States. (State employment agencies may omit the date the employee began employment.)

Signature of Employer or Authorized Representative	Print Name		Title
Business or Organization Name	Address (Street Name and Number, City, State, Zip Code)		Date (month/day/year)

Section 3. Updating and Reverification. To be completed and signed by employer.

A. New Name (if applicable)	B. Date of rehire (month/day/year) (if applicable)

C. If employee's previous grant of work authorization has expired, provide the information below for the document that establishes current employment eligibility.

Document Title:_____ Document #:_____ Expiration Date (if any): ___/___/___

I attest, under penalty of perjury, that to the best of my knowledge, this employee is eligible to work in the United States, and if the employee presented document(s), the document(s) I have examined appear to be genuine and to relate to the individual.

Signature of Employer or Authorized Representative	Date (month/day/year)

Form I-9 (Rev. 11-21-91)N Page 2

EXHIBIT 1.8 (CONTINUED)

LISTS OF ACCEPTABLE DOCUMENTS

LIST A		LIST B		LIST C
Documents that Establish Both Identity and Employment Eligibility	**OR**	Documents that Establish Identity	**AND**	Documents that Establish Employment Eligibility

LIST A — Documents that Establish Both Identity and Employment Eligibility

1. U.S. Passport (unexpired or expired)

2. Certificate of U.S. Citizenship (INS Form N-560 or N-561)

3. Certificate of Naturalization (INS Form N-550 or N-570)

4. Unexpired foreign passport, with I-551 stamp or attached INS Form I-94 indicating unexpired employment authorization

5. Permanent Resident Card or Alien Registration Receipt Card with photograph (INS Form I-151 or I-551)

6. Unexpired Temporary Resident Card (INS Form I-688)

7. Unexpired Employment Authorization Card (INS Form I-688A)

8. Unexpired Reentry Permit (INS Form I-327)

9. Unexpired Refugee Travel Document (INS Form I-571)

10. Unexpired Employment Authorization Document issued by the INS which contains a photograph (INS Form I-688B)

LIST B — Documents that Establish Identity

1. Driver's license or ID card issued by a state or outlying possession of the United States provided it contains a photograph or information such as name, date of birth, gender, height, eye color and address

2. ID card issued by federal, state or local government agencies or entities, provided it contains a photograph or information such as name, date of birth, gender, height, eye color and address

3. School ID card with a photograph

4. Voter's registration card

5. U.S. Military card or draft record

6. Military dependent's ID card

7. U.S. Coast Guard Merchant Mariner Card

8. Native American tribal document

9. Driver's license issued by a Canadian government authority

For persons under age 18 who are unable to present a document listed above:

10. School record or report card

11. Clinic, doctor or hospital record

12. Day-care or nursery school record

LIST C — Documents that Establish Employment Eligibility

1. U.S. social security card issued by the Social Security Administration (other than a card stating it is not valid for employment)

2. Certification of Birth Abroad issued by the Department of State (Form FS-545 or Form DS-1350)

3. Original or certified copy of a birth certificate issued by a state, county, municipal authority or outlying possession of the United States bearing an official seal

4. Native American tribal document

5. U.S. Citizen ID Card (INS Form I-197)

6. ID Card for use of Resident Citizen in the United States (INS Form I-179)

7. Unexpired employment authorization document issued by the INS (other than those listed under List A)

Illustrations of many of these documents appear in Part 8 of the Handbook for Employers (M-274)

Form I-9 (Rev. 10/4/00)Y Page 3

To complete the I-9 form, the employee fills out the Employee Information and Verification information in Section 1. This section must be signed by the employee; it may also require a preparer's or translator's signature if such a person assisted with the document. The employer fills out Section 2, which requires the examination of one or more original documents, as previously noted and as described in more detail on the second page of the exhibit. The reviewing person must then sign at the bottom of Section 2. Section 3 of the form is used only to update the information if an employee subsequently changed names, or quit and was rehired within three years of the original completion of the form, or has obtained a new work authorization.

Creating the Personnel File

When a new employee starts work, either the human resources or payroll staff should create a personnel folder in which all employee-related documents are stored. This folder should be capable of holding several hundred pages of documents and have multiple dividers so that information can be logically divided and easily accessed. Information can be grouped in a variety of ways within the folder; here are some common subsets of information to consider:

- *Deduction information.* One block of information will be the deductions related to all types of benefits, such as medical, life, and dental insurance. This means that the sign-up or waiver sheets for each type of insurance should be included in the folder.

- *Employee correspondence.* Employees may communicate with the payroll or human resources departments from time to time, perhaps to make complaints, to notify the company of time off for various reasons (such as jury duty), or to ask for special treatment in some manner. If these communications are in writing, they should be included in the folder. If they are verbal, the person receiving the information may include them in a memo, if the matter appears sufficiently important, and store the memo in the folder.

- *Employee reviews.* All employee reviews should be kept in the folder. They are particularly important if employees later file suit against the company in the event of a termination, since the company must be able to prove that an employee was

21

terminated for cause. Also, note whether both the reviewer and the employee have signed a review; if either one is missing, obtain these signatures if possible, so that additional proof of employee receipt is made.

- *Garnishment information.* If there are court orders for garnishing an employee's pay for any reason (e.g., tax levies, creditor levies, child support, or alimony) include a copy of each one in the folder.

- *Tax-related information.* Tax deductions can only be made from an employee's wages if prior written authorization has been made by the employee. The employer should retain proof of these requests (nearly always in the form of a W-4 form) in the folder.

It is absolutely essential that the entire set of personnel files for all employees be kept under the strictest security at all times. These files contain potentially damaging information about employees, such as job reviews, medical information, or court orders that could be embarrassing or job-threatening if the information were to become public knowledge. Employees rely on the employer to keep this information confidential, and the employer should meet this expectation.

Payroll Change System

There will be changes in employees' lives that require them to ask for alterations to the information used to create their paychecks. For example, an employee may have a baby, which requires an alteration in that person's medical insurance from two adults (which is at one price) to a family plan (which is at another price); this change will probably require a different payroll deduction for the employee's portion of the insurance expense, which must be reflected in his or her paycheck. As another example, an employee might be diagnosed with a long-term medical problem that will require a great deal of medication, so this person might enroll in a cafeteria plan in order to deduct the medication cost from his or her pretax wages.

These and other scenarios will occur regularly, so the payroll staff must have a procedure in place for handling them. One approach is to create a separate form for each type of payroll change, but this can result in a blizzard of paperwork. A better approach is to use a single, summary-level change document, such as the one shown in Exhibit 1.9.

EXHIBIT 1.9

The Employee Change/New Form

Employee Name: _____   Social Security #: _____

Reason: _____

Categories	Changes/New	Effective Date
Name		
Address		
Phone		
Gender		
Birthdate		
Hire Date		
Term Date		
Title		
Salary		
Status		
Married/Single		
Federal Exempt		
State lived in		
State worked in		
Medical Deduction		
Dental Deduction		
LTD		
STD		
Supp Life		
401K% or $		
Dependent Flex Deduction		
Dependent Flex Goal		
Medical Flex Deduction		
Medical Flex Goal		
Direct Deposit Routing #/account #		

Comments: _____
_____
_____

Completed by: Date:

This employee change form can be used as the source document for new employees, as well as for each incremental change requested by existing employees. In the latter case, enter just the information relating to a specific request (such as a change in short-term disability, supplemental life insurance, or a 401(k) deduction); then have the employee sign it, to confirm the transaction, and submit it to the payroll staff for processing. Finally, file the completed form in the employee's personnel folder.

IN THE REAL WORLD

Problems with Centralized Payroll Records

A printing company decided to conduct an industry "rollup," whereby it purchased a number of small regional printing plants around the country. As a cost-saving measure, the human resources files of the new subsidiaries were shifted to a central human resources location for administration by a single human resources group. This caused a problem for the payroll departments (which were retained in each location) because they had no access to the payroll deduction information that was contained within the personnel folders. The company considered digitizing all of the documents in these files and making them available to authorized users over a corporate intranet, but concluded that the risk of someone hacking into the system and accessing personal information was too great. As a less technologically intensive alternative, the company installed a private fax machine in the office of each subsidiary's payroll department so that requested documents could be sent directly to the requesting person's attention with minimal risk of interception.

Summary

The information in this chapter covers only the general process flow of several types of payroll systems, setting up new employees, and changing their information in the system over time. Other chapters contain a great deal of supplementary information. For example, Chapter 2, "Accumulating Time Worked," describes systems for collecting and summarizing employee hours in a variety of ways. Chapter 3, "Payroll Procedures and Controls," describes a number of payroll processing procedures in detail, as well as a number of key control points that will reduce the risk of payroll errors or fraud.

All of these chapters should be read in order to obtain a better understanding of the payroll process.

CHAPTER 2

Accumulating Time Worked[1]

After reading this chapter you will be able to

- Determine the appropriate amount of information to collect through a time-tracking system

- Determine the level of automation required to collect labor data in the most cost-effective manner

- Select appropriate timekeeping reports for management review

- Calculate the cost-effectiveness of a labor data collection system

In some industries, labor costs still comprise such a large proportion of total costs that it is mandatory to carefully track and evaluate these costs. This chapter explores the need for timekeeping, how to collect labor data, the costs to assign to the resulting data, and the kinds of reports that can be generated for further analysis. It also points out the problems inherent to timekeeping and explains how they can be avoided.

The Need for Time Tracking

Three types of costs are incurred by any organization: *direct materials*, *overhead*, and *direct labor*. Historically, the largest of these three types of cost was either direct materials or labor. This necessitated the creation of elaborate tracking mechanisms for these two cost categories, while over-head costs were largely ignored. Since the advent of technology advances, however, the cost of overhead has skyrocketed, while direct labor costs have shrunk. As a result, much of the accounting literature has advocated the complete elimination of direct labor cost tracking, on the grounds that the tracking mechanism is much too expensive in relation to the amount of direct labor cost that is now incurred.

In reality, a company's specific circumstances may still require the use of detailed direct labor tracking. This is certainly the case if the proportion of direct labor to total company costs remains high, such as 30 percent or more of total company costs. Given this large percentage, it is crucial that management know the variances that are being incurred and how to reduce them. Another case is when a company operates in such a competitive industry that shifts in costs of as little as 1 percent will have a drastic impact on overall profitability. Finally, the decision to use a detailed labor-tracking mechanism can be driven less by the total direct labor cost and more by the level of efficiency of the tracking system. For example, if a company's data-tracking costs reflect the relationship to the proportions of total company costs noted in Exhibit 2.1, then there is a strong need to reduce the labor-tracking system:

EXHIBIT 2.1

Data-Tracking Costs by Cost Type

Cost Type	Proportion of Total Costs	Proportion of Total Tracking Costs
Direct Materials	40%	15%
Direct Labor	10%	65%
Overhead	50%	20%
Totals	**100%**	**100%**

In the exhibit, the cost of direct labor is very low, while the cost of collecting all associated data is much higher than for the other two types of costs, even when they are combined. The proportions shown here are quite common. If a company is in this situation, then the data-tracking system for direct labor is probably not worth the cost of administration. That said, if this data-tracking system can be made more efficient, perhaps with the data collection methods described in the next section, then it may still be worthwhile to use a reasonably detailed timekeeping system.

In short, it makes sense to employ a relatively detailed time-tracking system for direct labor if the proportion of total company costs is heavily skewed in favor of direct labor costs, profit pressures are high, or the cost of the timekeeping system is relatively low in proportion to the amount of direct labor cost incurred.

Data Collection Methods

In most cases, a company's total direct labor cost is not so high that it warrants the creation of an elaborate data collection system. Instead, you can either focus on a simple system that collects only the most basic data or else install a system that utilizes a greater degree of automated data collection, thereby keeping costs low while still obtaining a high degree of detailed information.

If a simple data collection system is needed, the easiest possible system to implement is one in which employees are assumed to work 40 hours per week and the only need to log hours is to record any overtime, which is recorded on an exception basis and forwarded to the payroll staff; the staff then enters the additional overtime costs into the payroll system and generates payments to employees. This approach is most useful when a company has a relatively fixed base of direct labor employees who rarely work any additional hours and who also rarely work less than a fixed number of hours per week. A further justification for such a system is when a company has such a small amount of direct labor cost that a more elaborate timekeeping system would not be worth the effort to implement. This system yields no information whatsoever regarding how the cost of labor is being charged to various jobs. It has the singular benefit of being very inexpensive to maintain, but at the cost of providing no costing information to management.

A slightly more complex system is to have direct labor employees fill out time cards that itemize their hours worked each week. These time cards are reviewed by their supervisors for accuracy and then forwarded to the payroll staff, to compile the information and keypunch it into the payroll system. This approach is most useful when there is a significant amount of variation in the number of hours worked per week, resulting in continuing variations in employee pay from week to week. This approach requires considerably more administrative labor because of the large amount of data entry involved; additional labor is also needed to verify the entries made by employees and to investigate and correct any errors.

One step up from this entirely manual system is the addition of a time clock. In its simplest form, a $100 to $500 time clock can be mounted on a wall, into which employees can insert their time cards to have their "in" and "out" times recorded. This approach makes time cards easier to read and controls the recording of time worked, so that there is less chance of any deliberate alteration of time worked. This approach is highly recommended, since the additional cost is minimal and is easily justified by the increased level of data accuracy.

The next step up in system complexity involves the use of a computerized time clock. Like the time clock just described, this device is also mounted on a wall for employee access, but it contains two additional features. One is the use of a bar-coded or magnetically coded employee card that is "swiped" through a channel on the side of the clock whenever an employee clocks in or out. This card contains the employee's identifying number; the system records that number, and all associated time worked, with complete accuracy. The second innovation in the clock is a computer that is linked to a central payroll computer. This feedback mechanism allows the time clock to reject employee swipes if they are made at the wrong time (such as during the wrong break time) or are made for employees who are not supposed to be working during specified shifts (which may occur if one employee brings in someone else's card and attempts to record that person as being on the premises and, therefore, eligible to be paid). The system can reject swipes that fall into any number of violation parameters and require the override password of a supervisor to record those swipes. The benefits of this innovation are twofold: it yields a great improvement in a company's control over the timekeeping process, and all data swiped into it requires no further keypunching—all of the data is sent straight into the payroll system, where it is reviewed for errors and then used to pay employees. This eliminates the cost of extra data entry, as well as the risk of data entry errors. These innovations do come at a price, however, which is typically in the range of $2,000 to $3,000 per automated time clock. A large facility may require a number of these clocks if many employees must use them, so the cost of this addition must be carefully weighed against the benefits.

TIPS & TECHNIQUES

The prices quoted above for automated timekeeping systems were quite high. Additional research will uncover a variety of less expensive timekeeping systems on the market, systems that dispense with some of the backup, security, job costing, and other features of a high-end timekeeping system. That said, before making such a purchase, be careful to ensure that these lower-cost units integrate with the existing payroll system, otherwise, you may find that an alternative system with a low upfront cost does not automatically send data to the payroll database, thus requiring manual rekeying of the payroll data.

A larger volume of data can be obtained by using the just-described computerized time clocks at every workstation in the production area, or a modified version thereof. By doing so, employees can easily punch in information about which jobs they are working on at any given time, without having to walk to a centralized data entry station to do so. These workstations can be time clocks that are directly linked to the payroll system; but since these clocks are so expensive, this option is not normally used, especially if many workstations are required. A more common approach is to purchase a number of "dumb" terminals, which have no internal error-checking capacity at all, and link them to a central computer that does all the error checking for employee and job codes, as well as hours worked. This option is much less expensive, especially for very large facilities. However, it suffers from one significant flaw: If the central computer goes down, then the entire system is nonfunctional; this problem does not arise when using automated time clocks, for each one is a separately functioning unit that does not depend on the availability of a central computer. This problem is a particular issue in companies that have large amounts of machinery that generate electrical energy, for the extra radiation can interfere with the transmission of signals from the workstations to the central computer, usually either requiring the installation of heavily shielded cabling or the use of fiber optics, both of which are expensive options.

An employee uses the dumb terminal to enter his or her employee number, then the start time, and then the job number. All time accrued from that point forward will be charged to the entered job number, until the employee enters a different job number. This data entry process may require a large number of entries per day, which introduces the risk of a high degree of data inaccuracy. The problem can, however, be minimized by the use of bar-coded or magnetic-stripe employee cards, as previously described, as well as bar-code scanning of all current job numbers.

This last option is clearly much more expensive than any preceding option, since the cost of the central computer can be anywhere in the range of $10,000 to $250,000, and requires a large number of dumb terminals that cost at least $500 each. What is the reason for incurring this expense? This system enables a company to track the time worked on specific jobs. This is a very important capability when customers are charged based on the specific number of hours that employees work on their projects, especially when the customer has a right to investigate the underlying hourly records and to protest billings that do not match these detailed records. This is a particularly important issue for government work, where cost-plus contracts are still common, and the government has a right to closely review all supporting labor records. It may also be a major concern for any organization for which the cost of direct labor is still a relatively large proportion of total costs; otherwise, managers would have no valid information about how a large proportion of company costs are being incurred. Nonetheless, the data entry system required to support the collection of this information is very expensive, so you should conduct a cost-benefit analysis to see if the value of the supporting information is worth the cost of the system.

It is also possible to have employees manually track the time they charge to each job on which they are working. Though this option may seem much less expensive than the use of the data entry terminals described, this approach is not recommended unless the number of employees using it is very small. The reason is that the level of data errors will be extremely high, given the large number of jobs to which labor is charged each day (the time charged to a job may be wrong, as well as the job number to which the time is charged). As a result, the cost of the administration time required to track down and correct these problems will greatly exceed the cost of installing an automated time-tracking system; this correction cost will be so high for a large facility that the comparable cost of an automated system will be far lower.

A final timekeeping system to mention, one that is not frequently used, involves *backflushing*. In fact, this is not a real timekeeping system at all; instead, the standard labor hours are stored in the labor routings database for each product and multiplied by the amount of production completed each day, which yields a standard amount of labor that should have been completed for each workstation in order to complete the total amount of production issued. This method is only good for developing approximations of the amount of labor that was needed to complete each step in the production process. It is of no use for spotting labor inefficiencies and cannot be used to derive payroll (since it does not report hours worked at the employee level, nor would these numbers be accurate even if it did so). Thus, the backflushing method, though a simple way to derive approximate labor hours, does not yield accurate information for most purposes to which direct labor information is applied.

It should be apparent from this discussion that a higher degree of data accuracy and a lower cost of timekeeping on a per-transaction basis can only be achieved with a high degree of expensive automation— and the more information required from the system, the more expensive it will be to collect it. Accordingly, you must first determine how badly a company needs each possible type of direct labor data, then structure the data collection system based on the level of need. Before making this

TIPS & TECHNIQUES

Though the cost of an automated timekeeping unit is quite high, do not spend too little and buy too few of these units if you have to record the time for a large number of employees. If you do, employees will waste an inordinate amount of time queuing up in front of the units, waiting to enter their time. A more cost-effective approach over the long term is to buy extra units and position them near the most heavily used facility entry and exit points, with additional units on both sides of the highest-traffic areas. This will preclude employees standing in lines at the machines.

decision, it is best to review the following section, which describes the various types of data that can be collected through a timekeeping system.

Information to Collect through Timekeeping

The most obvious item that must be collected through a timekeeping system is the number of hours worked by each employee. This single data element actually involves the collection of two other data items: the employee's name (or identifying number) and the date on which the labor was completed. This set of information is the minimum required to do nothing more than calculate payroll for direct labor employees.

The next highest level of information that can be collected includes the identifying number of the job on which an employee is working. This additional data allows a company to accumulate information about the cost of each job. In some companies, where employees man a single workstation and perform processing on a multitude of jobs each day, the amount of data collected may be from 5 to 10 times greater than when only the direct labor hours per day are collected. This level of data collection is most necessary when customer billings are compiled from the number of employee hours charged to their jobs.

A higher level of detail that can be collected includes the workstation at which an employee is working. This data is collected when a company wants to track the amount of time spent on each of its machines, so that it can tell which ones are being utilized the most frequently. This information is of the greatest importance when a facility either has bottleneck operations or very expensive equipment whose utilization is an important factor in the determination of capital efficiency. However, this information can also be obtained by multiplying labor routings by production volumes, which yields an approximate level of machine utilization, or simply by visually examining the flow of production through a facility. Thus, this additional level of detail will be worth collecting only in select situations.

Another factor to track is the activities of each employee, in the absence of an identifying workstation. For example, an employee could be repairing faulty products, manning a machine as the primary operator, substituting for other workers during their lunch breaks, and sitting in on a quality circle—all in the same day. This added level of detail is quite useful if a company wants to track activities for an activity-based costing system, which in turn can be very useful for activity-based management or for tracking quality costs. But this represents a highly detailed level of data tracking that in many situations is not appropriate: picture a large number of employees moving through a facility, spending large parts of their day either writing down what they are doing at any given moment or trying to locate a data entry terminal into which they can enter this information. In many cases, it is more efficient to conduct a study that results in estimates of employee time spent in various activities; this is a much more cost-effective way to collect information.

In sum, a timekeeping system can collect information at the following levels of detail:

- Hours worked

- The jobs on which hours were worked

- The workstations used to work on jobs

- The activities used at each workstation to work on jobs

Each of these levels of data collection represents an increasing level of detail that can overwhelm the timekeeping system. For example, at the first level, there may be just one record per day that identifies the hours one employee worked. At the next level, an employee may work on five jobs in a day, which would increase the number of records to five. For each of those jobs, the employee might use two workstations, which would increase the number of records to 10. Finally, there may be three activities performed at each workstation, which would result in a total of 30 records per employee per day. It is evident that each level of additional detail collected through the timekeeping system results in massive jumps in the amount of data that employees must enter into the system, as well as to be processed by it. You must review the added utility of each level of data collected, compare this benefit to the cost of collecting it, and make a determination of what level of data is sufficient for a company's needs. In many cases, stopping at either the first or second level of data collection will be more than sufficient.

Timekeeping Reports

The reports issued from a timekeeping system should be directed toward the correction of data that has just been collected, comparisons to budgeted hours, and trends in hours. The reports should not include pay rates or the total dollar cost of direct labor, since this information is more appropriately reported through the payroll system, where all direct labor costs are stored.

A good timekeeping report that is designed to correct data entry errors should not present the entire (and, likely, voluminous) list of all employee times recorded in the current period, but rather just those that clearly require correction. These can be targeted at hours that are too high, entries with missing information, overtime, or hours worked during a weekend. A computer program can be created to sift through all direct labor data, pick out possibly incorrect data, and present it in a report format similar to the one shown in Exhibit 2.2.

In addition to error correction, it is also important to devise a report that lists expected direct labor hours for various functions and compares these hours to those actually incurred. By doing so, it is possible to see where operations are being conducted inefficiently or where the underlying standards are incorrect. The budgeted labor information is most easily obtained through a manufacturing resources planning (MRP II) system, which compiles from labor routings and the production schedule the hours that should be worked each day, by workstation. The budgeted labor information for this report must otherwise be compiled manually. An example of the report is shown in Exhibit 2.3.

Normally, there is no budget in the accounting system for the hours worked by each employee, since this requires an excessive degree of effort to compile a budget; furthermore, it must be recompiled every time employees leave or join the company. Instead, you can create a trend line report of hours worked by each employee, which is useful for determining any tendency to work an inordinate amount of overtime or to work less than a normal amount of hours. The example shown in Exhibit 2.4 covers only a few weeks, but this report can be reconfigured in landscape format to show the hours worked by employee for every week of a rolling 12-week period. Another approach is to report employee hours by month instead of by week, which makes it possible to fit the hours worked for an entire year into a single report.

EXHIBIT 2.2

Timekeeping Data Correction Report

Employee Number	Employee Name	Date Worked	Hours Worked	Job Number Charged	Comments
00417	Smith, J.	04/13/03	10	A-312	Overtime approval needed
00612	Avery, Q.	04/14/03	8	D-040	Invalid job number
00058	Jones, L.	04/13/03	8	—	No job number
01023	Dennison, A.	04/14/03	12	A-312	Overtime approval needed
03048	Grumman, O.	04/15/03	8	D-040	Invalid job number
03401	Smith, J.	04/16/03	8	A-310	Date is for a weekend
02208	Botha, T.L.	04/14/03	25	—	No job number

EXHIBIT 2.3

Comparison of Actual
to Budgeted Time Report

Date	Workstation ID Number	Budgeted Hours	Actual Hours	Variance
04/14/03	PL-42	142	174	-32
04/14/03	PL-45	129	120	+9
04/14/03	RN-28	100	100	0
04/14/03	RN-36	140	145	-5
04/14/03	TS-04	292	305	-7
04/14/03	ZZ-10	81	80	+1
04/14/03	ZZ-12	40	60	-20

EXHIBIT 2.4

Trend of Hours by Employee Report

Department	Employee Name	Hours, Week 1	Hours, Week 2	Hours, Week 3	Hours, Week 4
Drilling	Sanderson, Q.	40	40	40	40
Drilling	Underwood, C.	35	38	37	32
Drilling	Hecheveria, L.	32	32	32	32
Lathe	Anderson, B.	48	52	49	58
Lathe	Oblique, M.	47	45	50	52
Sanding	Masters, D.	40	40	40	40
Sanding	Bitters, I.M.	40	40	40	40

As illustrated in Exhibit 2.4, it is also useful to include a column that identifies the department in which an employee works, for over-time utilization frequently varies considerably by department, given the different workloads and capacities under which each one operates. By sorting in this manner, you can readily determine which departments are consistently under- or overutilized. In the exhibit, it is readily apparent that the Lathe Department is being overworked, which will require the addition of more equipment, more personnel, or both.

Problems with Timekeeping and Payroll

Despite your best efforts to create an accurate timekeeping system, there are several types of errors that will arise from time to time and that require special controls to avoid. One is the charging of time to an incorrect job. This is an easy error to make, typically caused by incorrect data entry by a direct labor person, who, for example, transposes numbers or leaves out a digit. To keep this problem from arising, the timekeeping system can be made an interactive one that accesses a database of currently open jobs to see if an entered job number matches anything currently in use. If not, the entry is rejected at once, forcing the employee to reenter the information. This control can be made even more precise by altering the database to associate only particular employees with each job, so that only certain employees are allowed to charge time to specific jobs; however, this greater degree of precision requires additional data entry by the job scheduling staff, who must enter the employee numbers into the database for all people who are scheduled to work on a job. If there are many jobs running through a facility at one time, this extra data entry will not be worth the improvement in data accuracy. If the existing data entry system involves only a simple rekeying of data from a paper-based time card submitted by employees, the data must be interpreted and then entered by the data entry staff.

But this generally results in the least accurate data of all, for now there are two people entering information (the employee and the data entry person), which creates two opportunities to make a mistake. In short, the best way to avoid charging time to the wrong job is to have an interactive data entry system.

Another problem is that a vastly inaccurate amount of hours will sometimes be charged to a job, usually through the incorrect recording of numbers. For example, an eight-hour shift might be entered incorrectly as 88 hours. To avoid such obvious mistakes, the timekeeping system can be altered to automatically reject any hours that clearly exceed normal boundaries, such as the number of hours in a shift or day. A more sophisticated approach is to have the timekeeping system automatically accumulate the number of hours already charged during the current shift by an employee, which yields an increasingly small number of hours that can still be worked through the remainder of the shift; any excess can either be rejected or require an override by a supervisor (indicating the presence of overtime being worked). This approach is not possible, however, if employees record their time on paper, since the information is entered after the fact, and any correction to an incorrect number will be a guess by the data entry person and hence may not be accurate.

Another possible problem is that an employee might charge an incorrect employee code to a job, resulting in the correct number of hours being charged to the job but at the labor rate for the employee whose number was used, rather than the rate of the person actually doing the work. To avoid this error, the timekeeping system should be set up to automatically access a list of valid employee numbers to at least ensure that any employee code entered corresponds to a currently employed person. Though this is a weak control point, it at least ensures that hours charged to a job will be multiplied by the hourly labor rate of *someone*, rather than by zero. A much stronger control is to require employees to use a bar-coded or magnetically encoded employee number that they carry with them on a card, which ensures that they enter the same employee code every time. A weaker control is to post a list of bar-coded or magnetically encoded employee numbers next to each data entry station—it is weaker because an employee can still scan someone else's code into the terminal. If a paper-based system is used, an employee normally writes his or her employee number at the top of a time report, which is then entered by a data entry person into the computer at a later date. The problem with this approach is that the data entry person may enter the employee number incorrectly, which will charge all of the data on the entire time report to the wrong employee number. Again, an interactive timekeeping system is crucial for the correct entry of information.

Yet another problem is that the cost per hour that is used by the timekeeping system may not be the same one used in the payroll system. This problem arises when there is no direct interface between the timekeeping and payroll systems, meaning that costs per hour are only occasionally (and manually) transferred from the payroll system to the timekeeping system. This results in costs per hour on timekeeping reports that are generally too low (on the grounds that employees generally receive pay increases, rather than decreases, so that any lags in data entry will result in costs per hour that are too low). One way to fix this problem is to create an automated interface between the payroll and timekeeping systems, so that all pay changes are immediately reflected in any timekeeping reports that track labor costs. It is important that this interface be fully automated, rather than one that requires operator intervention, otherwise there is still a strong chance that the cost data in the timekeeping system will not be updated, due to operator inattention.

An alternative approach is to keep all labor costs strictly confined within the payroll system and to import timekeeping data into it, rather than exporting payroll data to the timekeeping system. There are two reasons for taking this approach: First, exporting payroll data anywhere else in a company makes it easier for unauthorized employees to see confidential payroll information; second, the payroll system cannot generate many meaningful reports without data from the timekeeping system, whereas the timekeeping system can generate a number of reports that do not need labor cost data (see the earlier section on timekeeping reports). Thus, it may be better to leave the payroll data where it is and instead work on an automated interface that imports timekeeping data into the payroll system.

Not only is it entirely possible that any of the problems described in this section will occur, but it is also possible that they will go undetected for a substantial period of time. To avoid this happening, the internal auditing department should be asked to conduct a periodic review of the controls surrounding the timekeeping and payroll systems, as well as a test of transactions to see if any problems can be spotted. The resulting audit report can be used to further tighten the controls around these data collection systems.

IN THE REAL WORLD

Reducing the
Cost of Timekeeping

A routine analysis of the system costs at a large manufacturing facility discovered that the cost of administering the company's direct labor timekeeping system appeared to be inordinately high. Approximately 50 percent of the entire cost accounting function was devoted to the collection and interpretation of data related to direct labor. The controller asked a cost accountant, Ms. Anna North, to investigate the situation and recommend a revised system that would generate usable information, while costing as little as possible to administer.

The cost accountant's plan for this analysis was to, first, determine the level of detailed information collected by the timekeeping system, second, calculate the cost of collecting it, and then determine the benefit of using the resulting information. She would then see if costs could be reduced for the existing collection system, while losing no benefits from the system. If this was not possible, or if the costs could be reduced only by a modest amount, then she would investigate the possibility of reducing the level of information gathered, which in turn would reduce the cost of data collection.

Ms. North's first step was to determine the level of detailed information collected by the timekeeping system. She interviewed the facility's controller, Ms. Barbara MacCauley, who said that the timekeeping system required employees to write down on a time sheet the hours they worked each day on specific jobs, as well as the workstations where they worked on each job. The typical time sheet looked like the one shown in Exhibit 2.5.

EXHIBIT 2.5

Atlanta Facility Time Sheet

Employee Name: Mort Dulspice

Date of Time Card: 4/13/03

Time In	Time Out	Job	Work Center
08:00	08:45	004712	Lithograph
08:46	09:12	004712	Etching
09:13	10:48	004712	Lamination
10:49	12:00	004712	Glue
01:00	02:10	004799	Lithograph
02:11	03:04	004799	Etching
03:05	03:17	004799	Lamination
03:18	04:24	004799	Glue
04:25	05:00	004799	Packaging

It was apparent from the time sheet that each employee must carefully enter a large amount of information during the course of a shift. Also, the information entered by the employee in the example was not easy to read, making it likely that the person who entered this information into the computer would have a difficult time doing so correctly. Further, many time sheets were submitted each day by the 412 direct labor personnel at the facility, some of which were lost by employees or during the data entry process. This information had to be re-created, which could only be done through estimates of the work an employee completed during the period.

Ms. North found that these three issues gave rise to three different types of costs. The first cost was the time required by employees to enter their time worked onto each time sheet and then transport that time sheet to the payroll office for data entry. The second cost was for the data entry staff to initially enter the data into the computer; the third cost was to track down and correct any missing information or to correct data that was inaccurately entered. Ms. North calculated these costs for a typical month in the following manner:

❶ *Cost to initially record data.* She estimated that each employee required 10 minutes per day to complete and deliver his or her time sheets. Since the average burdened cost per hour for all 412 employees was $17.92, this resulted in a monthly cost of $25,869 to collect the information, assuming 21 business days per month (412 employees x 21 days x $2.99/day).

❷ *Cost to enter data into computer system.* She found that one and a half employees were required in the accounting department on a full-time basis to enter into the computer system the information from all 412 time sheets. These hourly employees earned a burdened wage of $12.05 per hour. This resulted in a monthly cost of $3,037 (1.5 employees x 21 days x 8 hours/day x $12.05/hour.)

❸ *Cost to correct data errors.* On average, the accounting staff spent three hours per day correcting errors that had been discovered on time sheets or created during data entry. These errors were investigated and corrected by a senior data entry clerk, whose hourly burdened pay was $15.28. This resulted in a monthly cost of $963 (3 hours x 21 days x $15.28).

The grand total of all these costs was $29,869 per month, or $358,428 per year.

Ms. North's next task, determining the value of the benefits derived from the timekeeping system, was much more difficult. She found that the number of daily hours worked was used by the payroll staff to calculate and pay weekly wages to the direct labor employees. She described this function as a mandatory one for which the system had to provide sufficient data to calculate the payroll, but she could not ascribe to it a monetary value.

Next she looked at the benefit of tracking hours by job worked. This information was used by the cost accounting staff to develop an income statement for each job, which the sales staff used to revise its pricing estimates for future jobs, to verify that pricing levels were sufficiently high to ensure a targeted profitability level per job of 30 percent. The proportion of direct labor to all job costs was about one-third, so this was considered a significant cost that must be tracked for this purpose. The pricing staff members assured the cost accountant that they frequently altered their pricing strategies in accordance with the information they received through the job income statements. Once again, Ms. North found herself unable to clearly quantify a benefit associated with the tracking of direct labor hours, this time in relation to job numbers, but it appeared that obtaining the information was mandatory.

Ms. North's last benefits-related task was to quantify the benefit of tracking labor hours by workstation within each job. She found that this information was only used by the industrial engineering staff, whose members summarized the information into a report that listed the total hours worked at each workstation, by day, so that they could determine when capacity utilization levels were reaching such heights that new equipment had to be purchased or when levels were so low that existing equipment could be sold. A brief discussion with the production scheduling staff revealed that standard capacity amounts per job were already stored in the labor routings of the facility's manufacturing resources planning (MRP II) system, which produced a similar report by multiplying the units in the production schedule by the hours per unit of production listed in the labor routings. This meant that an alternative system could be used to provide the industrial engineering staff with the information it needed, without resorting to additional data entry to provide this information.

Ms. North then perused sample time sheets submitted by employees and noted that an average of three workstations were referenced on each time sheet for each job on which work was performed. If she could convince the management staff to eliminate the tracking of time by workstation, she could cut the labor time spent by the direct labor employees on timekeeping by two-thirds, plus similar amounts by the data entry clerks who would otherwise have to enter and correct this information, since these additional entries would no longer have to be made. This worked out to a cost savings of $19,912 per month ($29,869 x 2/3), or $238,950 per year.

Ms. North realized that the industrial engineering staff would agree to this change only if she could prove that the data the staff received from the MRP II system was sufficiently accurate to replace the workstation capacity data it had been receiving from the timekeeping system. To ensure that the MRP II system maintained a high level of labor-routing accuracy (which was the prime driver of the accuracy of capacity information produced by the MRP II system), she added $50,000 back to her estimate of remaining timekeeping system costs, which would pay for an engineer whose sole purpose

Summary

The timekeeping function is coming under increasing attack as cost accountants realize that the costs of administering a detailed timekeeping system are exceeding the value of the resulting information. This issue can be resolved either by reducing the level of timekeeping effort until the effort expended equals the utility of the resulting information (which may result in the complete elimination of the timekeeping function) or by more fully automating the timekeeping and payroll functions so that the cost of the system administration is reduced to the point at which it is once again a cost-effective means of tracking labor activities.

Choosing which direction to take is based not only on the portion of total corporate costs devoted to direct labor, but also on how crucial it is to a company to wring out the highest possible profits from operations. Thus, the nature of the timekeeping system is driven not only by the total cost of direct labor, but also by the level of profitability of the business.

Endnotes

1. This chapter is derived with permission from Chapter 5 of Steven Bragg, *Cost Accounting* (New York: John Wiley & Sons, Inc., 2001).

CHAPTER 3

Payroll Procedures and Controls

After reading this chapter you will be able to

- Understand which procedures to use to process a payroll
- Know which controls to impose in the areas of employee advances, payroll checks, and payroll expenses
- Know when controls are not necessary, and can be safely eliminated

The payroll function is largely driven by procedures that should be followed consistently to ensure that work is completed properly and thoroughly. This also enables a payroll manager to exercise proper control over the function, since anyone following a procedure is also following the control points that have been built into them. In this chapter, we will cover the various types of procedures that should be used to run a payroll department, as well as address many of the control weaknesses and recommended control points that can offset them.

Payroll Procedures[1]

A payroll procedure is a written statement that itemizes the reason for an activity, notes who is responsible for it, and describes exactly how the activity is to be completed. It is highly applicable to the payroll function, which is full of activities that must be completed the same way, every time.

The first step in creating a set of payroll procedures is to construct a flowchart of the overall process, so that you can identify all activities, thereby ensuring that a procedure is written for each one. Also, each box in the flowchart contains an identifying index number for each procedure, which is later listed as the procedure number in the header for each procedure. Thus, you can first refer to a process flowchart for the specific procedure needed and then trace the index number to the detailed procedure. A sample payroll process flowchart is as shown in Exhibit 3.1.

The remainder of this section contains six payroll procedures that correspond to the activities noted on the payroll process flowchart. For consistency, they all have exactly the same format. The header contains a notation box on the right side that lists an index (or retrieval) number, the page number, the date on which the procedure was created, and the index number of any procedure that it has replaced. The main body of the procedure is in three sections: the "Purpose and Scope" section summarizes what the procedure is all about; the "Responsibilities" section item-

EXHIBIT 3.1

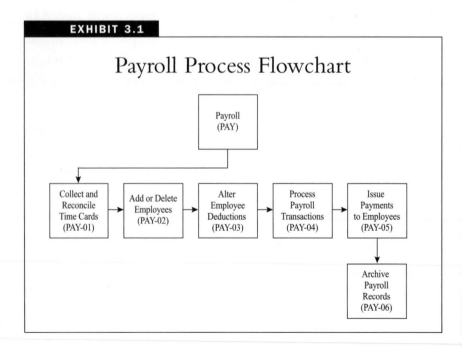

Payroll Process Flowchart

TIPS & TECHNIQUES

After a procedure has been written, instruct the most junior or least experienced person in the accounting department to walk through each step, to ensure that the described steps are clear, flow logically from one step to the next, and result in correct payroll outputs. Almost always, this person will find that instructions need to be added to a procedure. This is because the person writing a procedure is the most experienced at completing a specific task, and therefore makes assumptions about completing steps that a more junior person must have clearly written down.

izes which job positions must follow the procedure; and the "Procedures" section lists the exact steps to follow.

The procedures used here are designed for specific software packages and company procedures, hence are not meant to be copied; rather, they should be reviewed to grasp the general layout and terminology used in each procedure, and then used to design a customized set of procedures for the specific circumstances. Specific payroll procedures, shown in the preceding flowchart, are described individually throughout the remainder of this section.

Policy/Procedure Statement

Retrieval No.: PAY-01
Page: 1 of 1
Issue Date: 10/28/03
Supersedes: N/A

Subject: Collect and Reconcile Time Cards

1. PURPOSE AND SCOPE

This procedure is used by the payroll clerk to assemble time cards for all hourly employees, as well as to locate and resolve time-punching errors.

2. RESPONSIBILITIES

PR CLERK

Payroll Clerk

3. PROCEDURES

3.1 PR CLERK

Obtain Time Cards

1. Obtain time cards from all company locations. Check off the receipts against the standard list of company locations and contact the factory manager of each location from which no cards have been received.

3.2 PR CLERK

Review Time Cards

2. Add up the time on all time cards, circling those time punches that have no clock-ins or clock-outs. Note the total time on all error-free time cards and forward them to the payroll clerk for data entry into the payroll system.

3. Any time card containing overtime hours must also be initialed by a manager; those cards missing this approval must be returned and signed.

3.3 PR CLERK

Resolve Time Card Discrepancies

1. Review all time cards containing discrepancies with the responsible factory managers, who must initial all time cards for which there is an assumed clock-in or clock-out.

2. List the total time worked at the top of these time cards.

3. Forward the cards to the payroll clerk for data entry into the payroll system.

Policy/Procedure Statement

Retrieval No.: PAY-02
Page: 1 of 1
Issue Date: 10/28/03
Supersedes: N/A

Subject: Add or Delete Employees

1. PURPOSE AND SCOPE

This procedure is used by the payroll clerk to add or delete employees from the payroll system.

2. RESPONSIBILITIES

PR CLERK   **Payroll Clerk**

3. PROCEDURES

3.1 PR CLERK   **Obtain Addition or Deletion Documentation**

1. Receive documentation from the human resources department regarding the addition to or deletion from the payroll database of employees. Review the documentation for correct start or stop dates, extra pay, and (especially) the correct authorization signatures.

2. If any information is missing, return it to the sender for correction.

3.2 PR CLERK   **Update Payroll Database**

1. Go into the payroll software and access the EMPLOYEE menu. Go to the ADD screen if adding an employee. Enter the employee name and Social Security number, pay rate, and start date. If deleting an employee, go into the DELETE screen from the same menu, enter a Y in the TERMINATE field, and enter the final pay date, as well as the amount of any bonus payments.

2. Print the Updates Report from the option at the bottom of the screen to verify that the correct entries were made.

3.3 PR CLERK   **File Documentation**

1. Consult the document destruction policy to determine the date at which the filed documents can be destroyed for any terminated employees. Mark this date on the employee's folder and forward it to the document archiving area.

Policy/Procedure Statement

Retrieval No.: PAY-03
Page: 1 of 1
Issue Date:
10/28/03
Supersedes: N/A

Subject: Alter Employee Deductions

1. PURPOSE AND SCOPE

This procedure is used by the payroll clerk to alter employee deductions in the payroll system.

2. RESPONSIBILITIES

PR CLERK **Payroll Clerk**

3. PROCEDURES

3.1 PR CLERK **Obtain Deduction Information**

1. Obtain employee payroll deduction information from the human resources department.

2. Verify that all information on the deduction forms is clear and that each form has been authorized by the employee.

3.2 PR CLERK **Update Payroll Database**

1. Go into the payroll software and access the EMPLOYEE menu. Go to the DEDUCT screen; enter the deduction code and the amount of the deduction for each documented deduction. Be sure to enter a deduction termination code for those who are of limited duration.

2. Verify that deductions are correctly allocated to each payroll period, so that the total amount of each deduction is accurate on a monthly or annual basis.

3. Print the Updates Report from the option at the bottom of the screen to verify that the correct entries were made.

3.3 PR CLERK **File Documentation**

1. Return all employee documentation to the human resources department, so that they can file it in employee folders.

Policy/Procedure Statement

Retrieval No.: PAY-04

Page: 1 of 1

Issue Date: 10/28/03

Supersedes: N/A

Subject: Process Payroll Transactions

1. PURPOSE AND SCOPE

This procedure is used to guide the human resources coordinator or accounting staff through the payroll process.

2. RESPONSIBILITIES

HR COORD **Human Resources Coordinator**

3. PROCEDURES

3.1 HR COORD **Processing Steps**

1. Review all "Request for Time Off" forms that have been submitted during the most recent pay period.

2. Compare time-off requests to the accrued amounts for each employee, as noted in the payroll detail report for the last pay period. Notify employees if they do not have enough accrued vacation time available to fulfill their requests. Then process the portion of time they *do* have available into the payroll.

3. Collect all requests for employee transfers to different departments and enter this information into the payroll software.

4. Enter all manual check payments for the current period into the payroll software.

5. Collect all requests for pay changes. Verify that there are authorized signatures on the pay change forms, then enter the changes into the payroll software.

6. Collect all information regarding terminated employees. Calculate final payments due (if they have not already been paid with manual checks) and enter these final amounts into the payroll software.

7. Compare the garnishments file to the detailed payroll records from the last payroll period to see if any changes are needed to current employee deductions. If so, make those changes in payroll software.

8. On the Friday before the next payroll, clear out all old records from the electronic time clocks that relate back to the previous pay period. Review all electronic time cards for the current period and notify employees if they have incomplete time cards (such as having clocked in but never clocked out).

9. Manually transfer the totals from the electronic time clocks to the payroll processing software. To do this, enter the grand totals of regular and overtime hours into the HOURLY PAY BY EMPLOYEE screen.

10. Verify all data entry by printing the "Payroll Audit Report" and comparing all entered data to the source documents. If there are problems, go back and make the changes and then print this report again to ensure that all payroll data is correct.

11. Go to the PROCESS PAYROLL screen and process all employee pay. Be sure to match the check number on the check stock to the check number appearing in the computer.

12. Use a signature stamp to sign the checks. Then stuff them into envelopes, along with any special employee notices, and sort them by department.

13. Back up the payroll database twice. Leave one copy on-site and send the other copy to the off-site storage location.

14. Reset the software to begin processing the payroll for the next pay period.

15. For any off-site locations, send payroll checks by guaranteed overnight delivery.

16. Retrieve the check register from the data center and review it for possible errors. Then file it in the payroll data storage area.

3.1 HR COORD

Process Deductions

1. Move the cafeteria plan amount noted on the payroll summary from the corporate checking account to the cafeteria plan account.

2. Move the 401k amount noted on the payroll summary to the 401k fund management firm from the corporate checking account.

3. Update the corporate life insurance payment by adjusting it for the total number of employees now on the payroll, as noted in the payroll summary.

4. Issue a check to the United Way based on the amount shown on the payroll summary as having been deducted from employee paychecks.

5. Pay garnishments to the various court authorities. Verify that the amounts paid out match the deductions shown on the payroll summary.

Policy/Procedure Statement

Retrieval No.: PAY-05
Page: 1 of 1
Issue Date: 10/28/03
Supersedes: N/A

Subject: Issue Payments to Employees

1. PURPOSE AND SCOPE

This procedure is used by the payroll clerk to determine the locations of all employees in the company and to issue paychecks or deposit advices to them.

2. RESPONSIBILITIES

    PR CLERK   **Payroll Clerk**

3. PROCEDURES

3.1 PR CLERK   **Print Payroll Checks**

1. Go to the payroll software and access the PRINT option from the PAYMENTS menu.

2. Print the payroll test register and review it to ensure that all paychecks have been correctly calculated.

3. Insert check stock into the printer.

4. Use the TEST option to print a sample check and verify that the line spacing is correct. Repeat as necessary.

5. Print the entire batch of checks.

6. Reset the printer and print all deposit advices for those employees using direct deposit.

7. Print the check register.

8. Review the file of direct deposits, and export it to tape.

3.2 PR CLERK   **Issue Direct Deposit Data to Bank**

1. Include the direct deposits tape in a courier package to the bank.

2. Verify that the bank has received the tape, and that there are no errors in it.

3.3 PR CLERK   **Distribute Payment Notifications**

1. Have all checks signed by an authorized check signer.

2. Stuff all paychecks and deposit advices in envelopes.

3. Batch the envelopes by supervisor and deliver them to supervisors for delivery to employees.

Policy/Procedure Statement

Retrieval No.: PAY-06
Page: 1 of 1
Issue Date: 10/28/03
Supersedes: N/A

Subject: Archive Payroll Records

1. PURPOSE AND SCOPE

This procedure is used by the payroll clerk to properly label and archive all payroll records once they have been processed through the payroll system.

2. RESPONSIBILITIES

PR CLERK   **Payroll Clerk**

3. PROCEDURES

3.1 PR CLERK   **Index Payroll Records**

    1. Extract the personnel folders from the on-site files for all inactive employees.

    2. Batch all the time cards for prior work periods.

    3. Referring to the corporate document destruction policy, mark each item with the legally mandated earliest destruction date.

3.2 PR CLERK   **Archive Payroll Records**

    1. Box the records by destruction date; mark each box with an index number; and record the index number in the master index, along with the contents of each box.

    2. Send the boxes to the archiving center for storage.

The Need for Control Systems[2]

The most common situation in which a control point is needed is when an innocent error is made in the processing of a transaction. For example, a payroll clerk incorrectly calculates the number of hours worked by a nonexempt employee, resulting in a paycheck that is substantially larger than would normally be the case. This type of action may be caused by poor employee training, inattention, or the combination of a special set of circumstances that were unforeseen when the accounting processes were originally constructed. There can be an extraordinary number of reasons why a transactional error arises, which can result in errors that are not caught, and which in turn lead to the loss of corporate assets.

Controls act as review points at those places in a process where these types of errors have a habit of arising. The potential for some errors will be evident when a process flow expert reviews a flowchart that describes a process, simply based on his or her knowledge of where errors in similar processes tend to occur. Other errors will be specific to a certain industry; for example, the casino industry deals with enormous quantities of cash and so has the potential for much higher monetary loss through its cash-handling processes than do similar processes in other industries. Also, highly specific circumstances within a company may generate errors in unlikely places. For example, a manufacturing company that employs mostly foreign-born workers who do not speak English well or at all will experience more errors in any processes where these people are required to fill out paperwork, simply due to a reduced level of comprehension of what they are expected to do. Consequently, the typical process can be laced with areas in which a company has the potential for loss of assets.

Many potential areas of asset loss will involve such minor or infrequent errors that accountants can safely ignore them, hence avoiding the construction of any offsetting controls. Others have the potential for very high risk of loss, and so are shored up with not only one control point, but a whole series of multilayered cross-checks that are designed to keep all but the most unusual problems from arising or being spotted at once.

The need for controls is also driven by the impact of their cost and interference in the smooth functioning of a process. If a control requires the hiring of an extra person, then a careful analysis of the resulting risk mitigation is likely to occur. Similarly, if a highly efficient process is about to have a large and labor-intensive control point plunked down into the middle of it, it is quite likely that an alternative approach should be found that provides a similar level of control, but from outside the process.

The controls installed can be of the preventive variety, which are designed to spot problems as they occur (such as flagging excessive hourly amounts for the payroll data entry staff), or of the detective variety, which spot problems after they occur, so that the accounting staff can research the associated problems and fix them after the fact (such as a bank reconciliation). The former type of control is the best, since it prevents errors from ever happening, whereas the second type results in much more labor by the accounting staff to research each error and correct it. Consequently, the type of control point installed should be evaluated based on its cost of subsequent error correction.

All of these factors—perceived risk, cost, and efficiency—will have an impact on a company's need for control systems, as well as the decision to use the preventive or detective type of each control.

Key Payroll Controls

The types of payroll controls that you should consider implementing will vary by the type and size of the business, as well as whether the payroll is processed internally or by a supplier. Because the control risk will vary so significantly by a company's individual circumstances, it is best to review

TIPS & TECHNIQUES

There is a major difference between the number and type of payroll controls required for a single company location versus those required for a multilocation arrangement, especially if the accounting and internal auditing functions are centralized in just one of the locations. The risk of control problems increases in the latter scenario, because the people most concerned with maintaining proper levels of control are all situated in one place and cannot know what goes on elsewhere. This type of environment requires significant additional controls, such as the centralization of payroll check storage, occasional verification of the existence of employees, and close examination and approval of submitted time sheets.

the following list of controls and then select only those that will improve the control environment. The controls are described in the following subsections.

Employee Advances

Employees may ask for advances on their next paycheck, or to cover the cost of their next trip on the company's behalf. In either case, it is easy to lose track of the advance. The following controls are needed to ensure that an advance is eventually paid back.

- *Continually review all outstanding advances.* When advances are paid to employees, it is necessary to continually review and follow up on the status of these advances. Employees who require advances are sometimes in a precarious financial position and must be issued regular reminders to ensure that the funds are paid back in a timely manner. A simple control point is to have a policy that requires the company to automatically deduct all advances from the next employee paycheck, thereby greatly reducing the work of tracking advances.

- *Require approval of all advance payments to employees.* When
  employees request an advance for any reason—as a draw on the
  next paycheck or as funding for a company trip—it should
  always require formal signed approval from their immediate
  supervisors. The reason is that an advance is essentially a small
  short-term loan, which would also require management
  approval. The accounts payable supervisor or staff should only
  be allowed to authorize advances that are in very small
  amounts.

Payroll Checks

The storage, printing, and distribution problems associated with checks
of all types certainly apply to payroll checks. The following controls are
particularly applicable to those companies that process their payrolls in-
house, since they handle check stock. However, even companies that
outsource their payroll activities should consider the controls related to
bank reconciliations, uncashed checks, and signature cards. If employees
are paid solely through direct deposits, then these controls do not apply.
They are:

- *Control check stock.* The check stock cannot be stored in the
  supply closet along with the pencils and paper, because anyone
  can remove a check from the stack, and then they are only a
  forged signature away from stealing funds from the company.
  Instead, the check stock should be locked in a secure cabinet,
  to which only authorized personnel have access.

- *Add security features to check stock.* With today's advanced
  technologies, checks can be successfully modified or copied.
  To counteract this, purchase check stock with such security
  features as a "Void" logo that appears when a check is copied,
  microprinting that is difficult to copy, or holograms that are
  difficult to reproduce. A particularly effective method is to
  print a small lock icon on the face of a check, which warns a

bank teller that the check contains security features that are listed on the back. The teller can then check the list of features and verify that they exist.

- *Control signature plates.* If anyone can access the company's signature plates, then it is possible not only to forge checks, but also to stamp authorized signatures on all sorts of legal documents. Accordingly, these plates should always be kept in the company safe.

- *Fill in empty spaces on checks.* If the line on a check that lists the amount of cash to be paid is left partially blank, a forger can insert extra numbers or words that will result in a much larger check payment. Avoid this by having the software that prints checks insert a line or series of characters in the spaces.

- *Mutilate voided checks.* A voided check can be retrieved and cashed. To keep this from happening, use a stamping device that cuts the word "void" into the surface of the check, thereby sufficiently mutilating it so that it cannot be used again.

- *Perform bank reconciliations.* This is one of the most important controls anywhere in a company, for it reveals all possible cash inflows and outflows. The bank statement's list of checks cashed should be carefully compared to the company's internal records to ensure that checks have not been altered once they leave the company, or that the books have not been altered to disguise the amount of the checks. It is also necessary to compare the bank's deposit records to the books to spot discrepancies that may be caused by someone taking checks or cash from the batched bank deposits. Further, compare the records of all company bank accounts to see if any check kiting is taking place. In addition, it is absolutely fundamental that the bank reconciliation be completed by someone who is completely unassociated with the payroll function, so that there is no way for anyone to conceal their wrongdoings by altering the bank reconciliation. Finally, because it is now possible to retrieve bank records online through the Internet, a reconciliation can be conducted every day. This is a useful approach, since irregularities can be spotted and corrected much more quickly.

- *Review uncashed checks.* If checks have not been cashed, it is possible that they were created through some flaw in the payroll system that sent a check to a nonexistent employee. An attempt should be made to contact these employees to see if there is a problem.

- *Update signature cards.* A company's bank will have on file a list of check signatories that it has authorized to sign checks. If one of these people leaves the company for any reason, he or she still has the ability to sign company checks. To void this control problem, the bank's signature card should be updated as soon as a check signer leaves the company.

Payroll Expenses

The controls used for payroll cover two areas: the avoidance of excessive amounts of pay to employees, and the avoidance of fraud related to the creation of paychecks for nonexistent employees. Both types of controls are addressed here.

- *Verify hours worked.* Employees may pad their time sheets with extra hours, hoping to be paid for these amounts. Alternatively, they may have fellow employees clock them in and out on days that they do not work. These actions can be difficult to spot, especially when there are many employees for a supervisor to track or if employees work in outlying locations. Supervisors should review and initial all time sheets to ensure that the hours claimed have been worked, though they may not remember what hours were worked several days earlier in the reporting period. As noted in Chapter 2, an automated time clock can be used to block out the hours when an employee is allowed to clock in or out and to quickly create reports for managers that highlight timekeeping irregularities. Finally, it's essential to review the employee hours loaded into the payroll software to the amounts listed on employee time sheets to ensure that there have been no errors in the rekeying of hours data.

- *Require approval of all overtime hours worked by hourly personnel.* One of the simplest forms of employee fraud is to return to the company after hours and clock out at a later time, or have another employee do it on one's behalf, thereby creating false overtime hours. This can be resolved by requiring supervisory approval of all overtime hours worked. A more advanced approach is to use a computerized time clock that categorizes each employee by a specific work period, so that any hours worked after his or her standard time period will be automatically flagged by the computer for supervisory approval. It may not even allow an employee to clock out after a specific time of day without a supervisory code first being entered into the computer.

- *Require approval of all pay changes.* Pay changes can be made quite easily through the payroll system if there is collusion between a payroll clerk and any other employee. This can be spotted through regular comparisons of pay rates *paid* to the approved pay rates *stored* in employee folders. It is best to require the approval of a high-level manager for all pay changes, which should include that person's signature on a standard pay change form. It is also useful to audit the deductions taken from employee paychecks, since these can be altered downward to effectively yield an increased rate of pay. This audit should include a review of the amount and timing of garnishment payments, to ensure that these deductions are being made as required by court orders.

- *Require approval of all negative deductions.* A negative deduction from a paycheck is essentially a cash payment to an employee.

Though this type of deduction is needed to offset prior deductions that may have been too high, it can be abused by artificially increasing a person's pay. Consequently, all negative deductions should be reviewed by a manager.

- *Obtain computer-generated exception reports.* If the payroll software is sufficiently sophisticated, the programming staff can create exception reports that specify whether payments are being made to terminated employees, the amount of payments to new employees, whether negative deductions are being processed, or when unusually high base pay or overtime amounts are being processed. Any of these situations may call for a more detailed review of the flagged items to ensure that any intentional or unintentional errors will not result in incorrect payments.

- *Issue checks directly to recipients.* A common type of fraud is when the payroll staff either "creates employees" in the payroll system or carries on the pay of employees who have left the company, and then pockets the resulting paychecks. This practice can be stopped by ensuring that every paycheck is handed to an employee who can prove his or her identity. The only exception should be those cases when, due to disability or absence, an employee is unable to collect a check, and instead gives written authorization for it be to given to someone else, who brings it to the absent employee.

  For companies that have outlying locations for which it is impossible to physically hand a paycheck to employees, a reasonable alternative is to have the internal audit staff periodically travel to these locations with the checks on an unannounced basis and require physical identification of each recipient before handing over a check.

- *Provide lists of paychecks issued to department supervisors.* From time to time, it is quite useful to give supervisors a list of paychecks issued to everyone in their departments because they may be able to spot payments being made to employees who are no longer working there. This is a particular problem in larger companies, where any delay in processing termination paperwork can result in continuing payments to ex-employees. It also serves as a good control over any payroll clerk who may be trying to defraud the company by delaying termination paperwork and then pocketing the paychecks produced in the interim.

- *Compare the addresses on employee paychecks.* If the payroll staff is creating additional fake employees in the system and having the resulting paychecks mailed to their home addresses, then a simple comparison of addresses for all check recipients will reveal duplicate addresses. (Note, however, that employees can get around this problem by having checks sent to post office boxes. To control this, institute a policy to prohibit payments to post office boxes.)

The preceding set of recommended controls encompasses only the most common ones. Supplement these by reviewing the process flows used by a company to see if there is a need for additional (or fewer) controls, depending upon how the processes are structured. Thus, these controls should be considered only the foundation for a comprehensive set of controls that must be tailored to each company's specific needs.

When to Eliminate Controls

Notwithstanding the lengthy list of controls described in the last section, it is also possible—even advisable—to remove controls. By doing so, frequently you can eliminate extra clerical costs, or at least streamline the various accounting processes. To see if a control is eligible for removal, take the following steps:

1. *Flowchart the process.* Create a picture of every step in the entire process in which a control fits by creating a flowchart. This is needed in order to determine where other controls are located in the process flow. With a knowledge of redundant control points or evidence that there are no other controls available, you can then make a rational decision regarding the need for a specific control.

2. *Determine the cost of a control point.* Having used a flowchart to find controls that may no longer be needed, you must then determine their cost. This can be a complex calculation, for it may involve more than a certain amount of labor, material, or overhead costs that will be reduced. It is also possible that the control is situated in the midst of a bottleneck operation, so that its presence is directly decreasing the capacity of the process, thereby resulting in reduced profits. In such a situation, the incremental drop in profits must be added to the incremental cost of operating the control in order to determine its total cost.

3. *Determine the criticality of the control.* If a control point is merely one that supports another control, then taking it away may not have a significant impact on the ability of the company to retain control over its assets. However, if its removal can only be counteracted by a number of weaker controls, it may be better to keep it in operation.

4. *Calculate the control's cost/benefit.* The preceding two points can be compared to determine whether a control point's cost is outweighed by its criticality, or if the current mix of controls will allow it to be eliminated with no significant change in risk, while stopping the incurrence of its cost.

5. *Verify the use of controls targeted for elimination.* Even when there is a clear-cut case for the elimination of a control point, it is useful to notify everyone who is involved with the process in which it is embedded, in order to ascertain if there is some other use to

which it is being put. For example, a control that measures the cycle time of a manufacturing machine may no longer be needed as a control point, but may be an excellent source of information for someone who is tracking the percentage utilization of the equipment. In these cases, it is best to determine the value of the control to its alternate user before eliminating it. It may be necessary to work around the alternate use before the control point can be removed.

Repeat this control evaluation process whenever there is a significant change to a process flow. Even if there has not been a clear change for some time, it is likely that a large number of small changes have been made to a process, whose cumulative impact will necessitate a controls review. The period of time between these reviews will vary by industry, since some have seen little process change in many years, while others are constantly shifting their business models, which inherently requires changes to their supporting processes.

If there have been any significant changes to a business model, such as the addition of new technology, the implementation of different types of employment models, the opening of new company locations, or a shift to outsourcing or contracting out various types of labor, conduct a complete review of all associated process flows both prior to and immediately after the changes, so that unneeded controls can be promptly removed or so that weak controls can be enhanced.

Summary

Procedures and controls are critical components of the payroll process. Procedures are designed to increase the efficiency of the department by standardizing task steps; controls can have the opposite effect, by increasing the number of tasks in the procedures in order to ensure that there is no loss of assets. The payroll manager must reconcile the conflicting

IN THE REAL WORLD

Reducing Technology
to Improve Results

A sheet metal processing facility used a data entry software package to enter payroll changes to the payroll database, which was maintained by an outside supplier that processed all payrolls and printed checks for the company. One year, a number of payroll clerks came and went, resulting in a declining knowledge of how the data entry software worked. By the end of the year, the newest payroll clerk had only the most elementary knowledge of how to use the system, resulting both in widespread payroll processing errors and employees who were irritated because their paychecks were never correct. The problem was exacerbated by the lack of a procedure for this key function, which could only be created with difficulty, since no expert was available to write the procedure. To resolve the problem, the controller abandoned the more complex data entry software and instructed the clerk to simply call the supplier just before each payroll and tell the supplier's data entry staff which changes to make. Though this was technically a regression in the form of data entry used, the controller succeeded in matching the skill set of the payroll staff to the method of updating the database of payroll information. The change was a success, and payroll problems immediately declined.

goals of procedures and controls—efficiency versus asset control—by balancing the need for additional streamlining with any resultant loss of control. This is a balancing act and there is no one way to achieve it, since it will be based on the number of company locations, the skill level of the staff, the department's organizational structure, and other intangible factors. Also, once the payroll manager strikes a balance between the efficiency and control objectives, this issue must be revisited time and again, since the manner in which the payroll department operates will change over time; these changes must be incorporated into procedures and evaluated in terms of their impact on the control environment.

Endnotes

1. The flowchart and procedures used in this section were adapted with permission from Chapter 5 of Steven Bragg and Harry L. Brown, *Design and Maintenance of Accounting Manuals,* 4th Ed. (New York: John Wiley & Sons, Inc., 2002).

2. Much of the control-related discussion in this chapter is adapted with permission from Steven Bragg, *Accounting Reference Desktop* (New York: John Wiley & Sons, Inc., 2002), 303–319.

CHAPTER 4

Payroll Best Practices[1]

After reading this chapter you will be able to

- Understand how employees can alter their own payroll deduction data

- Know why bar-coded time clocks can automate the collection of payroll data

- Understand why fewer payroll cycles lead to less processing work by the payroll staff

- Learn how to streamline or eliminate the use of personal, vacation, and sick time tracking systems

Though anyone can cobble together a payroll system that operates moderately well, there are a number of steps that can be taken to greatly increase the efficiency of this operation. The steps are called "best practices," and are indicative of the work practices used by the operators of highly efficient payroll operations. Though some payroll best practices are clearly designed for larger companies with a multitude of employees, others can be used to improve the operations of companies of any size.

The following sections briefly describe a number of payroll best practices, including the pros and cons of their use, any problems with their implementation, and a graphical representation of their cost and installation time. The best practices are generally clustered, in order, by those relating to the gathering of payroll data, the processing of that data, and finally its distribution.

Automate Fax-Back of Payroll Forms

A payroll clerk is the unofficial keeper of the payroll and human resources forms. Employees come to this person to collect these sheets, which can vary from a request to change a payroll deduction to a request to change a pension deduction amount. If a company has many employees or many locations (which necessitates mailing forms to recipients), the chore of handing out forms can take up a large amount of staff time.

To avoid distributing forms to employees, you can set up an automated *fax-back system*. This best practice requires employees to contact a computer, either using a touch-tone phone or through the computer system, and request that the appropriate form be sent to a fax number accessible by the employee. If the employee has computer access, he or she can also download the form directly and either fill it out on his or her computer or print it, fill it out, and mail it back.

Because all of the forms are digitized and stored in the computer's memory, it is possible to make the transmission with no human intervention. For example, an employee accesses the system through a computer, scrolls through a list of available forms, highlights the needed item, enters the send-to fax number, and logs off. The form arrives a few moments later.

Under a manual distribution system, it is common practice to issue large quantities of forms to outlying locations, so that the payroll staff is not constantly sending them small numbers of additional forms; the disadvantage of this practice is that these forms end up being used for a long time, frequently past the date when they become obsolete. An automated fax-back system eliminates this problem by making available for transmission only the most recent version. This is a boon to the payroll staff, who might otherwise receive old forms that do not contain key information, thus requiring them to contact employees to gather the missing data, or even forcing employees to resubmit their requests on the current forms.

In addition, the system can automatically send along an extra instruction sheet with each distributed form so that employees can easily fill out forms without having to call the payroll staff for assistance.

An automated fax-back system can be expensive, so you should determine all costs before beginning an implementation. The system includes a separate file server linked to one or more phone lines (for receiving touch-tone phone requests, as well as for sending out forms to recipient fax machines), plus a scanner for digitizing payroll forms. The best way to justify these added costs when servicing a large number of employees is that the system saves a large amount of staff time. Without enough employees to justify costs, the system should not be installed.

Be sure to leave enough time in the implementation schedule to review the variety of fax-back systems on the market prior to making a purchase, as well as for configuring the system and testing it with employees. If the system has an option for document requests both by phone and computer, then implement one at a time to ensure that each variation is properly set up.

Cost: 💵💵💵

Installation time: 🕐 🕐 🕐

Give Employees Direct Access to Deduction Data

A major task for the payroll staff is to meet with employees to go over the effect of any deduction changes they wish to make, calculate the changes, and enter them into the payroll database. This can be a particularly time-consuming task if the number of possible deduction options is large, if employees are allowed to make deduction changes at any time, or if employees are not well-educated as to the impact of deduction changes on their net pay.

A particularly elegant best practice that resolves this problem is to give employees direct access to the deduction data so they can determine the impact of deduction changes themselves and enter the changes directly into the payroll database. To do so, it is necessary to construct an interface to the payroll database that lists all deductions taken from employee paychecks (with the exception of garnishments, which are set by law). However, this is not enough, for most deductions are usually tied to a benefit of some sort. For example, a deduction for a medical plan can only be changed if the underlying medical plan option is changed. Accordingly, an employee needs access to a "split screen" of information, with one side showing benefit options and the other side showing the employee's gross pay, all deductions, and net pay. This view allows the employee to modify deductions and see the impact on net pay. Examples of deductions for which this data view will work are federal and state tax deductions, medical and dental plan coverage, life and disability insurance coverage, and pension plan deductions.

Though the primary emphasis of this best practice is on allowing employees to alter their own deduction information, it can be used in other ways, too. For example, employees can alter the bank routing and account numbers used for the direct deposit of their pay into bank accounts, or change the amounts split between deposits to their savings and checking accounts. They can also use this approach to process requests for additional W-2 forms or to download files containing the employee manual or other relevant personnel information.

An example of this approach is the dental plan. Assume that on one side of the computer screen an employee is presented with five dental plan options, all with different costs. The employee can scroll through the list and select any option, while watching the selection automatically change the payroll calculation on the other side of the screen. Once the employee finds the selection that works best, he or she presses a button to enter the change into the payroll system. Such a system should include some selection "blocks" so that employees cannot constantly change deductions; for example, the software may limit employees to one health plan change per year.

This approach completely eliminates all work by the payroll staff to enter deduction changes into the computer. An added benefit is that employees are responsible for their own data entry mistakes. If they make an incorrect entry, they can go into the system themselves to correct it. The system can also be expanded to include other data items, such as employee names, addresses, and phone numbers. In addition, the deduction modeling system just described enables employees to determine precisely what their net pay will be, eliminating any surprises. In a more traditional system, an employee might make a deduction change without realizing the full impact of the change on his or her net pay and end up back in the payroll office, demanding a reversion to the old deduction level. By using the modeling system, the payroll staff can eliminate such repeat visits from employees.

This system will only work, however, if the organization is willing to invest a significant amount of software development effort to design an employee interface, as well as to provide either individual computers or central kiosks to employees so that they can use the system. Given its high cost, this system is usually found only in larger organizations with many employees, where the cost-benefit trade-off is obvious.

The software development effort required for this best practice is substantial, so it must be budgeted for well in advance and must gain the approval of the committee that schedules the order in which development projects will be completed. Also, be sure to carefully document all benefit plan rules related to changes in the plans, so that employees are not caught unawares; for example, many dental insurance plans only cover the costs for major dental surgery if participants have already been in the plan for at least one year; hence the computer system must alert employees of this requirement before they switch to a different plan.

Cost: 💵 💵 💵

Installation time: ⏰ ⏰ ⏰

Use Bar-Coded Time Clocks

The most labor-intensive task in the payroll area is calculating hours worked for hourly employees. To do so, a payroll clerk must collect all of the employee time cards for the most recently completed payroll period, manually accumulate the hours listed on the cards, and discuss missing or excessive hours with supervisors. This is a lengthy process with a high error rate, due to the large percentage of missing start or stop times on time cards. Any errors are usually found by employees as soon as they are paid, resulting in possibly confrontational visits to the payroll staff, from whom they demand an immediate adjustment to their pay in the form of a manual check. These changes disrupt the payroll department and introduce additional inefficiencies to the process.

The solution is to install a computerized time clock. This clock requires an employee to swipe a uniquely identified card through a reader installed on its side. The card is encoded with either a magnetic strip or a bar code that contains the employee's identification number. Once the swipe occurs, the clock automatically stores the date and time, and downloads this information upon request to the payroll department's computer, where special software automatically calculates the hours worked and highlights any problems for additional research (such as missed card swipes). Many of these clocks can be installed through a large facility or at outlying locations so that employees can conveniently record their time, no matter where they may be. More advanced clocks also track the time periods when employees are supposed to arrive and leave, and require a supervisor's password for card swipes outside of that time period; this feature allows for greater control over employee work hours. Many of these systems also issue absence reports, so that supervisors can tell who has not shown up for work. Thus, an automated time clock eliminates much low-end clerical work, while at the same time providing new management tools for supervisors.

But before purchasing such a clock, you should recognize its limitations. The most important one is cost. This type of clock costs $2,000 to $3,000 each; or they can be leased for several hundred dollars per month. If several clocks are needed, this can add up to a substantial investment. Moreover, outlying time clocks that must download their information to a computer at a distant location require their own phone lines, which represents an additional monthly payment to the phone company. There may also be a fee for using the software on the central computer that summarizes all the incoming payroll information. Given these costs, typically bar-coded time clocks are used only where there are so many hourly employees that a significant savings can be seen in the payroll department resulting from their installation.

Also, employees will lose their swipe cards. To encourage them to keep their cards in a safe place, the company can charge a small fee for replacing them.

Another issue to consider is that prior to the use of this type of clock, hourly employees will have gotten used to paper-based time cards that have their start and stop times punched onto them. When a bar-coded time clock is installed, they miss the security of seeing this record of the hours they worked. Instead, they swipe a card through the clock and never see any evidence of time worked. To overcome the discomfort that comes from this changeover, the accounting staff should show the hourly personnel how the new clock works and where the data is stored, to ensure employees that their time data will not be lost. If there is an option that allows them to look up information on the time clock's LCD display, they should receive training in how to do this; in addition, it's a good idea to post a procedure next to the clock that explains how to obtain this information. It is also useful to install a set of green and red lights next to the scanner, with the green light flashing when a successful scan has been completed (and the red light indicating the reverse).

Cost:

Installation time: 🕃 🕃

Use Biometric Time Clocks

The bar-coded time clocks described in the preceding best practice represent an excellent improvement in the speed and accuracy with which employee time data can be collected. However, it suffers from an

TIPS & TECHNIQUES

If you have the choice of purchasing a time clock that accepts either bar-coded cards or magnetic stripe cards, take the bar-coded card option. The reason is that bar codes can be manufactured in-house with a variety of bar-code-labeling software that is easy to obtain, whereas magnetic stripe cards must be purchased from a supplier. Printed bar codes can then be glued to the back of a scanning card and run through a lamination machine to permanently seal it. And to avoid the risk that employees might run the card through a copier to make multiple copies of an authorized bar code, just cover the card with a red-tinted plastic sheath when running it through the lamination machine, so that a copier cannot "see" the underlying bar code through the red overlay.

integrity flaw: Employees can use each other's badges to enter and exit from the payroll system, called "buddy punching." This means that some employees could be paid for hours when they were not on-site at all.

A division of Ingersoll-Rand called Recognition Systems has surmounted this problem with the use of biometric time clocks (which can be seen at *www.handreader.com*). This reader requires an employee to place his or her hand on a sensor, which matches its size and shape to the dimensions already recorded for that person in a central database. The time entered into the terminal will then be recorded against the payroll file of the person whose hand was just measured. Thus, only employees who are on-site can have payroll hours credited to them. The company sells a variation on the same machine, called the HandKey, which is used to control access to secure areas. These systems have a secondary benefit, which is that no one needs an employee badge or pass key, which tend to be lost or damaged over time, and so represent a minor headache for the accounting or human resources staffs, who must track them. In a biometric monitoring environment, all an employee needs is his or her hand.

These biometric monitoring devices are expensive, however, and require significant evidence of buddy punching to justify their cost. If these clocks are intended to replace bar-coded time clocks, then there is no projected labor savings from reducing the manual labor of the payroll personnel (since this advantage was already covered by the bar-coded clocks), leaving only the savings from buddy punching to justify their purchase.

For this system, too, you will have to address the lack of time-punched data as noted for the bar-coded time clock. Again, it can be resolved by meeting with the hourly personnel to show them how their time data is collected, stored, and summarized, and how to access this information on the time clock if the device has such data available.

Cost: 💵 💵

Installation time: ⏰

Prohibit Deductions for Employee Purchases

Many companies allow their employees to use corporate discounts to buy products through them. For example, a company may have obtained a large discount on furniture from a supplier, then allows its employees to buy at the discounted rate and have the deductions subtracted from their paychecks in convenient installments. Some employees will make excessive use of this benefit, purchasing all kinds of supplies through the company; accordingly, it is common to see a small minority of employees making the bulk of these purchases. The problem for the payroll staff is that they must keep track of the total amount that each employee owes the organization and gradually deduct the amount owed from successive paychecks. If an employee makes multiple purchases, the payroll staff must constantly recalculate the amount to be deducted. Depending on the number of employees taking advantage of discount shopping through the company, this can have a measurable impact on the efficiency of the payroll department.

The solution to this problem is to prohibit employee purchases through the organization. By doing so, all the extra paperwork associated with employee purchases is immediately swept away. That said, though this is a good best practice for most companies to implement, it should first be cleared with senior management. The reason is that some employees may be so accustomed to purchasing through the company that they will be upset, even angry, by the change, which may be a condition that management wants to avoid (especially if valuable employees will be among those upset). Also, some companies have valid reasons for allowing employee purchases, such as when, for example, steel-toed boots or safety clothing are necessary for performing their jobs.

As just noted, this best practice should be reviewed with all key department managers and senior management before being made public. Also, any employees who are currently having deductions taken from their paychecks for past purchases should be "grandfathered" into the new rule, so that they are not forced to suddenly pay off the remaining amounts due.

Cost:

Installation time:

Disallow Prepayments

Many employees do not have the monetary resources to see them through until the next payday. Their solution is to request a pay advance, which is deducted from their next paycheck. It is a humane gesture on the part of the payroll manager to comply with such requests, but it wreaks havoc with the efficiency of the payroll department. Whenever such a request is made, the payroll staff must manually calculate the taxes to take out of the payment, then manually cut a check and have it signed. And, that's not all: The staff must manually enter the pay advance in the computer system so that the amount is properly deducted from the next paycheck. For larger advances, it may be necessary to make deductions over several paychecks, which requires even more work. Furthermore, if an employee quits work before earning back the amount of the advance, the company has just incurred a loss. Clearly, paycheck prepayments do not help the efficiency of the payroll department. This is a particularly significant problem in organizations where the average pay level is near the minimum wage, since the recipients may not have enough money to meet their needs from pay day to pay day.

The best practice that solves this problem seems simple, but can be quite difficult to implement. You must establish a rule that no paycheck prepayments will be issued, which effectively ends the extra processing required of the payroll staff. The trouble with this rule is that a needy employee can usually present such a good case for a pay advance that exceptions will be made; this grinds away at the rule over time, until it is completely ignored. Other managers will assist in tearing down the rule by claiming that they will lose good employees if advances are not provided to them.

The best way to support this rule is to form an association with a local lending institution that specializes in short-term loans. Then, if an employee requests an advance, he or she can be directed to the lending institution, which will arrange for an interest-bearing loan to the employee. When this arrangement exists, it is common for employees to tighten their budgets rather than pay the extra interest charged for use of the lender's money. This improves employee finances while increasing the processing efficiency of the payroll staff.

It's important to arrange for alternative employee financing *before* setting up a no-advance rule, in order to be certain that alternative financing will be available to employees. Then go over the rule with all employees several weeks before it is to be implemented, so that they will have fair warning of the change. Also, make brochures available in the payroll department that describe the services of the lending institution, as well as contact information and directions for reaching it.

Cost:

Installation time:

Eliminate Personal Leave Days

A common task for the payroll staff is to either manually or automatically track the vacation time employees earn and use. Depending on the level of automation, this task can require some portion of staff time every week on an ongoing basis. Some companies then take the additional step of accruing and tracking the usage of personal leave days, which are essentially the same as vacation time, but tracked under a different name. By having both vacation and personal leave days, the payroll staff has to track data in both categories, which doubles the work required to simply track vacation time.

A reasonable, and easily implemented, best practice is to convert personal leave days into vacation days and eliminate the extra category of time off. By doing so, the payroll staff can cut in half the time required to analyze employee vacation time. The only resistance to this change usually comes from the human resources department, which likes to offer a variety of benefits to match those offered by other companies; for example, if a competitor offers personal leave days, then so should the company. Though only a matter of semantics, this can cause a problem with implementing the simpler system.

Cost:

Installation time: 🕑

Use Honor System to Track Vacation and Sick Time

It is common for the payroll staff to be in charge of tracking the vacation and sick time used by employees. This involves sending out forms for employees to fill out whenever they take time off, usually requiring their supervisor's signature. Upon receipt, the payroll staff logs the used time in the payroll system and files the forms in the employee personnel folders. If the payroll staff does not account for this information correctly in the payroll system, employees will probably spot the problem on their remittance advices the next time they are paid and will go to the payroll office to look into the matter. These inquiries take up accounting staff time, as does the paperwork-tracking effort.

When used with some control features, it is possible to completely eliminate the tracking of vacation and sick time by the payroll staff. In this scenario, employees are placed on the honor system of tracking their own vacation and sick time. Though this system keeps the payroll staff from having to do any tracking of this information, there is also a strong possibility that some employees will abuse the situation and take extra time. There are two ways to avoid this problem. One is to institute a companywide policy that automatically wipes out all earned vacation and sick time at the end of each calendar year, which has the advantage of limiting the amount of vacation and sick time to which an employee can claim that he or she is entitled. This step mitigates a company's losses if a dishonest employee leaves the company and claims payment for many hours of vacation and sick time that may go back for years. The other way to avoid the problem is to switch the tracking role to employee supervisors. These people are in the best position to see when employees are taking time off and can track their time off

 TIPS & TECHNIQUES

A common best practice is to merge different tracking systems for personal leave days, vacation days, and sick days into an enlarged number of vacation days, thereby reducing the number of tracking systems from three to one. However, this can meet with considerable resistance by employees, who feel that the company is trying to take away some of their time off. A good way to prevent this from happening is to grant an increased number of hours of vacation carryover time into the next year, at least for the first year or two of the transition, so that employees have an adequate time frame in which to use up excess leave days. This is seen as a particular benefit in companies that did not previously allow a carryover of unused sick time or personal leave days, but which will now roll into the vacation category, where the time may be carried forward.

much more easily than can the payroll staff. In short, with some relatively minor control changes, it is possible to use an honor system to track employee vacation and sick time.

Cost:

Installation time:

Switch to Salaried Positions

When processing payroll, it is evident that the labor required for a salaried person is significantly lower than for an hourly employee; there is no change in the payroll data from period to period for a salaried person, whereas the number of hours worked must be recomputed for an hourly employee every time the payroll is processed. Therefore, it is reasonable to shift as many employees as possible over to salaried positions from hourly ones in order to reduce the labor of calculating payroll.

Implementing this best practice can be a significant problem, though. First, it is not under the control of the accounting department, since it is up to the managers of other departments to switch people over to salaried positions, so the controller must persuade others to make the concept a reality. Second, this best practice is generally opposed by unions, which prefer to give their members the option to earn overtime pay. Finally, there may be government regulations that prohibit converting employees to salaried positions, with the main determining criterion being that a salaried person must be able to act with minimal supervision. This situation will vary by state, depending on local laws.

Given the three issues just noted, it may seem impossible to implement this best practice. However, it is quite possible in some industries. The main factor for success is that the industry have few hourly workers to begin with. For example, a company with many highly educated employees, or one that performs limited manufacturing, may already have so many salaried employees that it becomes a minor cleanup issue to convert the few remaining hourly employees to salaried positions.

Cost:

Installation time:

Minimize Payroll Cycles

Many payroll departments are fully occupied with processing some kind of payroll every week, and possibly even several times in one week. The latter situation occurs when different groups of employees are paid for different time periods. For example, hourly employees may be paid every week, while salaried employees may be paid twice a month. Processing multiple payroll cycles eats up any spare hours of the payroll staff, leaving them with little time for cleaning up paperwork or researching improvements to its basic operations.

To alleviate this problem, all of the various payroll cycles can be consolidated into a single, companywide payroll cycle. By doing so, the payroll staff no longer has to spend extra time on additional payroll processing, nor does it have to worry about the different pay rules that may apply to each processing period; instead, everyone is treated exactly the same. To make payroll processing even more efficient, it is useful to lengthen the payroll cycles. For example, a payroll department that processes weekly payrolls must run the payroll 52 times a year, whereas one that processes monthly payrolls only does so 12 times per year, which eliminates 75 percent of the processing that the first department must handle. These changes represent an enormous reduction in the payroll-processing time the accounting staff requires.

Any changes to the payroll cycles may, however, be met with opposition by the organization's employees. The primary complaint is that the employees have structured their spending habits around the timing of the former pay system and that any change will mean they won't have enough cash to continue those habits. For example, employees who currently receive a paycheck every week may have a great deal of difficulty in adjusting their spending when they receive a paycheck only once a month. If a company were to switch from a short to a longer pay cycle, it is extremely likely that the payroll staff would be deluged with requests for pay advances well before the next paycheck was due for release, requiring a large amount of payroll staff time to handle. To overcome this problem, increase pay cycles incrementally, perhaps to twice a month or once every two weeks, and tell employees that pay advances will be granted for a limited transition period. By making these incremental changes, it is possible to reduce the associated level of employee discontent caused by implementing this best practice.

Review the prospective change with the rest of the management team to make sure that it is acceptable to them. They must buy into the need for the change, because their employees will also be impacted, and the managers will receive complaints about it. This best practice requires a long lead time to implement as well as multiple notifications to the staff about its timing and impact on them. It is also useful to go over the granting of payroll advances with the payroll staff, so that they are prepared for the likely surge in requests for advances.

Cost: 🤑

Installation time: 🕐 🕐 🕐

Link Payroll Changes to Employee Events

There are many payroll changes that must be made to an employee's file when certain events occur. Many of these changes are never made, however, either because the payroll staff is so busy with the standard, daily processing of information that it has no time to address them or because the payroll staff does not possess enough knowledge to link the payroll changes to the employee events. For example, when an employee is married, this should trigger a change in that person's W-4 form, so that the amount of taxes withheld will reflect those for a married person.

Automation can create many of these linkages. Here are some examples:

- As soon as an employee reaches the age of 55, the system issues a notification to the pension manager to calculate the person's potential pension, while also notifying the employee of his or her pension eligibility. These notifications can be by letter, but a linkage between the payroll system and the e-mail system could result in more immediate notification.

- As soon as an employee has been with a company for 90 days, his or her period of probation has been completed. The system should then automatically include the employee in the company's dental, medical, and disability plans, and start deductions for these amounts from the person's paycheck. Similarly, the system can automatically enroll the employee in the company's 401(k) plan and enter that deduction in the payroll system. Since these pay changes should not come as a surprise to the employee, the system should also generate a message to the employee, detailing the changes made and the net payroll impact.

- When a company is informed of an employee's marriage, the computer system generates a notice to the employee that a new W-4 form should be filled out, as well as a new benefit enrollment form, in case the employee wishes to add benefits for the spouse or any children. Finally, a notification message can ask the employee if he or she wants to change the beneficiary's name on the pension plan to that of the spouse.

- When an employee notifies the company of an address change, the system automatically notifies all related payroll and benefit suppliers, such as the 401(k) plan administrator and health insurance provider, of the change.

- When a new employee is hired, the system sends a message to the purchasing department, asking that business cards be ordered for the person. Another message goes to the information systems department, requesting that the appropriate levels of system security be set up for the new hire. Yet another message goes to the training department, asking that a training plan be set up for the new employee.

Many of these workflow features are available on high-end accounting and human resources software packages. However, this software costs more than a million dollars in most cases, and so is well beyond the purchasing capability of many smaller companies. An alternative is to customize an existing software package to include these features, but the work required will be expensive. Accordingly, these changes should only be contemplated if there are many employees, since this would result in a sufficient volume of savings to justify the added expense.

Cost: 💵 💵 💵

Installation time: ⏰ ⏰

Link the 401(k) Plan to the Payroll System

A common activity for the payroll staff is to take the 401(k) deduction information from the payroll records as soon as each payroll cycle is completed, enter it into a separate database for 401(k) deductions, copy this information onto a diskette, and send it to the company's 401(k) administration supplier, who uses it to determine the investment levels of all employees, as well as to test for 401(k)discrimination. This can be a lengthy data entry process if there are many employees, and it is certainly not a value-added activity when the core task is simply to move data from one database to another.

The best way to avoid retyping 401(k) payroll deductions is to link the payroll system directly to a 401(k) plan. This is done by outsourcing the payroll-processing function to a supplier that also offers a 401(k) plan. A good example of this is Automated Data Processing (ADP), which offers linkages to a number of well-known mutual funds through its payroll system. When a company uses ADP's payroll and 401k services, a payroll department can record a 401(k) payroll deduction for an employee just once; ADP will then take the deduction and automatically move it into a 401(k) fund, with no additional bookkeeping required from the payroll staff. For those companies with many employees, this can represent a significant reduction in the workload of the payroll staff.

There are two problems with this best practice. One is that a company must first outsource its payroll function to a supplier that offers 401(k) administration services, which the company controller may not be willing to do. The second problem is converting to the new 401(k) plan. To do so, all employees in the old plan must be moved to the new plan. The associated paperwork may be great enough that the transition is not worthwhile; moreover, the 401(k) administrator may require a separation fee if the company is terminating its services inside of a minimum time interval, which may involve a small penalty payment. These issues should be considered before switching to a centralized payroll and 401(k) processing system.

Cost: 💵 💵

Installation time: ⏰ ⏰

Link the Payroll and Human Resources Databases

The payroll database shares many data elements with the human resources database. Unfortunately, these two databases are usually maintained by different departments—accounting for the first and human resources for the second. Consequently, any employee who makes a change to one database, such as to an address field in the payroll system, must then walk to the human resources department to have the same information entered again for other purposes, such as benefits administration or a pension plan. Thus, there is an obvious inefficiency for the employee who must go to two departments for changes; another inefficiency is that the accounting and human resources staffs duplicate each other's data entry efforts.

An alternative is to tie the two databases together. This can be done by purchasing a software package that automatically consolidates the two databases into a single one. But the considerable cost of buying and implementing an entirely new software package will grossly exceed the cost savings obtained by consolidating the data.

A less costly approach is to create an interface between the two systems that automatically stores changes made to each database and updates the other one as a daily batch program. However, creating this interface may still be expensive, as it involves a reasonable amount of customized programming work. Consequently, this best practice is a costly proposition and is usually only done when both computer systems are being brought together for other reasons than to simply reduce data entry work.

Furthermore, if the two databases are consolidated into a single system, the initial conversion of data from both originating systems into the new one can be a major operation: Someone must design an automated conversion program that shifts the old data into the format used by the new system, merge the data from both databases, and then import them into the new system. Also, the new system will probably have a number of processing steps, screens, and online forms that differ from the systems being replaced, so both the payroll and human resources staffs will require training prior to the "go live" date for the new system.

Cost: 💵 💵 💵

Installation time: ⏰ ⏰ ⏰

Consolidate Payroll Systems

A company that grows by acquisition is likely to have a number of payroll systems—one for each company it has acquired. This situation may also arise for highly decentralized organizations that allow each location to set up its own payroll system. Though this approach does enable each location to process payroll in accordance with its own rules and payment periods, while also allowing for local maintenance of employee records, there are several serious problems with this setup that can be solved by the consolidation of all these systems into a single, centralized payroll system.

One problem with multiple payroll systems in one company is that employee payroll records cannot be shifted through the company when, say, an employee is transferred to a different location. Instead, the employee first must be listed as having been terminated from the payroll system of the location he or she is leaving and then listed as a new hire in the payroll system of the new location. By repeatedly reentering an employee as a new hire, it is impossible to track the dates and amounts of pay raises; the same problem arises for the human resources staff, who cannot track eligibility dates for medical insurance or vesting periods for pension plans. In addition, every time employee data is reentered into a different payroll system, there is a risk of data inaccuracies that may result from the input of incorrect pay rates or checks sent to the wrong address. Also, a company cannot easily group data for companywide payroll reporting purposes. For all these reasons, it is common practice to consolidate payroll systems into a single, centralized location that operates with a single payroll database.

Before embarking on such a consolidation, however, you must consider the costs of implementation. One is that a consolidation of many payroll systems may require an expensive new software package that must run on a more powerful computer, which entails extra capital and software maintenance costs. Probably, too, a significant cost will be associated with converting the data from the disparate databases into the consolidated one. In addition, extra time may be needed to test the tax rate for all company locations in order to avoid penalties for improper tax withholdings and submissions. Finally, the timing of the implementation is of some importance. Many companies prefer to make the conversion on the first day of the new year, so there is no need to enter detailed pay information into the system for the prior year in order to issue year-end payroll tax reports to the government. In sum, the cost of consolidating payroll systems is considerable and must be carefully analyzed before deciding to convert.

Cost: 💵 💵

Installation time: ⏰ ⏰

Avoid Job Costing through the Payroll System

Some controllers have elaborate cost accounting systems set up to accumulate a variety of costs from many sources, sometimes to be used for activity-based costing and, more frequently, for job costing. One of these costs is labor, which is sometimes accumulated through the payroll system. When this is done, employees use lengthy time cards on which they record the time spent on many of their activities during the day, resulting in vastly longer payroll records than would otherwise be the case. This is a problem when the payroll staff is asked to sort through and add up all of the job-costing records, since this increases the workload of the payroll personnel by an order of magnitude. In addition, the payroll staff may be asked to enter the job-costing information that they have compiled into the job-costing database, yet another task that gets in the way of processing the payroll.

The obvious solution is to disallow job costing to be merged into the payroll function, thereby enabling the payroll staff to vastly reduce the amount of work they must complete, as well as shrink the number of opportunities for calculation errors. However, this step may meet with opposition from those people who need the job-costing records. Fortunately, there are several ways to avoid conflict over the issue. One is to analyze who is charging time to various projects or activities and determine if the proportions to time charged vary significantly over time; if they do not, there is no reason to continue tracking job-costing information for hours worked. Another possibility is to split the functions so that the payroll staff collects their payroll data independently of the job-costing data collection, which can be handled by someone else. Either option will keep the job-costing function from interfering with the orderly collection of payroll information.

Cost: 💸

Installation time: ⏰

Automate Vacation Accruals

The accounting topic that is of the most interest to the greatest number of employees is how much vacation time they have left. In most companies, this information is kept manually by the payroll staff, meaning that employees troop down to the payroll department once a month (and more frequently during the prime summer vacation months!) to see how

much vacation time they have left to use. When employees are constantly coming in to find out this information, it is a major interruption to the
payroll staff, because it happens at all times of the day, preventing them
from settling down into a comfortable work routine. When numerous
employees want to know about their vacation time in a single period, it
can mean a considerable loss of efficiency for the payroll staff.

A simple way to prevent employees from bothering the payroll staff
is to include the vacation accrual amount in employee paychecks. The
information appears on the payroll stub, showing the annual amount of
accrued vacation, net of any used time. By providing this information
to employees in every paycheck, they have no need to inquire about it
in the payroll office, thereby eliminating a major interruption to staff.

There are, however, several points to consider before implementing
this best practice. First, the payroll system must be equipped with a
vacation accrual option. If not, the software must be customized to
allow for the calculation and presentation of this information, and this
may cost more to implement than the projected efficiency savings.
Another problem is that the accrual system must be set up accurately
for each employee when it is originally installed; otherwise, there will
be a number of outraged employees crowding into the payroll office,
causing more disruption than was the case before. This is a problem
because employees have different numbers of allowed vacation days per
year, or may have unused vacation time from the previous year that
must be carried forward into the next year. If this information is not
accurately reflected in the automated vacation accrual system when it
is implemented, employees will hasten to the payroll department to
have this information corrected at once. Another problem is that the
accruals must be adjusted over time to reflect changes. Otherwise, once
again, employees will interrupt the staff to notify them of changes,
thereby offsetting the value of the entire system. For example, an

employee may be raised from two to three weeks of allowed vacation at the fifth anniversary of his or her hiring. The payroll department must have a schedule of when this person's vacation accrual amount changes to the three-week level or the employee will come in and complain about it. If these problems can be overcome, then showing vacation accruals on the paychecks becomes a relatively simple means of improving the efficiency of the payroll department.

To achieve this goal, have a schedule available in the payroll department that itemizes the dates on which employees with sufficient seniority are scheduled to have increases in their allowed vacation amounts; include a review of this document in the monthly departmental schedule of activities, so that accrual changes can be made in a timely manner. Also, train the payroll staff to properly enter data into the payroll system for any vacation hours taken by employees. Finally, create a procedure for making changes to the data in the automated vacation accrual system, so that the staff can correct errors in the system.

Cost:

Installation time:

Post Commission Payments on the Company Internet

A sales staff whose pay structure is heavily skewed in favor of commission payments, rather than salaries, will probably hound the accounting staff at month-end to see what their commission payments will be. This coincides to the time of the month when the accounting staff is trying to close the accounting books, and so increases their workload at the worst possible time of the month. But, by creating a linkage between the accounting database and a company's Internet site, it is now possible to shift this information directly to the Web page where the sales staff can view it at any time, and without involving the valuable time of the accounting staff.

There are two ways to post the commission information. One is to wait until all commission-related calculations have been completed at month-end, and then either manually "dump" the data into an HyperText Markup Language (HTML) format for posting to a Web page, or else run a batch program that does this automatically. Either approach will give the sales staff a complete set of information about their commissions. That said, this approach still requires some manual effort at month-end (even if only for a few minutes while a batch program runs).

An alternative approach is to create a direct interface between the accounting database and the Web page, so that commissions are updated constantly, including grand totals for each commission payment period. By using this approach, the accounting staff has virtually no work to do in conveying information to the sales staff. In addition, sales personnel can check their commissions at any time of the month and call the accounting staff with any concerns right away. This is a great improvement, as problems can be spotted and fixed at once, rather than waiting until the crucial month-end closing period to correct them.

No matter which method you use for posting commission information, a password system will be needed, since this is highly personal payroll-related information. There should be a reminder program built into the system, so that the sales staff is forced to alter their passwords on a regular basis, thereby reducing the risk of outside access to this information.

Cost: 💵💵

Installation time: ⏰ ⏰

Deposit Payroll into Credit Card Accounts

Some companies employ people who, for whatever reason, either are unable to set up personal bank accounts or do not choose to. In these cases, they must take their paychecks to a check-cashing service, which charges them a high fee to convert the check into cash. Moreover, the check-cashing service may have a long approval process. Also worrisome is that employees will be carrying large amounts of cash just after using this service, which increases their risk of theft. They also run the risk of losing their paychecks prior to cashing them. Thus, the lack of a bank account poses serious problems for a company's employees.

A good solution to this problem is to set up a Visa debit card, called the Visa Paycard, for any employees requesting one, and then shift payroll funds directly to the card. This allows employees to take any amount of cash they need from an ATM, rather than the entire amount at one time from a check-cashing service. The card can also be used like a credit card, so that employees have little need to make purchases with cash. Further, the fee to convert to cash at an ATM is much lower than the fee charged by a check-cashing service. There is also less risk of theft through the card, since it is protected by a personal identification number (PIN). Employees will also receive a monthly statement showing their account activity, which they can use to get a better idea of their spending habits.

Using this card can, however, be difficult for anyone who speaks English as a second language or who cannot understand ATM instructions. To help these users, Visa makes available multilingual customer service personnel, which reduces the severity of this problem.

The Paycard has only recently been rolled out by Visa, hence is currently available only through a few banks. Contact the company's bank to see if it has this option available; if not, an alternative is to switch the payroll function to the Paymaxx Internet site (*www.paymaxx.com*), which offers the Paycard option.

Cost:

Installation time: 🕐

Use Direct Deposit

A major task for the payroll staff is to issue paychecks to employees. This task breaks down as follows: First, the checks must be printed (though this seems easy, it is all too common for the check run to fail, resulting in the manual cancellation of the first batch of checks, followed by a new print run). Next, the checks must be signed by an authorized check signer, who may have questions about payment amounts, which may require additional investigation. Third, the checks must be stuffed into envelopes and then sorted by supervisors (since they generally hand out paychecks to their employees). Fourth, the checks are distributed, usually with the exception of a few checks being held for later pick-up for those employees who are not currently on-site. If checks are stolen or lost, the payroll staff must cancel them and manually issue replacements. Finally, the person in charge of the bank reconciliation must track those checks that have not been cashed and follow up with employees to remind them to cash their checks (there are usually a few employees who prefer to cash checks only when they need the money, surprising though this may seem). In short, there are a number of steps involved in issuing payroll checks to employees. How can we eliminate some of them?

We can eliminate the printing and distribution of paychecks by using direct deposit. This best practice involves issuing payments directly to employee bank accounts. In addition to eliminating the steps involved with issuing paychecks, it carries the additional advantage of putting money in employee bank accounts immediately, so that those employees who are off-site on payday do not have to worry about how they will receive their money—it will appear in their checking accounts automatically, with no effort on their part. Also, this practice eliminates the effort of asking employees to cash their checks, since it is done automatically.

It can be difficult to get employees to switch over to direct deposit. Though the benefits to them may seem obvious, some will prefer to cash their own checks; then there are those who do not have bank accounts. To solve this problem, an organization can either force all employees to accept direct deposit, or implement the practice only with new hires while allowing existing employees to continue to receive paychecks. If employees are forced to accept direct deposit, the company can either arrange with a local bank to give them bank accounts or issue the funds to a debit card (see the preceding best practice).

Another problem for the company is the cost of this service. A typical charge by the bank is $1.00 for each transfer made, which can add up to a considerable amount if there are many employees and/or many pay periods per year. This problem can be reduced by shrinking the number of pay periods per year.

Implementing direct deposit requires the company to transfer payment information to the company's bank in the correct direct deposit format, which the bank uses to transfer money to employee bank accounts. This information transfer can be accomplished either by purchasing an add-on to a company's in-house payroll software or by paying extra to a payroll outsourcing company to provide the service; either way, there is an expense associated with starting up the service. If you have trouble finding an intermediary to make direct deposits, it can also be done through a Web site that specializes in direct deposits. For example, *www.directdeposit.com* provides this service, along with upload links from a number of popular accounting packages, such as ACCPAC, DacEasy, and Great Plains.

And because some paper-based form of notification should still be sent to employees, so that they know the details of what they have been paid, keep in mind that using direct deposit will not eliminate the steps of printing a deposit advice, stuffing it in an envelope, or distributing it (though this notification can be mailed instead of handed out in person).

An alternative is to send e-mails to employees that contain this information, though some employees may not have e-mail, or may have concerns that other people can access their e-mail messages.

Cost: 💸

Installation time: ⏰ ⏰

Use a Forms/Rates Data Warehouse for Automated Tax Filings

Any organization that operates in a number of states will have to file an inordinate number of sales and income tax returns, not to mention a plethora of lesser forms. The traditional way to meet these filing requirements is to either hire a staff of tax preparation personnel, or outsource some or all of these chores to a supplier. Either approach represents a significant cost. An alternative worth exploring is to store tax rates and forms in a database that can be used to automatically prepare tax returns in conjunction with other accounting information that is stored in either a general ledger or a data warehouse.

To make this best practice operational, you must first have a common database containing all of the information that would normally be included on a tax return. This may call for some restructuring of the chart of accounts, as well as the centralization of companywide data into a data warehouse (see the preceding best practice). This is no small task, since the information needed by each state may vary slightly from the requirements of other states, requiring subtle changes in the storage of data throughout the company that will yield the appropriate information for reporting purposes.

The second step is to obtain tax rate information and store it in a central database. This information can be located by accessing the tax agency web sites of all 50 states; but it is more easily obtained in electronic format from any of the national tax reporting services. This information can then be stored in the forms/rates data warehouse.

The next step is to create a separate program for each of the tax reports, so that the computer report issued mimics the reporting format used by each state. Then the information can be manually transferred from the computer report to a printout of the Portable Document Format (PDF) file of each state's tax form. Those programming staffs that have the time, may also want to create a report format that mirrors each state tax form. These forms then can be printed out, with all tax information on them, and immediately mailed out.

The trouble with this best practice is the exceptionally high programming cost associated with developing a completly automated solution, because there are so many tax forms to be converted to a digital format. Accordingly, it is more cost-effective to determine which tax forms share approximately the same information, and then develop an automated solution for them first. Any remaining tax forms that require special programming to automate should be reviewed on a case-by-case basis to determine whether it is cost-beneficial to complete further programming work or to leave a few reports for the tax preparation staff to complete by hand.

Cost: 💵 💵 💵

Installation time: 🕐 🕐 🕐

Reducing Staff Efforts with an Automated Clock

A major candy manufacturing facility employed hundreds of hourly employees in its operations. They all punched in their time using a manual time clock, which required the services of a full-time payroll clerk to calculate hours worked, as well as to track down employees who had forgotten to punch in or out. She also had to consult with supervisors about employees who appeared to be clocking out much later than they should, as well as those who did not take mandatory breaks. This effort became overwhelming as the facility continued to grow and add more employees.

To keep the problem from worsening, the plant controller bought an automated time clock, which had a direct linkage to the payroll clerk's computer. The plant's security officer was taught how to create bar codes with a simple bar-code label printer and accompanying lamination machine. After a brief training period for the staff and supervisors, the payroll clerk found that the bulk of her work had been eliminated—the new clock prevented employees from clocking in too early or too late, and required a supervisory override if any employees tried to do so. The system also alerted the payroll clerk when anyone had failed to clock in or out on an exception basis, and even gave the clerk the name of the employee's supervisor, so that she could track down the person immediately and correct the situation. Of course, the system also summarized all hours worked by employee, so there was no need to laboriously summarize this data.

The payroll manager concluded that the installation of just one barcoded time clock had probably saved the company from hiring a second payroll clerk to perform menial data collection and correction activities.

Summary

If improperly managed, the payroll function can require an inordinate amount of labor to run. But by using some of the best practices described in this chapter, you can streamline the function to a considerable extent, requiring far less effort by a smaller staff. Before implementing any change discussed in this chapter, be sure to run cost-benefit calculations to ensure that the contemplated changes will indeed result in increased efficiencies; a number of these best practices are expensive to implement, and so are feasible only for larger organizations with many employees.

Endnotes

1. This chapter is largely adapted with permission from Chapter 16, "Payroll Best Practices," in *Accounting Best Practices*, 2nd Ed., by Steven Bragg (New York: John Wiley & Sons, Inc., 2001).

CHAPTER 5

Compensation

After reading this chapter you will be able to

- Compute overtime pay earned under the provisions of a piece-rate plan

- Complete and submit Form 8027 to the IRS, which summarizes tip income reported by employees to the employer

- Know the paperwork to submit to the government following the end of a calendar year

- Know the types of fringe benefits that must be recorded as taxable income to employees

This chapter covers a multitude of issues surrounding employee compensation, with a particular emphasis on the types of compensation that are taxable income to employees. The chapter begins with guidelines for determining whether an employer can designate someone as an employee or contractor; next it offers guidelines for differentiating between salaried and hourly employees. The chapter then covers a number of general compensation-related topics, such as activities for which wages must be paid, the standard workweek, and payments made to temporary work agencies. The bulk of the chapter, however, is devoted to a discussion of a variety of compensation types, as well as business expenses that can be reported as gross income to employees for tax purposes. The chapter finishes with coverage of several forms used to report employee and supplier income to the government.

Employee or Contractor Status

A key compensation issue is whether someone is an employee or a contractor, since the reporting of income to the IRS varies considerably for each one, as do the tax withholding requirements of the employer. The defining criteria that establishes a person as an employee is when the company controls not only the types of work done by the person, but also *how* the work is done. An employer also controls the type of work done by a contractor, but not how the work is done. Other supporting evidence that defines an individual as a contractor is the presence of a contract between the parties; whether the contractor provides similar services to other clients; and whether the contractor is paid based on the completion of specific tasks, rather than on the passage of time.

An employer may be tempted to categorize employees as contractors even when it knows this is not the case, since the employer can avoid matching some payroll taxes by doing so. However, taking this approach leaves an employer liable for all the federal income, Social Security, and Medicare taxes that should have been withheld. Consequently, strict adherence to the rules governing the definition of an employee and contractor should be followed at all times.

Wage Exemption Guidelines

You should be aware of the general rules governing whether an employee is entitled to an hourly wage or a salary, since this can avoid complaints from employees who wish to switch their status from one to the other. The key guidelines for designating a person as being eligible for a salary are as follows:

- *Administrative.* Those in charge of an administrative department, even if they supervise no one, and anyone assisting management with long-term strategy decisions.

- *Executive.* Those who manage more than 50 percent of the time and supervise at least two employees.

- *Professional.* Those who spend at least 50 percent of their time on tasks requiring knowledge obtained through a four-year college degree (including systems analysis, design, and programming work on computer systems), even if a degree was not obtained. The position must also allow for continued independent decision making and minimal close supervision.

Wage Payment Guidelines

A number of special activities fall within the standard workday for which an employee earning an hourly wage must be compensated. The most frequently encountered activities are as follows:

- Employer-mandated charitable work
- Employer-mandated meal times when employees are required to stay in their work locations
- Employer-mandated training programs
- Employer-mandated travel between work locations
- Employer-mandated work activities
- Rest periods equal to or less than 20 minutes

Special activities falling outside the standard workday for which an employee earning an hourly wage must be compensated include the following items:

- Attendance at an employer-mandated training session
- Emergency work for the employer
- Equipment start-up or shut-down work

- Maintenance work
- Overlapping work related to shift-change problems

Workers Paid by a Temporary Agency

It is common for companies to ask a temporary agency to send workers to complete short-term jobs. The temporary agency is considered the employer of these workers if it screens and hires them and can fire them. Under these conditions, the temporary agency is liable for all tax withholdings from their pay. The company paying the temporary agency for these services is liable only for prearranged fees paid to the agency; it is not responsible for their payroll taxes.

The Workweek

The workweek is a fixed period of 168 consecutive hours that recur on a consistent basis. The start and stop times and dates can be set by management, but they should be consistently applied. And whatever the workweek is defined to be, it should be listed in the employee manual to avoid confusion about which hours worked fall into which workweek, not only for payment purposes but also for the calculation of overtime.

It is unwise to alter the stated workweek, since it may be construed as avoidance to pay overtime. For example, assume a company has a history of requiring large amounts of overtime at the end of the month in order to make its delivery targets. Suddenly company management elects to change the workweek from Monday through Sunday to Wednesday through Tuesday right in the middle of the final week in a month, thereby reducing much of the overtime hours that employees would otherwise earn to regular hours. This would be a highly suspect change of workweek that might be construed by the government as a way to avoid overtime payments.

It is, however, perfectly legitimate for different workweeks to be assigned for different departments and locations. This is particularly common when a company is acquired and elects not to conform to the acquiree's workweek. If there are many of these acquisitions, a centralized payroll department may find itself tracking every conceivable variation on a workweek, all within the same organization.

The Minimum Wage

The minimum wage is the minimum amount of money per hour that must be paid to all employees—with some restrictions by type of industry. The minimum wage is set by the federal government, though it can be overridden by local law with a higher minimum wage requirement. Consult with your state wage enforcement division to determine the local rate.

To determine if an employer is paying at least the minimum wage, summarize all forms of compensation earned during a workweek and divide it by the number of hours worked. The most common forms of compensation include *base wages, commissions, shift differentials, piece-rate pay*, and *performance bonuses*. If the calculation results in an average rate that drops below the minimum wage, then the employer must pay the difference between the actual rate paid and the minimum wage.

Example. The Close Call Company, which specializes in making rush deliveries, pays its delivery staff at a rate of $8 per delivery made. In the last week, one employee completed 25 deliveries, which entitled him to $200 in wages. However, because the minimum wage of $5.15 for the 40 hours worked should have entitled him to a base wage of $206, the company must pay him an additional $6 in order to be in compliance with the law.

Computing Pay under the Hourly Rate Plan

The hourly rate plan is by far the most common method for calculating wages for hourly employees. This involves simply multiplying the wage rate per hour times the number of hours worked during the workweek. It can be complicated by adding shift differentials, overtime, and other forms of bonus pay to the base wage rate. (The overtime calculation is covered in a later section.)

Example. Manuel Eversol works the second shift at a manufacturing facility, where he earns an extra $0.25 per hour as a shift differential, as well as a base wage of $12.50 per hour. He worked a standard 40 hours in the most recent workweek. The calculation of his total wages earned is:

($12.50 base wage + $0.25 shift differential) x 40 hours = **$510** weekly pay

Computing Pay under the Piece-Rate Plan

The piece-rate pay plan is used by companies that pay their employees at least in part based on the number of units of production completed. To calculate wages under this method, multiply the rate paid per unit of production by the number of units completed in the workweek. An employer that uses this approach must still pay its staff for overtime hours worked; to calculate this, divide the total piece-rate pay by the hours worked, then add the overtime premium to the excess hours worked. An employer can avoid this extra calculation by computing wages earned during an overtime period using a piece rate that is at least 1.5 times the regular piece rate.

Example. The Alice Company makes miniature Alice dolls and pays its staff a piece rate of $0.75 for each doll completed. One worker completes 320 dolls in a standard 40 hour workweek, which entitles her to pay of $240 (320 dolls x $0.75 piece rate). The worker then labors an extra five hours, during which time she produces an additional 42 dolls. To calculate her pay for this extra time period, her employer first calculates her regular piece-rate pay, which is $31.50 (42 dolls x $0.75 piece rate). The employer then calculates the overtime due by calculating the standard wage rate during the regular period, which was $6 per hour ($240 total pay/40 hours), resulting in a premium of $3 per hour. The employee's overtime pay is therefore $15 ($3 overtime premium x 5 hours).

The employer could also have simply set the piece rate 50 percent higher for work performed during the overtime period, which would have been $1.13 ($0.75 x 1.5). In this example, the higher piece rate would have resulted in a slightly higher payment to the employee, since the person produced slightly more than the standard number of dolls during the period.

Paying Salaries for Partial Periods

Many salaried employees begin or stop work partway through a pay period, so the payroll staff must calculate what proportion of their salary has been earned. This calculation also must be done when a pay change has been made that is effective as of a date partway through the person's pay period.

To determine the amount of a partial payment, calculate the salaried employee's hourly rate, then multiply this rate by the number of hours worked. A common approach for determining the hourly rate is to divide the total annual salary by 2,080 hours, which is the total number of work hours in a year.

Example. The Pembrose Company pays its employees on the fifteenth and last day of each month, which amounts to 24 pay periods per year. One employee, Stephanie Ortiz, has been hired partway through a pay period at an annual salary of $38,500. She starts work on the twentieth of the month, and there are seven business days left in the pay period. The payroll staff first determines her hourly rate of pay, which is $38,500/2,080 hours, or $18.51. They then calculate the number of hours left in the pay period, which is 8 hours a day x 7 working days, or 56 hours. Consequently, Ms. Ortiz's pay for her first pay period will be $18.51 x 56 hours, or $1,036.56.

Overtime Pay

Overtime is a pay premium of 50 percent of the regular rate of pay that is earned by employees on all hours worked beyond 40 hours in a standard workweek. This calculation can vary for individual states, so be sure to check with the local state agency that tracks wage law issues to see if there are variations from the federally mandated rule.

When calculating overtime, the employer does not have to include in the 40 base hours such special hours as vacations, holidays, sick time, or jury duty.

Example. Ahmad Nefret is a welder who works 47 hours during a standard workweek at an hourly wage of $22 per hour. The overtime premium he will be paid is 50 percent of his hourly wage, or $11. The calculation of his total pay is as follows:

47 hours x regular pay rate of $22/hour = $ 1,034

7 hours x overtime premium of $11/hour = $ 77

Total pay = **$ 1,111**

Example. Jamie Hildebrandt worked 33 hours during the four-day workweek following Labor Day. Though her employer will pay her for 41 hours worked (eight hours of holiday time plus 33 hours worked), there will be no overtime paid out, since eight of the hours were not actually worked.

Commissions

An employee earns a commission when he or she secures a sale on behalf of a business. The commission may be earned when an invoice is issued or when cash is received from the customer. The commission calculation may be quite complex, involving a percentage of the dollar amount sold, a fixed fee per sale, a bonus override for the sale of specific items, or perhaps a commission-sharing arrangement with another member of the sales force. In any case, commissions are considered regular wages for tax withholding purposes, so all normal income tax withholdings, as well as taxes for Social Security, Medicare, and FUTA must be deducted from them.

Example. Mr. Charles Everson is a salesperson for the Screaming Fiddler Company. His basic compensation deal is a 6 percent commission on all sales at the time they are invoiced, plus $25 each for any fiddle that is currently overstocked. He sells two of the Melodic series fiddles for $600 each, and three of the overstocked Kid's Mini models for $450 each. His compensation is as follows:

2 x $600 Melodic series fiddles = $1,200 x 6% commission = $72

3 x $450 Kid's Mini series fiddles = $1,350 x 6% commission = $81

Bonus on sales of overstocked Kid's Mini models = $75

Total = **$228**

Tips

Tips are paid directly to employees by customers for services performed. Employees who receive tips must report them to the employer by the tenth day of the month after the month in which the tips were received, except when total tips for the month are less than $20. This information should be reported to the employer on Form 4070, "Employee's Report of Tips to Employer".

The employer is required to withhold income, Social Security, and Medicare taxes from employee tips. These deductions are frequently made from employee base wages, rather than their tips, since employees do not usually contribute their tip income back to the employer so taxes can be withheld from it. If, by the tenth day of the following month there are insufficient employee funds from which to withhold the designated amount of taxes, the employer no longer has to collect it. If there are some employee funds on hand but not enough to cover all taxes to be withheld, then the withholdings should be first for Social Security and Medicare on all regular wages, then for federal income taxes on regular wages, next for Social Security and Medicare taxes on tips, and finally on income taxes for tips. Also, if the employer does not have enough reportable wages for an employee to withhold the full amount of required taxes, the employer must still provide the full amount of matching taxes.

Example. Alice Mane is a waitress at the Bowers Café. In the past month, she reported $390 in tip income, while her employer paid $120 in base wages. The Bowers Café needs to deduct the following amounts from her total pay:

	Tips	Wages	Total Income
Gross Pay	$390.00	$120.00	$510.00
Federal income tax	78.00	24.00	102.00
Social Security	24.18	7.44	31.62
Medicare	5.66	1.74	7.40
Net Pay	**282.16**	**86.82**	**368.98**

The employer finds that the total withholdings on both tip and wage income for Ms. Mane is $141.02. However, only $120 was paid out as wages, so the entire $120 must be deducted. The first types of taxes to be deducted from the $120 will be the Social Security and Medicare taxes on her regular pay, which total $9.18 and leave $110.82 available for other taxes. Next in line are the federal income taxes on her regular pay, which are for $24, leaving $86.82 available for other taxes.

Next in order of priority are Social Security and Medicare taxes on her tip income, which total $29.84 and leave $56.98 available for the last deduction, which is the federal income tax withholding on her tip income. By allocating the remaining $56.98 to her federal income tax withholding, the company has paid off all her other taxes, leaving her responsible for $21.02 in unpaid federal income taxes.

Back Pay

Back pay is frequently paid to an employee as part of an arbitration award, perhaps related to an unjustified termination or an incorrectly delayed wage increase. Whatever the reason for the back pay, it should be treated as regular wages for tax withholding purposes. However, some recent court cases have more tightly defined the types of back pay awards that are subject to withholding, so consult with a lawyer to determine the correct treatment.

Business Expense Reimbursements

If an employee submits substantiation of all expenses for which reimbursement is requested, then the corresponding payment from the employer to the employee is not considered income to the employee. Substantiation can take the following forms:

- A receipt that clearly indicates the amount of the expense.
- Per diem rates that do not exceed the per diem rates listed in IRS Publication 1542, which itemizes per diems for a variety of locations throughout the country. If an acceptable per diem rate is used, then travel, meals, and entertainment expense receipts for those days do not have to be submitted. If an employee is traveling to or from the home office, then the IRS allows a per diem on travel days of up to three-fourths of the normal rate.

Meals and entertainment present a special situation from the employer's perspective. Only 50 percent of these costs are allowed as tax deductions on the employer's tax return, though all of the expenses claimed by employees can be reimbursed to them without it being listed as income to them. Also, meal expenses incurred by the company on behalf of an employee are not wages to the employee if they are incurred for the employer's convenience and are provided on the employer's premises.

Health insurance costs, including expenses incurred for an employee's family, are not considered employee wages, but must be recorded as wages in Subchapter S corporations for those employees who own more than 2 percent of the business.

If an employee lives away from home for less than one year on company business, the living costs paid to the employee for this period are not considered taxable income. However, once the duration exceeds one year, the employee is considered to have permanently moved to the new location, rendering all such subsequent payments taxable income to the employee.

Such fringe benefits as tickets to entertainment events, free travel, and company cars should be recorded as employee gross income. The amount of incremental gross income added should be the fair market value of the fringe benefit, minus its cost to the employee, minus any deductions allowed by law.

Example. Brad Harvest obtains discounted season tickets to the local baseball team through his company. The market price for the tickets is $2,500, but he only pays his employer $750 for them. The difference of $1,750 is considered income to Mr. Harvest, and should be reported as such to the IRS.

Club Memberships

Club dues are taxable income to the employee, except for that portion of the dues that are business related, which must be substantiated. Clubs that fall into this category are airline and hotel clubs, as well as golf, athletic, and country clubs. The portion of the club dues that are personal income to the employee can be treated as a wage expense to the employer for tax purposes.

Example. Brad Harvest is a member of an airline club, which allows him access to club facilities at a variety of airports around the country. He estimates that he uses these facilities 70 percent of the time while he is traveling on company business. He can substantiate this estimate with travel records. The annual cost of the membership is $400. Accordingly, only 30 percent of the cost, or $120, is recognizable as his personal income.

Education Reimbursement

The reimbursement of an employee's educational expenses by the employer is not income to the employee if the education being reimbursed is related to his or her current job and will either serve to maintain or improve the person's skills for conducting that job. However, the payments *are* income if the education is undertaken to promote the person or shift him or her into an unrelated position requiring different skills.

An employer can change the reportable income situation somewhat by creating an educational assistance plan (EAP). This is a written plan that an employer creates on behalf of its employees, who are the only recipients of educational assistance under the plan. The plan is only acceptable to the IRS if it does not favor highly compensated employees or shareholders, does not give employees the option to receive cash instead of educational assistance, and is launched with a reasonable amount of notice to employees. For this plan, employees are considered to be current staff; long-term leased staff; former staff who retired, were laid off, or who left due to disability; or a sole proprietor or business partner. Expenses covered under the plan include school fees, supplies, books, and equipment related to training; they do not include expenses for lodging, meals, and transportation, nor education related to sports or hobbies unless this education is both related to the business and is part of a degree program. If all of these conditions are met, then using an EAP will allow each employee to exclude up to $5,250 per year for educational assistance paid by the employer.

Employee Achievement Awards

Employee achievement awards can be excluded from employee gross income, but only if the awards are tangible property, given in recognition of length of service with the business or for safety achievement and as part of a meaningful presentation. This exclusion is up to $400 per year. A higher limit of $1,600 applies if the awards are made under a written plan that does not favor highly compensated employees. The total exclusion for both types of awards is $1,600, not the combined total of $2,000.

Example. Marion Smith receives achievement awards for every quarter during which she works in a meat-packing plant without being injured. Every quarter, she is paid a bonus of $50 during a formal achievement ceremony. This payment is taxable gross income to her, because it is a cash award instead of a tangible award.

Golden Parachute Payments

So-called golden parachute payments are made to employees or officers as a result of a change in corporate control or ownership. This type of payment is subject to all normal payroll tax withholdings. In addition, if the payment is more than three times a person's average annual compensation for the past five years, the employer must also withhold a 20 percent excise tax for the incremental amount exceeding this limit.

Example. The Golden Egg Company has laid one by being sold to a large international conglomerate. Under the terms of a golden parachute agreement, its president, Jason Fleece, is awarded a payment of $500,000. His average pay for the past five years was $125,000. Three times this amount, or $375,000, is the limit above which a 20 percent excise tax will be imposed. The amount subject to this tax is $125,000, so the company must deduct $25,000 from the total payment, in addition to all normal payroll taxes on the full $500,000 paid.

Life Insurance

The value of group term life insurance paid for by the employer is excluded from income for the first $50,000 of life insurance purchased. The excess value of life insurance coverage over this amount must be included in employee income. This income is only subject to Social Security and Medicare taxes. Use the IRS table in Exhibit 5.1 to determine the fair market value of group term life insurance per $1,000 of insurance for a range of age brackets.

EXHIBIT 5.1

Fair Market Value Multiplier for Group Term Life Insurance

Age Bracket	Value per $1,000 per Month
Under age 25	$0.05
Age 25–29	$0.06
Age 30–34	$0.08
Age 35–39	$0.09
Age 40–44	$0.10
Age 45–49	$0.15
Age 50–54	$0.23
Age 55–59	$0.43
Age 60–64	$0.66
Age 65–69	$1.27
Age 70 and above	$2.06

Example. Group term insurance in the amount of $80,000 is purchased for a 54-year-old employee, who contributes $2 per month to this benefit. The first $50,000 of this amount is excluded from the employee's gross income. To calculate the value of the remaining $30,000, divide it by 1,000 and multiply the result by $0.23 (as taken from the table in Exhibit 5.1 for the 50–54 age bracket), which yields a fair value of $6.90 per month. Then subtract the employee's $2 monthly contribution to arrive at a net monthly value received of $4.90. Next multiply the monthly value of $4.90 by 12 in order to obtain the full-year value of the life insurance, which is $58.80. The $58.80 should be reported as the employee's gross income.

The preceding scenario does not apply if the employer is the beneficiary of the life insurance. This would not be a benefit to the employee, and therefore its fair value should not be included in his or her gross income.

IN THE REAL WORLD

Route Recommendations through Your Auditors

The controller of a private, family-owned business was concerned about the family's reaction if he took a hard stand on reporting a number of expenses as gross income to the family members, since the family had a history of reacting poorly to these suggestions. Specific issues were extensive personal use of company cars and club memberships, as well as large amounts of life insurance on family members paid for by the company. The controller asked the external auditors for advice, and they elected to include these issues in their management letter to the family. This step gave the controller a source of authority for implementing the changes, which were now grudgingly accepted by the affected family members.

Meal Breaks

Some organizations will pay employees for a fixed amount of time off for a meal break if they work more than a set number of hours in a day. For example, if employees work more than 10 hours in a day, they are awarded an extra half-hour of pay as long as they turn in a receipt as evidence of having purchased a meal. This extra amount is typically paid at an overtime pay rate.

If an employer gives time off for a meal break partway through a shift, such as lunch, this does not have to be paid time as long as the employees are relieved from all work responsibilities during the time period. If they are required to be on call during this period, then the employer would otherwise have had to pay someone else to take that position, so employees should receive compensation for this type of meal break.

TIPS & TECHNIQUES

Though it may be company policy to automatically deduct some amount of time from the reported working time of its nonexempt employees to account for a lunch break, there should be a system in place that verifies the actual absence of employees from their places of work. This is necessary in case employees claim they had to work through their lunch breaks and were not compensated for this effort. Possible verification techniques to require employees to log themselves in and out of the payroll system at lunch time (though this tends to result in a number of missing card punches), to lock down the work area during the lunch break, or to have substitutes take their places and record for whom they were working during the lunch break.

Moving Expenses

Employers may ask employees to move to a different company location. If the employer pays a third party or reimburses the moving employee for actual costs incurred, there is no reportable income to the employee. This applies only if the employee's new workplace is at least 50 miles further from his or her residence than the former workplace; and the employee must work out of the new location for at least 39 weeks during the 12-month period following the move. Otherwise, the move transaction will have the appearance of being a simple compensation by the employer to the employee, who uses the funds to move to a new location while still working at the same place.

If the employer pays the employee a fixed amount to complete the move, and if the actual expenses incurred are less than the payment, then the difference is reported as income to the employee.

Example. The Fragrant Perfume Company asks its lead software developer to move to New York City, where she can create a new logistics system for herbs being shipped through the New York port facilities. The new location is 250 miles away from her previous position at company headquarters. The company pays her $20,000 to complete the move, against which she can substantiate incurred expenses of $16,000. The difference of $4,000 is gross income, from which the company must deduct payroll taxes.

Outplacement Services

An employer may offer resumé assistance, counseling, and other outplacement services to employees it has terminated. The value of these services is not recorded as income for the affected employees, unless the employer receives a substantial business benefit from providing the services and the services would have been reimbursable business expenses to the employees if they had paid for them directly. These rules will usually apply, since an employer can claim a business benefit in the form of good morale of the remaining employees, who can see that terminated employees are being well taken care of. If these rules do not apply, then the employer must withhold taxes on the fair market value of the services.

If the services are provided in exchange for severance pay, then the employer must withhold taxes on them. This latter situation arises when employees ask that the services be provided in an attempt to mask the offsetting compensation, so they can avoid paying payroll taxes.

Personal Use of Company Vehicles

A number of taxation rules apply if an employee drives a company vehicle for personal use. The basic rule is that personal use of this asset is taxable income to the employee. The following rules apply:

- If the vehicle is a specialty one, such as a garbage truck, then there is an assumption that no personal use will occur, so using this type of vehicle will never result in taxable income to the employee.

- If the employer requires the employee to use the vehicle to commute to work, an enforced company policy prohibits the vehicle from all other personal use, and the employee is not a highly compensated employee, director, or officer, then the employee will be charged $1.50 of taxable income for each commute in each direction.

- If the employee can substantiate the amount of business use to which the vehicle was put, including dates, miles, and the purpose of each trip, all remaining miles are assumed to be for personal use. In this scenario, it is possible to determine the income charged to the employee by multiplying the IRS-designated rate of 34.5¢ per mile (which is revised annually) by the number of miles of personal use, less 5.5¢ per mile if the employee pays for all fuel. This approach is only allowable if the fair market value of the vehicle is approximately $15,000 or less (also revised annually) and the car is driven at least 10,000 miles per year in total. If the situation exceeds these restrictions, then the alternative approach is to multiply the proportion of personal miles used on the vehicle by its annual lease value (which is a percentage of a vehicle's fair market value, as supplied by the IRS) and record this amount as personal income to the employee.

Example. The president of Hot Rod Custom Modifiers, Inc. drives a company-owned Ferrari. The value of the car is clearly beyond $15,000, so he must record as personal income the proportion of his personal use of the car multiplied by its annual lease value of $28,000. The proportion of his personal use was 78 percent, so the company must record 78 percent of $28,000, or $21,840, as his gross income associated with his use of the car.

Reduced Interest Loans

An employer may loan money to employees. When this happens, if the amount of the loan is greater than $10,000 and is at an interest rate less than the Applicable Federal Rate (AFR), the difference is taxable income to the employee. This income is subject to Social Security and Medicare taxes, but not income tax withholding. The current AFR is available on the IRS web site at *www.irs.gov* or by calling 800-829-1040.

Example. An employer loans $1,000,000 to one of its officers so the individual can purchase a new home. The stated interest rate on the loan is 3 percent, while the AFR is 7 percent. The amount of income reportable by the employee is the 4 percent difference between the two rates, or $40,000.

Travel Time

The time spent to travel back and forth from work to home, and vice versa, is not time for which the employer is liable to pay compensation, unless an employee is called away from home for emergency work and must travel for a significant period of time to reach the location specified.

If an employee is traveling among multiple locations as part of his or her job, such as is experienced by a traveling salesperson, then this travel time is paid time. However, the amount of paid time only corresponds to those hours during which an employee works during a regular work day.

Example. Herbert Bailes normally works from 8:00 A.M. to 4:00 P.M., Monday through Friday. However, a special project requires him to stay at an off-site location and travel home on Saturday, which occupies him from 7:00 A.M. to noon. Of the five hours spent traveling on Saturday, the hours in the time period from 8:00 A.M. to noon can be claimed for wage reimbursement, since they fall within his regularly scheduled workday.

Annual Paperwork Reminders

There are several documents that the payroll department must issue or process at the end of a calendar year. Place the following paperwork-related items on the payroll activities calendar so they are not forgotten:

- Remind employees to review their withholding status and submit a new W-4 form if changes are in order.
- Remind employees who claimed total exemption from income tax withholding to submit a new W-4 form by the end of December.
- Give a completed W-2 form to all employees by the end of January.
- Give a completed 1099 form to all qualifying suppliers by the end of January.

- Send Copy A of all completed W-2 forms to the Social Security Administration by the end of January.

- Send a copy of all completed 1099 forms to the IRS with a transmittal Form 1096 by the end of January.

- Verify that all Forms W-2 and W-3 sum up to the totals listed on the Form 941, or be aware of the differences between the two sets of numbers.

The W-2 Form

The W-2 form contains the information needed by employees to file their annual income tax returns with the government. It itemizes the various types of income paid by the employer to the employee during the past calendar year. If an employee works for several employers during a year, then each one must provide a completed W-2 form. Also, if an employer changes payroll systems during the year, it is not uncommon to issue a separate W-2 form from each system for that period of the year during which each payroll system was recording compensation paid to employees.

An employer can send W-2 forms to its employees either in a paper or electronic format. However, if it uses the electronic format, it must first obtain permission from each employee to do so, which may be withdrawn with 30 days notice. No matter which format is used, the W-2 form must be sent to employees no later than January 31 following the year for which the form is being provided. Copies of these completed forms must also be sent to the IRS, along with a transmittal form. An example of the W-2 form is shown in Exhibit 5.2.

The employer fills out the form by listing the employer's name, address, and identifying information in the upper left corner of the form, followed by the same information for the employee in the lower left corner. The right side contains many numbered blocks in which the

EXHIBIT 5.2

W-2 Form

a Control number	22222	Void ☐	For Official Use Only ▶ OMB No. 1545-0008		

b Employer identification number		1 Wages, tips, other compensation $	2 Federal income tax withheld $
c Employer's name, address, and ZIP code		3 Social security wages $	4 Social security tax withheld $
		5 Medicare wages and tips $	6 Medicare tax withheld $
		7 Social security tips $	8 Allocated tips $
d Employee's social security number		9 Advance EIC payment $	10 Dependent care benefits $
e Employee's first name and initial Last name		11 Nonqualified plans $	12a See instructions for box 12 $
		13 Statutory employee ☐ Retirement plan ☐ Third-party sick pay ☐	12b $
		14 Other	12c $
			12d $
f Employee's address and ZIP code			

15 State	Employer's state ID number	16 State wages, tips, etc. $	17 State income tax $	18 Local wages, tips, etc. $	19 Local income tax $	20 Locality name
		$	$	$	$	

Form **W-2** Wage and Tax Statement (99)

2002

(Rev. February 2002)

Cat. No. 10134D

Department of the Treasury—Internal Revenue Service

For Privacy Act and Paperwork Reduction Act Notice, see separate instructions.

Copy A For Social Security Administration—Send this entire page with Form W-3 to the Social Security Administration; photocopies are **not** acceptable.

Do Not Cut, Fold, or Staple Forms on This Page — Do Not Cut, Fold, or Staple Forms on This Page

various types of wages paid are listed. The following list describes the most commonly used boxes in the form:

Box 1: Wages, tips, other compensation.

Include in this box the total amount of all wages, salaries, tip income, commissions, bonuses, and other types of compensation paid to the employee.

Box 2: Federal income tax withheld.

The federal income taxes withheld by the company from the employee's pay are recorded here. *Only* federal taxes should be included here, since state income taxes withheld are listed in Box 17 at the bottom of the report.

Box 3: Social Security wages.

The total amount of compensation paid that is subject to Social Security taxes should be listed here. This means that anyone's pay that exceeds the statutory limit set for Social Security wages in any given year will see only the statutory limit listed in this box.

Box 4: Social Security tax withheld.
List the total amount of Social Security taxes withheld for the calendar year in this box.

Box 5: Medicare wages and tips.
The total amount of all compensation paid during the year should be listed here. Unlike Social Security, there is no upper limit on the wages on which Medicare taxes are paid, so in most cases the number listed in this box will be the same as the one listed in Box 1.

Box 6: Medicare tax withheld.
List the total amount of Medicare taxes withheld for the calendar year in this box.

Box 12c: Cost of group term life insurance over $50,000.
As explained earlier in the "Life Insurance" section, the value of all life insurance purchased by an employer on behalf of its employees in excess of $50,000 must be reported as income. This portion of total compensation is itemized in Box 12 next to a signifying letter "G." There is also room for additional special payments in this box.

Box 12k: Excise tax on golden parachute payments.
As explained earlier in the "Golden Parachute Payments" section, the employer must withhold a 20 percent excise tax on excessively large golden parachute payments. The total excise tax is listed in Box 12 next to a signifying letter "K."

In addition, state and local wage and income tax withholding information is listed across the bottom of the form in Boxes 15 through 20.

Employer's Annual Tip Income Tax Return

An employer is required to submit a Form 8027, "Employer's Annual Information Return of Tip Income and Allocated Tips," to the IRS no later than February 28 of each year following the reporting calendar year. This form is used by large eating establishments to report tips earned by employees. If an employer runs multiple eating establishments, a separate form must be completed for each one. The form is not used to submit any taxes, but rather to give the IRS an idea of the amount of employee tip income as a proportion of total receipts for an establishment. A sample Form 8027 is shown in Exhibit 5.3.

What the IRS is trying to determine with this form is whether an establishment's tipped employees are failing to report some portion of their tip income to the business. To do this, lines 1 and 2 of the form are used to determine the proportion of tips that customers are charging through their credit cards, which can be easily proven by a review of the underlying charge receipts. This proportion is then compared to the proportion of actual total receipts reported to the business by its employees to the total amount of gross receipts for the business. Ideally, the two percentages should match. If the latter percentage is lower, this indicates that employees are not reporting all of their tip income. If this appears to be a problem, the business owner can call the IRS at 800-829-1040 or search for "Voluntary Compliance Agreements" on the IRS web site at *www.irs.gov*. This program gives assistance in educating employees about their obligations in reporting tip income.

The 1099 Form

The 1099 form is issued to all suppliers to whom a business pays (to quote the IRS):

> . . . at least $600 in rents, services (including parts and materials), prizes and awards, other income payments, medical and health care payments, crop insurance proceeds, cash payments for fish (or other aquatic life) . . .

EXHIBIT 5.3

Employer's Annual Tip Income Return Form

Form **8027**	**Employer's Annual Information Return of Tip Income and Allocated Tips**	OMB No. 1545-0714
Department of the Treasury Internal Revenue Service	► See separate instructions.	**2001**

		Type of establishment **(mark only one checkbox)**
Use IRS label. Make any necessary changes. Otherwise, please type or print.	Name of establishment Number and street (see instructions)　　　Employer identification number City or town, state, and ZIP code	☐ 1 Evening meals only ☐ 2 Evening and other meals ☐ 3 Meals other than evening meals ☐ 4 Alcoholic beverages

Employer's name (same name as on Form 941)	**Establishment number** (see instructions)

Number and street (P.O. box, if applicable)	Apt. or suite no.

City, state, and ZIP code (if a foreign address, see instructions)

Does this establishment accept credit cards or other charges?	Yes ☐ (lines 1 and 2 **must** be completed) No ☐	Mark **if:** Amended Return ☐ Final Return ☐

1	Total charged tips for calendar year 2001	**1**	
2	Total charge receipts showing charged tips (see instructions)	**2**	
3	Total amount of service charges of less than 10% paid as wages to employees	**3**	
4a	Total tips reported by indirectly tipped employees	**4a**	
b	Total tips reported by directly tipped employees . . . . **Note:** *Complete the Employer's Optional Worksheet for Tipped Employees on page 4 of the instructions to determine potential unreported tips of your employees.*	**4b**	
c	Total tips reported (add lines 4a and 4b)	**4c**	
5	Gross receipts from food or beverage operations (see instructions)	**5**	
6	Multiply line 5 by 8% (.08) or the lower rate shown here ► _____ granted by the IRS. (Attach a copy of the IRS determination letter to this return.) . . . . **Note:** *If you have allocated tips using other than the calendar year (semimonthly, biweekly, quarterly, etc.), mark an "X" on line 6 and enter the amount of allocated tips from your records on line 7.*	**6**	
7	Allocation of tips. If line 6 is more than line 4c, enter the excess here . . . . ► This amount must be allocated as tips to tipped employees working in this establishment. Mark the checkbox below that shows the method used for the allocation. (Show the portion, if any, attributable to each employee in box 8 of the employee's Form W-2.)	**7**	
a	Allocation based on hours-worked method (see instructions for restriction). . . . . ☐ **Note:** *If you marked the checkbox in line 7a, enter the average number of employee hours worked per business day during the payroll period. (see instructions)* _____		
b	Allocation based on gross receipts method . . . . ☐		
c	Allocation based on good-faith agreement (Attach a copy of the agreement.) . . . ☐		

8 Enter the total number of directly tipped employees at this establishment during 2001 ►

Under penalties of perjury, I declare that I have examined this return, including accompanying schedules and statements, and to the best of my knowledge and belief, it is true, correct, and complete.

Signature ►　　　　　　　　　　　Title ►　　　　　　　　　　Date ►

For Privacy Act and Paperwork Reduction Act Notice, see page 4 of the separate instructions. 　Cat. No. 49989U　 Form **8027** (2001)

✱

As with the W-2 form, this form must be issued to suppliers as well as to the IRS, no later than January 31 of the year following the reporting year.

This form is not issued if the supplier is a corporation or if the payments are for rent to real estate agents; telegrams, telephone, freight or storage; wages paid to employees; business travel allowances paid to employees; and payments made to tax-exempt organizations. An example of the 1099 form is shown in Exhibit 5.4.

The 1099 form is similar to the W-2 form in that the upper left corner of the form contains employer contact information and the lower left corner contains supplier contact information. The right side of the report contains a number of boxes for itemizing the types of payments made to suppliers. The most commonly used box is number 7, "Nonemployee

EXHIBIT 5.4

1099 Form

9595	☐ VOID ☐ CORRECTED		
PAYER'S name, street address, city, state, ZIP code, and telephone no.	**1** Rents $	OMB No. 1545-0115	**Miscellaneous Income**
	2 Royalties $	**2002**	
	3 Other income $	Form **1099-MISC**	**Copy A**
PAYER'S Federal identification number	RECIPIENT'S identification number	**4** Federal income tax withheld $	**For Internal Revenue Service Center**
		5 Fishing boat proceeds $	**6** Medical and health care payments $	**File with Form 1096.**
RECIPIENT'S name		**7** Nonemployee compensation $	**8** Substitute payments in lieu of dividends or interest $	For Privacy Act and Paperwork Reduction Act
Street address (including apt. no.)		**9** Payer made direct sales of $5,000 or more of consumer products to a buyer (recipient) for resale ▶ ☐	**10** Crop insurance proceeds $	Notice, see the **2002 General Instructions for**
City, state, and ZIP code		**11**	**12**	**Forms 1099, 1098, 5498,**
Account number (optional)	2nd TIN not. ☐	**13** Excess golden parachute payments $	**14** Gross proceeds paid to an attorney $	**and W-2G.**
15		**16** State tax withheld $ $	**17** State/Payer's state no.	**18** State income $ $

Form **1099-MISC** Cat. No. 14425J Department of the Treasury - Internal Revenue Service

Do Not Cut or Separate Forms on This Page — Do Not Cut or Separate Forms on This Page

133

compensation," which is a catchall for the majority of payments made, unless they are specified in one of the other boxes. Box 4 is also needed if the company cannot obtain a taxpayer identification number (see next paragraph) from a supplier, in which case it must withhold 30 percent on payments made and report the withheld amount here.

The key factor for the average business is to determine if its suppliers are corporations. This is most easily done by issuing a W-9 form, "Request for Taxpayer Identification Number and Certification," on which the supplier states its form of legal organization and identification number, which the company can then use to issue a Form 1099, if necessary. A sample W-9 form is shown in Exhibit 5.5.

The W-9 is a simple form. The supplier fills out the identification information in the top block, enters an identification number in Part I, and signs the document in Part II. Suppliers may change their form of legal organization from time to time, so a company seeking to be in complete compliance with the law may want to consider making an annual W-9 mailing to all of its suppliers, so it has documentary proof of why it is (or is not) issuing 1099 forms.

TIPS & TECHNIQUES

Rather than go to the expense of making an annual mailing of W-9 forms to suppliers, you can simply e-mail them a PDF file that contains the form's image. Suppliers can then print the form directly from the e-mail program and either mail or fax back the completed form. To take advantage of this tip, however, you must compile a database of e-mail addresses for the accounting contacts at all suppliers. If this information is not available for some suppliers, then a supplemental mailing is typically required to account for them.

EXHIBIT 5.5

W-9 Form

Form **W-9** (Rev. January 2002) Department of the Treasury Internal Revenue Service	**Request for Taxpayer** **Identification Number and Certification**	Give form to the requester. Do not send to the IRS.

Name

Business name, if different from above

Check appropriate box: ☐ Individual/Sole proprietor ☐ Corporation ☐ Partnership ☐ Other ▶ .... ☐ Exempt from backup withholding

Address (number, street, and apt. or suite no.)

Requester's name and address (optional)

City, state, and ZIP code

List account number(s) here (optional)

Print or type — See Specific Instructions on page 2.

Part I   Taxpayer Identification Number (TIN)

Enter your TIN in the appropriate box. For individuals, this is your social security number (SSN). **However, for a resident alien, sole proprietor, or disregarded entity, see the Part I instructions on page 2.** For other entities, it is your employer identification number (EIN). If you do not have a number, see **How to get a TIN** on page 2.

Note: *If the account is in more than one name, see the chart on page 2 for guidelines on whose number to enter.*

Social security number

or

Employer identification number

Part II   Certification

Under penalties of perjury, I certify that:

1. The number shown on this form is my correct taxpayer identification number (or I am waiting for a number to be issued to me), **and**

2. I am not subject to backup withholding because: **(a)** I am exempt from backup withholding, or **(b)** I have not been notified by the Internal Revenue Service (IRS) that I am subject to backup withholding as a result of a failure to report all interest or dividends, or **(c)** the IRS has notified me that I am no longer subject to backup withholding, **and**

3. I am a U.S. person (including a U.S. resident alien).

Certification instructions. You must cross out item **2** above if you have been notified by the IRS that you are currently subject to backup withholding because you have failed to report all interest and dividends on your tax return. For real estate transactions, item **2** does not apply. For mortgage interest paid, acquisition or abandonment of secured property, cancellation of debt, contributions to an individual retirement arrangement (IRA), and generally, payments other than interest and dividends, you are not required to sign the Certification, but you must provide your correct TIN. (See the instructions on page 2.)

Sign Here	Signature of U.S. person ▶	Date ▶

Purpose of Form

A person who is required to file an information return with the IRS must get your correct taxpayer identification number (TIN) to report, for example, income paid to you, real estate transactions, mortgage interest you paid, acquisition or abandonment of secured property, cancellation of debt, or contributions you made to an IRA.

Use Form W-9 only if you are a U.S. person (including a resident alien), to give your correct TIN to the person requesting it (the requester) and, when applicable, to:

1. Certify the TIN you are giving is correct (or you are waiting for a number to be issued),

2. Certify you are not subject to backup withholding, or

3. Claim exemption from backup withholding if you are a U.S. exempt payee.

If you are a foreign person, use the appropriate Form W-8. See **Pub. 515,** Withholding of Tax on Nonresident Aliens and Foreign Entities.

Note: *If a requester gives you a form other than Form W-9 to request your TIN, you must use the requester's form if it is substantially similar to this Form W-9.*

What is backup withholding? Persons making certain payments to you must under certain conditions withhold and pay to the IRS 30% of such payments **after** December 31, 2001 (29% **after** December 31, 2003). This is called "backup withholding." Payments that may be subject to backup withholding include interest, dividends, broker and barter exchange transactions, rents, royalties, nonemployee pay, and certain payments from fishing boat operators. Real estate transactions are not subject to backup withholding.

You will **not** be subject to backup withholding on payments you receive if you give the requester your correct TIN, make the proper certifications, and report all your taxable interest and dividends on your tax return.

Payments you receive will be subject to backup withholding if:

1. You do not furnish your TIN to the requester, or

2. You do not certify your TIN when required (see the Part II instructions on page 2 for details), or

3. The IRS tells the requester that you furnished an incorrect TIN, or

4. The IRS tells you that you are subject to backup withholding because you did not report all your interest and dividends on your tax return (for reportable interest and dividends only), or

5. You do not certify to the requester that you are not subject to backup withholding under 4 above (for reportable interest and dividend accounts opened after 1983 only).

Certain payees and payments are exempt from backup withholding. See the instructions on page 2 and the separate **Instructions for the Requester of Form W-9.**

Penalties

Failure to furnish TIN. If you fail to furnish your correct TIN to a requester, you are subject to a penalty of $50 for each such failure unless your failure is due to reasonable cause and not to willful neglect.

Civil penalty for false information with respect to withholding. If you make a false statement with no reasonable basis that results in no backup withholding, you are subject to a $500 penalty.

Criminal penalty for falsifying information. Willfully falsifying certifications or affirmations may subject you to criminal penalties including fines and/or imprisonment.

Misuse of TINs. If the requester discloses or uses TINs in violation of Federal law, the requester may be subject to civil and criminal penalties.

Cat. No. 10231X   Form **W-9** (Rev. 1-2002)

Summary

The wage rules described in this chapter cover the majority of situations in which an employer will find itself. In cases where more detailed explanation of the rules is required for specific industries or for scenarios not described here, go to the IRS web site at *www.irs.gov* and download its *Publication 15-B, Employer's Tax Guide to Fringe Benefits*. As its name implies, this publication covers a wide range of fringe benefit exclusion rules, ranging from accident and health benefits to working condition benefits. It also addresses fringe benefit valuation rules and rules for withholding, depositing, and reporting taxes.

CHAPTER 6

Benefits

After reading this chapter you will be able to

- Know what proportion of medical payments to highly compensated employees should be considered taxable income to them

- Know the terms under which COBRA insurance must be offered to terminated employees

- Learn how the payment of disability insurance by a company or through employee pretax income will impact the taxability of any benefits received from the insurance

- Learn how to potentially reduce the cost of workers' compensation insurance

Though it may appear that the extension of benefits to employees is more a paperwork-laden human resources function than a payroll function, there are a number of payroll issues involving the amount and limitation of related payroll deductions, the taxability of benefits received, and the reporting of those benefits to the IRS. This chapter addresses these issues, and more, in respect to cafeteria plans, various types of medical insurance, leaves of absence, life insurance, pension plans, sick and disability pay, stock options, and workers' compensation insurance.

Cafeteria Plans

A cafeteria plan allows employees to pay for some benefits with pretax dollars, so that the amount of taxable income to them is reduced. In its simplest form, a *Premium-Only Plan* (POP) allows employees to take employer-required medical insurance deductibles from their pretax income. This version of the cafeteria plan requires almost no effort to administer, and is essentially invisible to employees. The primary impact to them is that the amount of taxes taken out of their paychecks is slightly reduced.

A more comprehensive cafeteria plan includes a Flexible Spending Account (FSA), which allows employees to have money withheld from their pay on a pretax basis and stored in a fund, which they can draw down by being reimbursed for medical or dependent care expenses.

Example. Allison Schoening has a long-term medical condition that she knows will require a multitude of prescriptions over the plan year. She knows the prescription co-pays will cost her at least $800 during the year. Accordingly, at the beginning of the year, she elects to have a total of $800 deducted from her pay in equal installments over the course of the year. When she pays for a co-pay, she keeps the receipt and forwards it to the payroll department, which reimburses her for it from the funds that she has already had deducted from her pay.

By having funds withdrawn from their pay prior to the calculation of taxes, employees will not pay any taxes (e.g., income taxes, Social Security taxes, or Medicare taxes) on the withdrawn funds.

Example. To continue the previous example, Allison Schoening earns $40,000 per year. The total of all taxes taken out of her pay, including federal and state income taxes, Social Security, and Medicare taxes, is 27 percent. Her net take-home pay, after also taking out $800 for the previously described medical expenses, is $28,400, which is calculated as

(($40,000 x (1–27%)) - $800). When she enrolls in the cafeteria plan and has $800 removed from her pay on a pretax basis to pay for the medical expenses, her take-home pay, net of medical costs, increases to $28,616, which is calculated as (($40,000 - $800) x (1–27%)). The increase in her take-home pay of $216 is entirely attributable to the removal of medical costs from her pay before tax calculations and deductions are made.

The cafeteria plans appears to be a sure-fire way to increase employee take-home pay. However, it has some built-in restrictions that, if not managed carefully, can result in a *reduction* in take-home pay. One issue is that employees are only allowed to choose the total amount of their annual cafeteria plan deductions at the beginning of the plan year; they cannot change it again until the plan year has concluded. This "lock-down" provision can only be altered when there have been changes in an employee's marital status, number of dependents (including adoptions) or the status of those dependents, residential address, or the employment status of the employee or a spouse or dependent. Furthermore, these changes must also result in a change in employee status in the underlying coverage before the amount of the cafeteria plan deduction can be altered.

Example. To continue the previous example, Allison Schoening's long-term medical condition clears up part-way through the year, and she can stop purchasing prescriptions. Consequently, she wants to reduce the amount of the cafeteria plan deductions being removed from her pay. She claims that there has been a change in her status because she changed residences midway through the year. This claim is denied by the cafeteria plan administrator, because the change in residence did not alter her eligibility for coverage under the terms of the underlying medical insurance plan.

Example. Allison Schoening decides to adopt a baby after the plan year has begun. This results in a change in her eligibility under the rules of the underlying medical insurance plan, which allows her to add the baby as a dependent. Since this is also an allowable change in status under the cafeteria plan, she is permitted to alter the amount of her cafeteria plan deductions to more closely match her altered medical expenses resulting from the adoption.

The reason it is so important to closely match the amount of actual expenses incurred to the amount withheld under a cafeteria plan, is that if an employee does not submit a sufficient amount of qualified expenses to be reimbursed from the withheld funds, the remaining funds will be lost at the end of the plan year. Only those expenses billed to the employee prior to year-end can be reimbursed through the plan. When a reimbursement request is made, an employee must provide a receipt from the health care provider, and make a written statement that he or she has not received reimbursement for this expense from any other source. Consequently, it is best for employees to make a low estimate of the total amount of qualified expenses that they expect to incur by the end of the year, rather than have too much withheld and then lose the unused portion.

Example. Allison Schoening receives a periodic statement from the FSA plan administrator, informing her that she still has $250 of funds left in her cafeteria plan account with one month to go before the plan year-end. Accordingly, she accelerates the purchase of several prescriptions at the local pharmacy on the last day of the plan year, even though she will not need the medication for some time to come. Because this action is acceptable under the cafeteria plan rules, reimbursement of the late purchases from the fund are approved, and she does not lose any funds from her FSA account.

Another problem for employees is that contributions to an FSA plan are treated as separate pools of funds if they are intended for medical expense reimbursements or for dependent care reimbursements. Cash from these two types of funds cannot be mixed. For example, if an employee contributes too much money to a dependent care account and cannot use it all by the end of the plan year, these funds cannot be shifted to other uses, such as the reimbursement of medical expenses.

A problem for employers offering an FSA cafeteria plan is that employees may legally make claims against the fund that exceed the amount they have thus far contributed to the plan and then quit the company. When this happens, the business cannot seek recompense from the individual for the difference between the amount contributed into the fund and the amount paid out. Nor can a company alleviate this potential problem by forcing employees to accelerate the amount of their contributions beyond the preset amount.

Example. Mr. Adolph Armsbrucker contributes $100 per month into the company's FSA fund, which will result in a total contribution of $1,200 at the end of the year. However, he submits expenses to the plan administrator of $550 in February, for which he is reimbursed. He has only contributed $200 to the fund at this point, so the company is essentially supporting the fund for the difference between $550 in expenses and $200 in funding, or $350. Mr. Armsbrucker leaves the company at the end of February, leaving the company with this liability.

The favorable tax treatment accorded to participants in a cafeteria plan is only available if the plan passes several nondiscrimination tests. First, a plan must have the same eligibility requirements for all employees; this means plan participation cannot be offered solely to highly compensated employees, nor require more than three years employment with the company prior to participation in the plan. Second, all plan participants must have equal access to the same nontaxable benefits offered under the plan. Finally, no more than one-quarter of all nontaxable benefits provided under the plan can be given to key employees.

Insurance Benefits

Insurance benefits may include medical, dental, vision, and life insurance. Deductions are usually taken from every paycheck to help defray the cost of the insurance, either in part or in total. A company may contribute to this cost by paying for some portion or all of the insurance itself. Even if employees pay the entire amount of the insurance, it is still usually less expensive than if they had obtained it themselves, since insurance companies generally quote lower prices to businesses employing a number of people. The contribution made by the company to defray the cost of medical insurance is *not* considered income to employees. Furthermore, if the company has a medical expense reimbursement plan under which employees can be reimbursed for any out-of-pocket medical expenses incurred by them, these additional payments also are not considered income to employees.

Example. In a sudden burst of generosity, the president of the Humble Pie Company announces at the company business party that all co-payments and deductibles on its medical insurance plan for the upcoming year will be paid by the company. These reimbursements are not taxable income to the employees.

The most common ways to provide medical insurance are through the Health Maintenance Organization (HMO), Preferred Provider Organization (PPO), and Point of Service (POS) plan.

- The HMO arrangement requires employees to go to designated doctors who have signed up to participate in the plan.

- The PPO option allows employees to consult with doctors outside of the group of designated doctors, but at a higher cost in terms of co-payments and deductibles.

- The POS plan requires employees to choose a primary care doctor from within the HMO network of doctors, but they can then see doctors outside the HMO's network, as long as the primary care doctor is still the primary point of contact.

Given the high cost of medical insurance provided by third parties, some organizations are turning to self-insurance plans. Under this approach, employee medical claims are submitted directly to the company or a third-party administrator, with the claims in either case being paid by the company. Once total claims reach a certain point, a *stop-loss* insurance policy takes over and pays all remaining claims. This stop-loss coverage prevents the company from incurring inordinate losses by providing umbrella coverage for major insurance claims. This approach eliminates the profit that would otherwise be charged by a third-party medical provider, while also allowing the company to exert more control over employee claims.

A key drawback to this arrangement is that if the plan's benefits are skewed in favor of highly compensated employees, the excess medical payments made on behalf of this group will be considered income to them for tax reporting purposes. Excess payments are considered to be those paid that exceed the level of payments made to other employees in the plan. In order not to be considered discriminatory, a self-insured plan should include at least 70 percent of all employees.

Example. The management team of the Humble Pie Company is offered free corrective eye surgery; it is not offered to other employees. The Chief Financial Officer (CFO) has this surgery, which costs $2,200. The entire cost of this surgery should be added to the CFO's reportable income, since the benefit was not made available to the rest of the company.

Insurance Continuation Subsequent to Employment

Under the terms of the Consolidated Omnibus Budget Reconciliation Act, employees of private sector, state, and local governments who lose their jobs have the right to accept continuing health insurance coverage,

TIPS & TECHNIQUES

Many third-party medical insurance providers do not allow partial-month insurance coverage. This is an important issue when an employee leaves a company near the beginning of a month, since the company will still pay its share of the medical cost for the remainder of the month, even if the employee is no longer working there. The payroll staff should be sure to charge the departing employee his or her full share of the medical insurance for the full month of medical coverage; this deduction is frequently missed in companies where more than one payroll is generated per month, since the employee share of the expense is spread over several paychecks. Despite the additional manual effort involved in altering the medical insurance deduction on an employee's final paycheck, this can result in significant cost savings to the company.

as long as the former employer had 20 or more employees in the prior year. If an employee is terminated, then he or she can accept coverage for an additional 18 months. If an employee becomes entitled to Medicare coverage or becomes divorced, then the coverage period extends to 36 months. If a spouse or dependent child of an employee loses coverage due to the death of an employee, then they can obtain coverage for up to 36 months. If a dependent child of an employee loses dependent status, then that person can obtain coverage for up to 36 months.

An employer is required to give notice of potential COBRA coverage to employees when a qualifying event occurs. (Employees are required to inform the health plan administrator of any divorce, disability, or dependent issues that would bring about qualification for benefits under COBRA.) The affected people then have up to 60 days to elect to take COBRA coverage.

If an employee chooses coverage, he or she can be required to pay up to 102 percent of the cost of the insurance. And if the employee fails to make timely payments under the terms of the insurance plan (within 30 days of the due date), the COBRA coverage can be terminated. COBRA coverage also will end if the employer stops providing medical coverage to its regular employees, if the covered individual obtains coverage under another health insurance plan subsequent to taking the COBRA coverage, or if the covered individual becomes covered by the Medicare program.

Example. A cook at the Humble Pie Company is laid off at the end of March. She is given paperwork to fill out at the time of termination for COBRA coverage. She submits the documentation accepting coverage after 55 days. The company is required to keep her on COBRA, since she filed in a timely manner. After three months, she obtains work with another company and enrolls in its medical insurance program. Because she is now covered by a different insurance program subsequent to her election to accept COBRA coverage, the Humble Pie Company no longer has to provide her COBRA coverage, and so terminates it.

Life Insurance[1]

It is common practice for a company to provide group term life insurance to its employees as part of a standard benefit package. This requires some extra reporting from a tax perspective, however. If the amount of the life insurance benefit exceeds $50,000, the company must report the incremental cost of the life insurance over $50,000 (to the extent that the employee is not paying for the additional insurance) on the employee's W-2 form as taxable income. In the less common case, where the company provides life insurance that results in some amount of cash surrender value, then the cost of this permanent benefit to the employee must also be included in the employee's W-2 form. The only case in which these costs are not included on an employee's W-2 form is when the company is the beneficiary of the policy, rather than the employee. The opposite situation arises if the company is providing life insurance only to a few key employees, rather than to all employees; in this case, the entire cost of the insurance must be reported on the employee's W-2 form as taxable income.

Leaves of Absence

The Family and Medical Leave Act (FLMA) entitles employees at companies with 50 or more employees to take up to 12 weeks of unpaid leave (which may be taken sporadically) each year for a specified list of family and medical reasons. Only those employees who have worked for the employer for a total of at least 12 months, and for at least 1,250 hours in the last 12 months, are covered by the act. A further restriction is that an employee must work at a company location where at least 50 employees are employed within a 75-mile radius of the facility. Valid reasons for taking the leave of absence include the birth of a child, serious illness, or caring for a family member with a serious illness.

During their absence, an employer must continue to provide medical insurance coverage if it had been taken by the employee prior to the leave of absence, though the employee can be charged for that portion of the expense that had been deducted from his or her pay prior to the leave. If the employee does not pay this portion of the expense within 30 days, the insurance can be cancelled for the remainder of the leave (though 15 days written notice must be provided), but it must be restored once the employee returns to work. If the terms of the medical insurance plan are changed by the company during the leave of absence, then the new terms will apply to the person who is on leave. Only medical insurance is subject to these provisions; other types of insurance, such as life and disability insurance, do not have to be maintained during the leave of absence.

Example. Samuel Lamont had a sick mother and took FMLA leave from the Humble Pie Company in order to care for her. Prior to his leave of absence, he paid $120 per month as his share of the cost of a company-provided medical insurance plan. During the leave, the company changed the employee share of the insurance for all employees to $160. Mr. Lamont concluded that he could not afford this additional cost and stopped paying for his share of the insurance. The company accordingly warned him in writing that coverage would be dropped, and then did so after payment became 30 days overdue. When he returned from leave, the company was required to restore his medical coverage.

Because of the large number of provisions of the FMLA and its cost impact on both the employer and employee, it is recommended that the employer fill out a formal, detailed response to a request for a leave of absence, copies of which should go into the employee's file as well as to the employee. The Department of Labor has issued a sample report that covers the key provisions of the FMLA, which is reproduced in Exhibit 6.1. This form, Number WH-381, may be downloaded in Acrobat PDF format from the Department of Labor's web site at *www.dol.gov*.

Upon returning from a leave of absence, an employee must be given the same or equivalent job, with the same level of pay and benefits that he or she had before the leave. However, no additional leave or seniority accrues during the term of an employee's leave of absence. In certain cases, where job restoration would cause significant economic damage to an employer, *key positions* will not be restored to returning employees. A key position is defined as a salaried employee whose pay is in the top 10 percent of all employees.

EXHIBIT 6.1

Employer Response Form for FMLA Leave Request

Employer Response to Employee
Request for Family or Medical Leave
(Optional Use Form — See 29 CFR § 825.301)

(Family and Medical Leave Act of 1993)

U.S. Department of Labor
Employment Standards Administration
Wage and Hour Division

OMB No. : 1215-0181
Expires : 06-30-02

Date:

To: _____
(Employee's Name)

From: _____
(Name of Appropriate Employer Representative)

Subject: REQUEST FOR FAMILY/MEDICAL LEAVE

On _____ , you notified us of your need to take family/medical leave due to:
(Date)

☐   The birth of a child, or the placement of a child with you for adoption or foster care; or

☐   A serious health condition that makes you unable to perform the essential functions for your job: or

☐   A serious health condition affecting your ☐ spouse, ☐ child, ☐ parent, for which you are needed to provide care.

You notified us that you need this leave beginning on _____ and that you expect
(Date)
leave to continue until on or about _____ .
(Date)

Except as explained below, you have a right under the FMLA for up to 12 weeks of unpaid leave in a 12-month period for the reasons listed above. Also, your health benefits must be maintained during any period of unpaid leave under the same conditions as if you continued to work, and you must be reinstated to the same or an equivalent job with the same pay, benefits, and terms and conditions of employment on your return from leave. If you do not return to work following FMLA leave for a reason other than: (1) the continuation, recurrence, or onset of a serious health condition which would entitle you to FMLA leave; or (2) other circumstances beyond your control, you may be required to reimburse us for our share of health insurance premiums paid on your behalf during your FMLA leave.

This is to inform you that: *(check appropriate boxes; explain where indicated)*

1. You are ☐ eligible ☐ not eligible   for leave under the FMLA.

2. The requested leave ☐ will ☐ will not   be counted against your annual FMLA leave entitlement.

3. You ☐ will ☐ will not be required to furnish medical certification of a serious health condition. If required, you must furnish certification by _____ *(insert date)* (must be at least 15 days after you are notified of this requirement), or we may delay the commencement of your leave until the certification is submitted.

4. You may elect to substitute accrued paid leave for unpaid FMLA leave. We ☐ will ☐ will not   require that you substitute accrued paid leave for unpaid FMLA leave. If paid leave will be used, the following conditions will apply: *(Explain)*

Form WH-381
Rev. June 1997

EXHIBIT 6.1 (CONTINUED)

5. (a) If you normally pay a portion of the premiums for your health insurance, these payments will continue during the period of FMLA leave. Arrangements for payment have been discussed with you, and it is agreed that you will make premium payments as follows: *(Set forth dates, e.g., the 10th of each month, or pay periods, etc. that specifically cover the agreement with the employee.)*

(b) You have a minimum 30-day *(or, indicate longer period, if applicable)* grace period in which to make premium payments. If payment is not made timely, your group health insurance may be cancelled, *provided* we notify you in writing at least 15 days before the date that your health coverage will lapse, or, at our option, we may pay your share of the premiums during FMLA leave, and recover these payments from you upon your return to work. We will ☐ ☐ will not pay your share of health insurance premiums while you are on leave.

(c) We ☐ will ☐ will not do the same with other benefits *(e.g., life insurance, disability insurance, etc.)* while you are on FMLA leave. If we do pay your premiums for other benefits, when you return from leave you ☐ will ☐ will not be expected to reimburse us for the payments made on your behalf.

6.   You ☐ will ☐ will not be required to present a fitness-for-duty certificate prior to being restored to employment. If such certification is required but not received, your return to work may be delayed until certification is provided.

7. (a) You ☐ are ☐ are not a "key employee" as described in § 825.217 of the FMLA regulations. If you are a "key employee:" restoration to employment may be denied following FMLA leave on the grounds that such restoration will cause substantial and grievous economic injury to us as discussed in § 825.218.

(b) We ☐ have ☐ have not determined that restoring you to employment at the conclusion of FMLA leave will cause substantial and grievous economic harm to *us. (Explain (a) and/or (b) below. See §825.279 of the FMLA regulations.)*

8.   While on leave, you ☐ will ☐ will not be required to furnish us with periodic reports every _____ _____ *(indicate interval of periodic reports, as appropriate for the particular leave situation)* of your status and intent to return to work *(see § 825.309 of the FMLA regulations).* If the circumstances of your leave change and you are able to return to work earlier than the date indicated on the reverse side of this form, you   ☐ will ☐ will not be required to notify us at least two work days prior to the date you intend to report to work.

9.   You ☐ will ☐ will not be required to furnish recertification relating to a serious health condition. *(Explain below. if necessary, including the interval between certifications as prescribed in §825.308 of the FMLA regulations.)*

This optional use form may be used to satisfy mandatory employer requirements to provide employees taking FMLA leave with Written notice detailing spectfic expectations and obligations of the employee and explaining any consequences of a failure to meet these obligations. (29 CFR 825.301(b).)

Note: Persons are not required to respond to this collection of information unless it displays a currently valid OMB control number.

Public Burden Statement

We estimate that it will take an average of 5 minutes to complete this collection of information, including the time for reviewing instructions. searching existing data sources, gathering and maintaining the data needed, and completing and reviewing the collection of information. If you have any comments regarding this burden estimate or any other aspect of this collection of information, including suggestions for reducing this burden. send them to the Administrator, Wage and Hour Division, Department of Labor, Room S-3502. 200 Constitution Avenue, N.W., Washington. D.C. 20210.

DO NOT SEND THE COMPLETED FORM TO THE OFFICE SHOWN ABOVE.

TIPS & TECHNIQUES

A company could be laying itself open to a lawsuit if it makes some types of deductions from employee pay checks without their authorization. The best way to avoid this problem is to have employees sign an authorization notice that clearly specifies the amount and type of any deductions, as well as the start and stop dates for the deductions. An example of such a form is noted in Exhibit 6.2.

Pension Plan Benefits[2]

There is an enormous variety of retirement plans available, each of which has a slightly different treatment under the tax laws, resulting in varying levels of investment risk to the employee or different levels of administrative activity. In this section, we will give a brief overview of each type of retirement plan.

Qualified Retirement Plan

A *qualified retirement plan* is one that is designed to observe all of the requirements of the Retirement Income Security Act (ERISA), as well as all related IRS rulings. By observing these requirements, an employer can immediately deduct allowable contributions to the plan on behalf of plan participants. Also, income earned by the plan is not taxable to the plan. In addition, participants can exclude from taxable income any contributions they make to the plan, until such time as they choose to withdraw the funds from the plan. Finally, distributions to participants can, in some cases, be rolled over into an Individual Retirement Account (IRA), thereby prolonging the deferral of taxable income. There are two types of qualified retirement plans, which are as follows:

EXHIBIT 6.2

Deduction Authorization Form

I hereby authorize that the following deductions be made from my pay:

Deduction Type	Deduction Amount	Start Date	Stop Date
☐ Cafeteria Plan—Dependent Care	_____	_____	_____
☐ Cafeteria Plan—Medical	_____	_____	_____
☐ Dental Insurance	_____	_____	_____
☐ Dependent Life Insurance	_____	_____	_____
☐ Long-Term Disability Insurance	_____	_____	_____
☐ Medical Insurance	_____	_____	_____
☐ Short-Term Disability Insurance	_____	_____	_____
☐ Supplemental Life Insurance	_____	_____	_____

_____   _____
Signature   Date

These forms should be kept in employee payroll files for immediate access in case an employee later challenges the amount of a deduction. To keep these challenges from occurring, it is useful to have all deductions identified separately on the remittance advice that accompanies each paycheck. For example, if there are deductions for short-term disability and long-term disability insurance, the amount of these deductions should be separately listed.

Defined Contribution Plan. This is a plan in which the employer is liable for a payment into the plan of a specific size, but not for the size of the resulting payments from the plan to participants. Thus, the participant bears the risk of the results of investment of the monies that have been deposited into the plan. The participant can mitigate or increase this risk by having control over a number of different investment options. The annual combined contribution to this type of plan by both the participant and employer is limited to the greater of $35,000 or one-fourth of a participant's compensation (though this is restricted in several cases—see the following specific plan types). Funds received by participants in a steady income stream are taxed at ordinary income tax rates, and cannot be rolled over into an IRA, whereas a lump-sum payment can be rolled into an IRA. Some of the more common defined contribution plans are as follows:

- *401(k) plan.* This is a plan set up by an employer into which employees can contribute the lesser of $11,000 or 15 percent of their pay, which is excluded from taxation until such time as they remove the funds from the account. All earnings of the funds while held in the plan will also not be taxed until removed from the account. Employers can also match the funds contributed to the plan by employees, and contribute the results of a profit sharing plan to the employees' 401(k) accounts. The plan typically allows employees to invest the funds in their accounts in a number of different investment options, ranging from conservative money market funds to more speculative small cap or international stock funds; the employee holds the risk of how well or poorly an investment will perform—the employer has no liability for the performance of investments. Withdrawals from a 401(k) are intended to be upon retirement or the attainment of age 59 1/2, but can also be distributed as a loan (if the specific plan document permits it) or in the event of disability or death.

Example. The Humble Pie Company matches the contributions of its employees for the first 3 percent of pay they contribute into a 401(k) plan. Sally Reed elects to have 8 percent of her pay contributed to the 401(k) plan each month. Her monthly rate of pay is $3,500. Accordingly, the company deducts $280 from her pay, which is 8 percent times $3,500. The company then adds $105 to her contribution, which is 3 percent times $3,500. Consequently, the total contribution to her 401(k) plan is $385, which is composed of $280 contributed by Ms. Reed and $105 contributed by the company.

- *403(b) plan.* This is similar to a 401(k) plan, except that it is designed specifically for charitable, religious, and educational organizations that fall under the tax-exempt status of 501(c)(3) regulations. It also varies from a 401(k) plan in two other ways: participants can only invest in mutual funds and annuities, and contributions can exceed the limit imposed under a 401(k) plan to the extent that participants can catch up on contributions that were below the maximum threshold in previous years.

- *Employee stock ownership plan (ESOP).* The bulk of the contributions made to this type of plan are in the stock of the employing company. The employer calculates the amount of its contribution to the plan, based on a proportion of total employee compensation, and uses the result to buy an equivalent amount of stock and deposit it in the ESOP. When an employee leaves the company, he or she will receive either company stock or the cash equivalent of the stock in payment of his or her vested interest.

- *Money purchase plan.* The employer must make a payment into each employee's account in each year that is typically based on a percentage of total compensation paid to each participant. The payments must be made, irrespective of company profits (see next item).

- *Profit sharing plan.* Contributions to this type of plan are intended to be funded from company profits, which is an incentive for employees to extend their efforts to ensure that profits will occur. However, many employers will make contributions to the plan even in the absence of profits. This plan is frequently linked to a 401(k) plan, so that participants can also make contributions to the plan.

Defined Benefit Plan. This plan itemizes a specific dollar amount that participants will receive, based on a set of rules that typically combine the number of years of employment and wages paid over the time period that each employee has worked for the company. An additional factor may be the age of the participant at the time of retirement. Funds received by participants in a steady income stream are taxed at ordinary income tax rates and cannot be rolled over into an IRA, whereas a lump-sum payment can be. This type of plan is not favorable to the company, which guarantees the fixed payments made to retirees, and so bears the risk of unfavorable investment returns that may require additional payments into the plan in order to meet the fixed payment obligations. Some of the more common defined benefit plans are as follows:

- *Cash balance plan.* The employer contributes a *pay credit* (usually based on a proportion of that person's annual compensation) and an *interest credit* (usually linked to a publicly available interest rate index or well-known high-grade investment such as a U.S. government security) to each participant's account within the plan. Changes in plan value based on these credits do not impact the fixed benefit amounts to which participants are entitled.

- *Target benefit plan.* Under this approach, the employer makes annual contributions into the plan based on the actuarial assumption at that time regarding the amount of funding needed to achieve a targeted benefit level (hence the name of the plan). However, there is no guarantee that the amount of the actual benefit paid will match the estimate upon which the contributions were based, since the return on invested amounts in the plan may vary from the estimated level at the time when the contributions were made.

A plan that can fall into either the defined contribution or defined benefit plan categories is the Keogh plan. It is available to self-employed people, partnerships, and owners of unincorporated businesses. When created, a Keogh plan can be defined as either a defined contribution or defined benefit plan. Under either approach, the contribution level is restricted to the lesser of 25 percent of taxable annual compensation (or 20 percent for the owner) or $35,000. It is not allowable to issue loans against a Keogh plan, but distributions from it can be rolled over into an IRA. Premature withdrawal penalties are similar to those for an IRA.

Nonqualified Retirement Plans

All the preceding plans fall under the category of qualified retirement plans. However, if a company does not choose to follow ERISA and IRS guidelines, it can create a *nonqualified retirement plan*. By doing so, it can discriminate in favor of paying key personnel more than other participants, or to the exclusion of other employees. All contributions to the plan and any earnings by the deposited funds will remain untaxed as long as they stay within the trust. The downside of this approach is that any contribution made to the plan by the company cannot be recorded as a taxable expense until the contribution is eventually paid out of the trust into which it was deposited and to the plan participant (which may be years in the future). Proceeds from the plan are taxable as ordinary income to the recipient and cannot be rolled over into an IRA.

An example of a nonqualified retirement plan is the 457 plan, which allows participants to defer up to $8,500 of their wages per year.

It is restricted to the use of government and tax-exempt entities. Distributions from the plan are usually at retirement, but can also be at the point of the employee's departure from the organization, or a withdrawal can be requested on an emergency basis. A key difference between the 457 plan and the qualified retirement plans is that the funds deposited in the trust by the employer can be claimed by creditors, unless the employer is a government entity.

Personal Retirement Accounts

An employer may not want to deal with the complex reporting requirements of a qualified retirement plan, nor set up a nonqualified plan. A very simple alternative is the *personal retirement account* (PRA), of which the most common is the individual retirement arrangement. The primary types of PRAs are the *individual retirement arrangement* and the *simplified employee pension*.

Individual Retirement Account (IRA). This is a savings account that is set up for the specific use of one person who is less than 70 1/2 years old. Contributions to an IRA are limited to the lesser of $2,000 per year or a person's total taxable compensation (which can be wages, tips, bonuses, commissions, and taxable alimony). There is no required minimum payment into an IRA. Contributions to an IRA are not tax deductible if the contributor also participates in an employer's qualified retirement plan and his or her adjusted gross income is greater than $42,000 if a single filer, $62,000 if filing a joint return, or $10,000 if married and filing a separate return. The deductible amount begins to decline at a point $10,000 lower than all of these values. If a working spouse is not covered by an employer's qualified retirement plan, then he or she may make a fully deductible contribution of up to $2,000 per year to the IRA, even if the other spouse has such coverage. This deduction is eliminated when a couple's adjusted gross income reaches

$160,000, and begins to decline at $150,000. Earnings within the plan are shielded from taxation until distributed from it.

It is mandatory to begin withdrawals from an IRA as of age 70 1/2; if distributions do not occur, then a penalty of 50 percent will be charged against the amount that was not distributed. When funds are withdrawn from an IRA prior to age 59 1/2 they will be taxed at ordinary income tax rates, and will also be subject to a 10 percent excise tax. However, the excise tax will be waived if the participant dies, is disabled, is buying a home for the first time (to a maximum of $10,000), is paying for some types of higher education costs or medical insurance costs that exceed 7.5 percent of the participant's adjusted gross income (as well as any medical insurance premiums following at least one-quarter year of receiving unemployment benefits). The following list reveals the wide range of IRA accounts that can be set up:

- *Education IRA.* This type of IRA is established for the express purpose of providing advanced education to the beneficiary. Though contributions to this IRA are not exempt from taxable income, any earnings during the period when funds are stored in the IRA will be tax-free at the time when they are used to pay for the cost of advanced education. The annual contribution limit on this IRA is $500, and is limited to the time period prior to the beneficiary reaching the age of 18. The maximum contribution begins to decline at the point when joint household income reaches $150,000 (and is eliminated at $160,000), and $95,000 for a single tax filer (and is eliminated at $110,000). The amount in this IRA can be moved to a different family member if the new beneficiary is less than 30 years old. The amount in the IRA must be distributed once the beneficiary reaches the age of 30. If a distribution is not for the express purpose of offsetting education expenses, then the distribution is taxable as ordinary income, and will also be charged a 10 percent excise tax.

- *Group IRA.* Though the intent of an IRA is for it to be the sole possession of one person, it can also be set up and contributed to by another entity. In the case of a group IRA, an employer, union, or other entity can set up a cluster of IRAs for its members or employees and make contributions into each of the accounts.

- *Individual retirement annuity.* This is an IRA that is composed of an annuity that is managed through and paid out by a life insurance company.

- *Inherited IRA.* This is either a Roth or traditional IRA that has been inherited from its deceased owner, with the recipient not being the deceased owner's spouse. After the owner's death, no more than five years can pass before the beneficiary receives a distribution; or an annuity can be arranged that empties the IRA no later than the beneficiary's life expectancy. This IRA is not intended to be a vehicle for ongoing contributions from the new beneficiary, so tax deductions are not allowed for any contributions made into it. Also, the funds in this IRA cannot be shifted into a rollover IRA, since this action would circumvent the preceding requirement to distribute the funds within five years.

- *Rollover IRA.* This is an IRA that an individual sets up for the express purpose of receiving funds from a qualified retirement plan. There are no annual contribution limits for this type of IRA, since its purpose is to transfer a preexisting block of funds that could be quite large. Funds deposited in this account, as well as any earnings accumulating in the accounts, are exempt from taxation until removed from it. Rollover funds can also be transferred (tax-free) into another qualified retirement plan. A common use of the rollover account is to "park" funds from the qualified plan of a former employer until the individual qualifies for participation in the plan of a new employer, at which point the funds are transferred into the new employer's plan.

- *Roth IRA.* Under this IRA, there are offsetting costs and benefits. On the one hand, any contribution to the IRA is not deductible; on the other hand, withdrawals from the account (including earnings) are not taxable at all, as long as the recipient is at least 59 1/2 years old, is disabled, or is made a beneficiary following the death of the IRA participant, or uses the money to buy a first-time home. Contributions are limited to $2,000 per year and can be continued indefinitely, irrespective of the participant's age. However, no contribution is allowed once the participant's adjusted gross income reaches $160,000 for a joint filer, or $110,000 for a single filer, and will gradually decline beginning at $150,000 and $95,000, respectively.

There are special rules for transferring funds into a Roth IRA from any other type of IRA. It is only allowed if the adjusted gross income of the transferring party is $100,000 or less in the year of transfer (the same limitation applies to both single and joint filers). Distributions from the Roth IRA that come from these rolled-over funds will not be taxable, but only if they have been held in the Roth IRA for at least five years following the date of transfer.

- *Savings incentive match plan for employees (SIMPLE).* Under this IRA format, an employer that has no other retirement plan and employs fewer than 100 employees can set up IRA accounts for its employees, into which they can contribute up to $6,500 per year. The employer commits to make a matching contribution of up to 3 percent of the employee's pay, depending upon how much the employee has chosen to contribute. The combined employee/employer contribution to the plan cannot exceed $13,000 per year. The employer also has the option of reducing its contribution percentage in two years out of every five consecutive years, or can commit to a standard 2 percent contribution for all eligible employees, even if they choose not to contribute to the plan. Vesting in the plan is immediate. The downside to this plan from an employee's perspective is that the excise tax assessment for a withdrawal within the first two years of participation is 25 percent, rather than the usual 10 percent that is assessed for other types of IRA accounts.

- *Spousal IRA*. This is an IRA that is funded by one spouse on behalf of the other, but only if the spouse being funded has less than $2,000 in annual taxable income. This contribution is only valid if the couple files a joint tax return for the year in which the contribution took place.

Simplified Employee Pension (SEP). This plan is available primarily for self-employed persons and partnerships, but is available to all types of business entities. It can be established only if no qualified retirement plan is already in use. The maximum contribution that an employer can make is the lesser of 15 percent of an employee's compensation, or $30,000. The amount paid is up to the discretion of the employer. The contribution is sent at once to an IRA that has been set up in the name of each employee, and which is owned by the employee. Once the money arrives in the IRA, it falls under all of the previously noted rules for an IRA.

Sick/Disability Pay

A typical company benefit plan allows for the accrual of a fixed number of sick days per year. When an illness forces an employee to stay home, the sick time accrual is used in place of work hours, so an employee is compensated for a normal number of working hours during his or her time off. Once all the accrued sick time is used up, an employee can use any remaining vacation time in order to continue being paid, but thereafter must take an unpaid leave of absence.

Additional wages may be paid from either short-term or long-term disability insurance plans, which are generally offered through third-party insurance providers. If an employer pays the entire cost of these insurance plans, then any benefits received from them by employees are taxable income to the employer. However, if the employees pay some portion of the cost of these plans with after-tax dollars, then only the employer-paid portion is recognized as taxable income to them. Alternatively, if employees pay for their share of these plans through a cafeteria plan, then they are doing so with before-tax dollars, which makes the proceeds from the insurance taxable.

Example. Molly Hatcher mistakenly ate a piece of the Humble Pie Company's namesake product and is out sick with a severe case of meekness. She had been paying for 40 percent of the cost of short-term disability insurance, with the company paying for the remainder of this cost. Under the policy, she is entitled to $350 per week. Of this amount, 60 percent will be recognized as taxable income to her, which is $210 per week.

Example. Molly Hatcher has elected to pay for half of her 40 percent share of the short-term disability insurance through the corporate cafeteria plan, which means that 20 percent of the total payments are made with pretax funds, 20 percent with after-tax funds, and 60 percent by the company. Under this scenario, 80 percent of the weekly short-term disability payments are subject to income taxes, thereby increasing her proportion of taxable income to $280.

Under a third-party liability insurance plan, the insurance carrier is responsible for all withholding, if the recipient asks it to do so by filing a Form W-4S. If the insurance carrier transfers this responsibility to the company, then the company must report the amount of taxable liability income received by an employee on its W-2 form at year-end.

Stock Options[3]

A stock option gives an employee the right to buy stock at a specific price within a specific time period. Stock options come in two varieties: the *incentive stock option* (ISO) and the *nonqualified stock option* (NSO).

Incentive stock options are not taxable to the employee at the time they are granted, nor at the time when the employee eventually exercises the option to buy stock. If the employee does not dispose of the stock within two years of the date of the option grant or within one year of the date when the option is exercised, then any resulting gain will be taxed as a long-term capital gain. However, if the employee sells the stock within one year of the exercise date, then any gain is taxed as ordinary income. An ISO plan typically requires an employee to exercise any vested stock options within 90 days of his or her voluntary or involuntary termination of employment.

The reduced tax impact associated with waiting until two years have passed from the date of option grant presents a risk to the employee that the value of the related stock will decline in the interim, thereby offsetting the reduced long-term capital gain tax rate achieved at the end of this period. To mitigate the potential loss in stock value, the employee can make a Section 83(b) election to recognize taxable income on the purchase price of the stock within 30 days following the date when an option is exercised, and withhold taxes at the ordinary income tax rate at that time. The employee will not recognize any additional income with respect to the purchased shares until they are sold or otherwise transferred in a taxable transaction, and the additional gain recognized at that time will be taxed at the long-term capital gains rate. It is reasonable to make the Section 83(b) election if the amount of income reported at the time of the election is small and the potential price growth of the stock is significant. That said, it is not reasonable to take the election if there is a combination of high reportable income at the time of election (resulting in a large tax payment) and a minimal chance of growth in the stock price, or that the company can forfeit the options. The Section 83(b) election is not available to holders of options under an NSO plan.

The alternative minimum tax (AMT) must also be considered when dealing with an ISO plan. In essence, the AMT requires that an employee pay tax on the difference between the exercise price and the stock price at the time an option is exercised, even if the stock is not sold at that time. This can result in a severe cash shortfall for the employee, who may only be able to pay the related taxes by selling the stock. This is a particular problem if the value of the shares subsequently drops, since there is now no source of high-priced stock that can be converted into cash in order to pay the required taxes. This problem arises frequently after a company has just gone public, and employees are restricted from selling their shares for some time after the IPO date, thus run the risk of losing stock value during that interval. Establishing the amount of the gain reportable under AMT rules is especially difficult if a company's stock is not publicly held, since there is no clear consensus on the value of the stock. In this case, the IRS will use the value of the per-share price at which the last round of funding was concluded. When the stock is eventually sold, an AMT credit can be charged against the reported gain, but there can be a significant cash shortfall in the meantime. In order to avoid this situation, an employee could choose to exercise options at the point when the estimated value of company shares is quite low, thereby reducing the AMT payment; however, the employee must now find the cash to pay for the stock that he or she has just purchased, and runs the risk that the shares will not increase in value and may become worthless.

An ISO plan is only valid if it follows these rules:

- *Incentive stock options can only be issued to employees.* A person must have been working for the employer at all times during the period that begins on the date of grant and ends on the day three months before the date when the option is exercised.

- *The option term cannot exceed 10 years from the date of grant.* The option term is only five years in the case of an option granted to an employee who, at the time the option is granted, owns stock that has more than 10% of the total combined voting power of all classes of stock of the employer.

- *The option price at the time it is granted is not less than the fair market value of the stock.* However, it must be 110 percent of the fair market value in the case of an option granted to an employee who, at the time the option is granted, owns stock that has more than 10 percent of the total combined voting power of all classes of stock of the employer.

- *The total value of all options that can be exercised by any one employee in one year is limited to $100,000.* Any amounts exercised that exceed $100,000 will be treated as a nonqualified stock option (to be covered shortly).

- *The option cannot be transferred by the employee and can only be exercised during the employee's lifetime.*

If the options granted do not include these provisions, or are granted to individuals who are not employees under the preceding definition, then the options must be characterized as nonqualified stock options.

A nonqualified stock option is not given any favorable tax treatment under the Internal Revenue code (hence the name). It is also referred to as a *nonstatutory stock option.* The recipient of an NSO does not owe any tax on the date when options are granted, unless the options are traded on a public exchange. In that case, the options can be traded at once for value, and so tax will be recognized on the fair market value of the options on the public exchange as of the grant date. An NSO option will be taxed when it is exercised, based on the difference between the option price and the fair market value of the stock on that day. The resulting gain will be taxed as ordinary income. If the stock appreciates in value after the exercise date, then the incremental gain is taxable at the capital gains rate.

There are no rules governing an NSO, so the option price can be lower than the fair market value of the stock on the grant date. The option price can also be set substantially higher than the current fair market value at the grant date, which is called a *premium grant*. It is also possible to issue *escalating price options*, which use a sliding scale for the option price that changes in concert with a peer group index, thereby stripping away the impact of broad changes in the stock market and forcing the company to outperform the stock market in order to achieve any profit from granted stock options. Also, a *heavenly parachute* stock option can be created that allows a deceased option holder's estate up to three years in which to exercise his or her options.

Company management should be aware of the impact of both ISO and NSO plans on the company, not just employees. A company receives no tax deduction on a stock option transaction if it uses an ISO plan. However, if it uses an NSO plan, the company will receive a tax deduction equal to the amount of the income that the employee must recognize. If a company does not expect to have any taxable income during the stock option period, then it will receive no immediate value from having a tax deduction (though the deduction can be carried forward to offset income in future years), and so will be more inclined to use an ISO plan. This is a particularly common approach for companies that have not yet gone public. In contrast, publicly held companies, which are generally more profitable and so must search for tax deductions, will be more inclined to sponsor an NSO plan. Research has shown that most employees who are granted either type of option will exercise it as soon as possible, which essentially converts the tax impact of the ISO plan into an NSO plan. For this reason also, many companies prefer to use NSO plans.

Stock Purchase Plans

Some companies offer stock purchase plans that allow employees to buy company stock at a reduced price. The purchases are typically made through ongoing deductions from employee paychecks, and are usually capped at a specified percentage of employee pay, such as 15 percent.

Example. The Humble Pie Company offers its stock to employees at a 20 percent discount from the market price. Deductions are made from employee paychecks to cover the cost of shares. Sally Reed has chosen to have $10 deducted from her pay on an ongoing basis in order to buy this stock. During the first pay period, company stock is publicly traded at $17.50, so the price at which Ms. Reed can buy it from the company is $14, or ($17.50 market price x (1–20%)). However, the deduction is not sufficient to purchase a share, so the company places the funds in a holding account until the next pay period, when another $10 brings the total available funds to $20. The company then deposits one share of stock in the account of Ms. Reed and transfers $14 to its equity account, leaving $6 on hand for the next stock purchase.

Workers' Compensation Benefits

Businesses are required by law to obtain workers' compensation insurance, which provides their employees with wage compensation if they are injured on the job. This insurance may be provided by a state-sponsored fund or by a private insurance entity. The key issue from the payroll perspective is in calculating the cost of the workers' compensation insurance. This calculation occurs once a year, when the insurer sends a form to the company asking it to list the general category of work performed by the various groups of employees (such as clerical, sales, or manufacturing), as well as the amount of payroll attributable to each category. It behooves the person filling out the form to shift as many employees as possible out of high-risk manufacturing positions, since the insurance cost of these positions is much higher than for clerical positions. It's also important to reduce the amount of payroll attributable to each group by any expense reimbursements or nonwage benefits that may be listed as wages, as well as the overtime premium on hours worked. By reducing the total amount of reported payroll expense, the total cost of the workers' compensation insurance will also be reduced.

Example. The payroll manager of the Humble Pie Company was responsible for managing the cost of workers' compensation. In the previous year, she was aware that the 58 manufacturing positions reported to the insurance company were subject to a four-times multiplier for insurance pricing purposes, because they worked in risky jobs, while the clerical staff only had a one-times multiplier. Thus, by legitimately shifting employees from the manufacturing category to the clerical category, she could reduce the cost of workers' compensation insurance for those positions by 75 percent. In reviewing the payroll records, she found that three production supervisors and one security guard were classified as manufacturing positions. She shifted the classification of these positions to clerical ones.

IN THE REAL WORLD

Reclassify Employees to Reduce Insurance Costs

A telemarketing firm had been classifying its employees largely as sales personnel on its workers' compensation application, because they were primarily engaged in "push" sales calls over the phone. However, the firm found that this classification resulted in a one-third increase in the cost of its worker's compensation insurance, because the assumption by the insurance company was that people in this position traveled constantly and so were more likely to be injured in traffic accidents while on company business. After discussions with the insurer, the telemarketing firm reclassified its entire sales staff as clerical positions, thereby dropping the cost of its workers' compensation insurance by one-third.

Summary

The payroll manager is required to have an increasingly in-depth knowledge of the rules associated with a wide range of benefits, partially because they impact record-keeping, withholding, and tax reporting issues, and partially because the payroll department is generally perceived to be similar to the human resources department, hence may be asked detailed questions about many of these topics by employees. Consequently, it behooves the payroll staff to obtain a high degree of knowledge of benefits-related issues.

Endnotes

1. This section is reprinted with permission from Steven Bragg, *Accounting Reference Desktop* (New York: John Wiley & Sons, Inc., 2002), 521.

2. *Ibid.*, 532–537.

3. *Ibid.*, 540–542.

CHAPTER 7

Payroll Taxes and Remittances

After reading this chapter you will be able to

- Determine how frequently your business must remit payroll taxes to the federal government, and by what means

- Fill out Form W-4 "Employee Withholding Allowance Certificate" and Form 941 "Employer's Quarterly Federal Tax Return"

- Calculate employee income tax withholdings using either the wage bracket or alternative formula methods

- Determine when withholdings should or should not be made from the pay of employees working abroad

alculating and remitting a variety of payroll taxes is a function central to the payroll department. In this chapter, we cover the purpose and instructions for filling out several tax-related IRS forms, as well as the calculation methodologies and remittance instructions for federal and state income taxes, Medicare taxes, and Social Security taxes. The discussion also addresses how to register with the federal government to remit taxes and specialized issues related to the withholding of payroll taxes for aliens or employees working abroad.

Definition of an Employee

The definition of an employee is extremely important to a business, since it directly impacts whether taxes are to be withheld from a person's pay, which also must be matched in some cases by the business. The basic rule is that a person doing work for a company is an employee if the employer controls both the person's work output *and* also the manner in which the work is performed. The second part of the definition is crucial, since the first part could also define a contractor who can choose to produce a deliverable for a company in any manner he or she chooses. This definition identifies two classes of workers:

- *Employee.* An employee is paid through the payroll system; the employing business is responsible for withholding taxes and paying matching tax amounts where applicable.

- *Contractor.* A contractor is paid through the accounts payable system; the business that uses the contractor's services is only responsible for issuing a Form 1099 at the end of the calendar year to both the IRS and contractor, stating the total amount paid to the contractor during the year. The contractor is liable for remitting all payroll taxes to the government.

If a company incorrectly defines an employee as a contractor, it may be liable for all payroll taxes that should have been withheld from that person's pay. Consequently, when in doubt as to the proper definition of a worker, it is safer from a payroll tax law perspective to assume that the person is an employee.

W-4 Form

When an employee is hired, he or she is required by law to fill out a W-4 form, which can be done either on paper or in an electronic format. An employee uses this form to notify the payroll staff of his or her marital status and the number of allowances to be taken; this information has a direct impact on the amount of income taxes withheld from the employee's pay. The form is readily available in Adobe Acrobat form through the Internal Revenue Service's web site. An example is shown in Exhibit 7.1.

There are two pages associated with the Form W-4. In the middle of the first page is a personal allowances worksheet; the actual form is at the bottom. The second page is used only by those taxpayers who plan to itemize their deductions, claim certain credits, or claim adjustments to income on their next tax return.

On the first page of the form, an employee generally should accumulate one allowance for him- or herself, another for a working spouse, and one for each dependent. Additional allowances can be taken for "head of household" status or for certain amounts of child or dependent care expenses. The total of these allowances is then entered on line 5 of the form at the bottom of the page, along with any *additional* amounts that an employee may want to withhold from his or her paycheck. (Note: They cannot base withholdings on a fixed dollar amount or percentage, but they can add fixed withholding amounts to withholdings that are based on their marital status and number of allowances.) An employee can also claim exemption from tax withholding on line 7 of the form. This lower portion of the form should be filled out, signed, and kept on file every time an employee wants to change the amount of an allowance or additional withholding, in order to maintain a clear and indisputable record of changes to the employee's withholdings.

If an employee has claimed exemption from all income taxes on line 7 of the form, this claim is only good for one calendar year, after which a new claim must be made on a new W-4 form. If an employee making this claim has not filed a new W-4 by February 15 of the next year, the payroll staff is required to begin withholding income taxes on the assumption that the person is single and has no withholding allowances.

EXHIBIT 7.1

Form W-4

Form W-4 (2002)

Purpose. Complete Form W-4 so your employer can withhold the correct Federal income tax from your pay. Because your tax situation may change, you may want to refigure your withholding each year.

Exemption from withholding. If you are exempt, complete only lines 1, 2, 3, 4, and 7 and sign the form to validate it. Your exemption for 2002 expires February 16, 2003. See **Pub. 505**, Tax Withholding and Estimated Tax.

Note: *You cannot claim exemption from withholding if (a) your income exceeds $750 and includes more than $250 of unearned income (e.g., interest and dividends) and (b) another person can claim you as a dependent on their tax return.*

Basic instructions. If you are not exempt, complete the **Personal Allowances Worksheet** below. The worksheets on page 2 adjust your withholding allowances based on itemized deductions, certain credits, adjustments to

income, or two-earner/two-job situations. Complete all worksheets that apply. **However, you may claim fewer (or zero) allowances.**

Head of household. Generally, you may claim head of household filing status on your tax return only if you are unmarried and pay more than 50% of the costs of keeping up a home for yourself and your dependent(s) or other qualifying individuals. See line E below.

Tax credits. You can take projected tax credits into account in figuring your allowable number of withholding allowances. Credits for child or dependent care expenses and the child tax credit may be claimed using the **Personal Allowances Worksheet** below. See **Pub. 919**, How Do I Adjust My Tax Withholding? for information on converting your other credits into withholding allowances.

Nonwage income. If you have a large amount of nonwage income, such as interest or dividends, consider making estimated tax payments using **Form 1040-ES**, Estimated Tax for Individuals. Otherwise, you may owe additional tax.

Two earners/two jobs. If you have a working spouse or more than one job, figure the total number of allowances you are entitled to claim on all jobs using worksheets from only one Form W-4. Your withholding usually will be most accurate when all allowances are claimed on the Form W-4 for the highest paying job and zero allowances are claimed on the others.

Nonresident alien. If you are a nonresident alien, see the **Instructions for Form 8233** before completing this Form W-4.

Check your withholding. After your Form W-4 takes effect, use Pub. 919 to see how the dollar amount you are having withheld compares to your projected total tax for 2002. See Pub. 919, especially if you used the **Two-Earner/Two-Job Worksheet** on page 2 and your earnings exceed $125,000 (Single) or $175,000 (Married).

Recent name change? If your name on line 1 differs from that shown on your social security card, call 1-800-772-1213 for a new security card.

Personal Allowances Worksheet (Keep for your records.)

A Enter "1" for **yourself** if no one else can claim you as a dependent . . . . **A** _____

B Enter "1" if:
- You are single and have only one job; or
- You are married, have only one job, and your spouse does not work; or
- Your wages from a second job or your spouse's wages (or the total of both) are $1,000 or less.

. . **B** _____

C Enter "1" for your **spouse**. But, you may choose to enter "-0-" if you are married and have either a working spouse or more than one job. (Entering "-0-" may help you avoid having too little tax withheld.) . . . . **C** _____

D Enter number of **dependents** (other than your spouse or yourself) you will claim on your tax return . . . . **D** _____

E Enter "1" if you will file as **head of household** on your tax return (see conditions under **Head of household** above) . **E** _____

F Enter "1" if you have at least $1,500 of **child or dependent care expenses** for which you plan to claim a credit . . **F** _____
(**Note:** *Do* not *include child support payments. See **Pub. 503**, Child and Dependent Care Expenses, for details.*)

G **Child Tax Credit** (including additional child tax credit):
- If your total income will be between $15,000 and $42,000 ($20,000 and $65,000 if married), enter "1" for each eligible child plus **1 additional** if you have three to five eligible children or **2 additional** if you have six or more eligible children.
- If your total income will be between $42,000 and $80,000 ($65,000 and $115,000 if married), enter "1" if you have one or two eligible children, "2" if you have three eligible children, "3" if you have four eligible children, or "4" if you have five or more eligible children. **G** _____

H Add lines A through G and enter total here. **Note:** *This may be different from the number of exemptions you claim on your tax return.* ▶ **H** _____

For accuracy, complete all worksheets that apply.
- If you plan to **itemize or claim adjustments to income** and want to reduce your withholding, see the **Deductions and Adjustments Worksheet** on page 2.
- If you have **more than one job** or are **married and you and your spouse both work** and the combined earnings from all jobs exceed $35,000, see the **Two-Earner/Two-Job Worksheet** on page 2 to avoid having too little tax withheld.
- If **neither** of the above situations applies, **stop here** and enter the number from line H on line 5 of Form W-4 below.

.... Cut here and give Form W-4 to your employer. Keep the top part for your records. ....

Form **W-4**	**Employee's Withholding Allowance Certificate**		OMB No. 1545-0010
Department of the Treasury Internal Revenue Service	▶ **For Privacy Act and Paperwork Reduction Act Notice, see page 2.**		2002

1 Type or print your first name and middle initial	Last name		2 Your social security number

Home address (number and street or rural route)	3 ☐ Single ☐ Married ☐ Married, but withhold at higher Single rate. **Note:** *If married, but legally separated, or spouse is a nonresident alien, check the "Single" box.*

City or town, state, and ZIP code	4 If your last name differs from that on your social security card, check here. You must call 1-800-772-1213 for a new card. ▶ ☐

5 Total number of allowances you are claiming (from line H above **or** from the applicable worksheet on page 2) **5** _____

6 Additional amount, if any, you want withheld from each paycheck . . . . **6** $ _____

7 I claim exemption from withholding for 2002, and I certify that I meet **both** of the following conditions for exemption:
- Last year I had a right to a refund of **all** Federal income tax withheld because I had **no** tax liability **and**
- This year I expect a refund of **all** Federal income tax withheld because I expect to have **no** tax liability.
If you meet both conditions, write "Exempt" here . . . . ▶ **7**

Under penalties of perjury, I certify that I am entitled to the number of withholding allowances claimed on this certificate, or I am entitled to claim exempt status.

Employee's signature
(Form is not valid unless you sign it.) ▶ _____ Date ▶ _____

8 Employer's name and address (Employer: Complete lines 8 and 10 only if sending to the IRS.)	9 Office code (optional)	10 Employer identification number

Cat. No. 10220Q

EXHIBIT 7.1 (CONTINUED)

Form W-4 (2002)   Page **2**

Deductions and Adjustments Worksheet

Note: Use this worksheet only if you plan to itemize deductions, claim certain credits, or claim adjustments to income on your 2002 tax return.

1   Enter an estimate of your 2002 itemized deductions. These include qualifying home mortgage interest, charitable contributions, state and local taxes, medical expenses in excess of 7.5% of your income, and miscellaneous deductions. (For 2002, you may have to reduce your itemized deductions if your income is over $137,300 ($68,650 if married filing separately). See **Worksheet 3** in Pub. 919 for details.) . . .   **1** $ _____

2   Enter: { $7,850 if married filing jointly or qualifying widow(er)
$6,900 if head of household
$4,700 if single
$3,925 if married filing separately }   . . . .   **2** $ _____

3   **Subtract** line 2 from line 1. If line 2 is greater than line 1, enter "-0-" . . . .   **3** $ _____
4   Enter an estimate of your 2002 adjustments to income, including alimony, deductible IRA contributions, and student loan interest   **4** $ _____
5   **Add** lines 3 and 4 and enter the total. Include any amount for credits from **Worksheet 7** in Pub. 919. .   **5** $ _____
6   Enter an estimate of your 2002 nonwage income (such as dividends or interest) . . . .   **6** $ _____
7   **Subtract** line 6 from line 5. Enter the result, but not less than "-0-" . . . .   **7** $ _____
8   **Divide** the amount on line 7 by $3,000 and enter the result here. Drop any fraction . . . .   **8** _____
9   Enter the number from the **Personal Allowances Worksheet**, line H, page 1 . . . .   **9** _____
10   **Add** lines 8 and 9 and enter the total here. If you plan to use the **Two-Earner/Two-Job Worksheet**, also enter this total on line 1 below. Otherwise, **stop here** and enter this total on Form W-4, line 5, page 1 . .   **10** _____

Two-Earner/Two-Job Worksheet

Note: Use this worksheet only if the instructions under line H on page 1 direct you here.

1   Enter the number from line H, page 1 (or from line 10 above if you used the **Deductions and Adjustments Worksheet**)   **1** _____
2   Find the number in **Table 1** below that applies to the **lowest** paying job and enter it here . . . . .   **2** _____
3   If line 1 is **more than or equal to** line 2, subtract line 2 from line 1. Enter the result here (if zero, enter "-0-") and on Form W-4, line 5, page 1. **Do not** use the rest of this worksheet . . . .   **3** _____

Note: If line 1 is **less than** line 2, enter "-0-" on Form W-4, line 5, page 1. Complete lines 4–9 below to calculate the additional withholding amount necessary to avoid a year end tax bill.

4   Enter the number from line 2 of this worksheet . . . .   **4** _____
5   Enter the number from line 1 of this worksheet . . . .   **5** _____
6   **Subtract** line 5 from line 4   . . . .   **6** _____
7   Find the amount in **Table 2** below that applies to the **highest** paying job and enter it here . .   **7** $ _____
8   **Multiply** line 7 by line 6 and enter the result here. This is the additional annual withholding needed . .   **8** $ _____
9   Divide line 8 by the number of pay periods remaining in 2002. For example, divide by 26 if you are paid every two weeks and you complete this form in December 2001. Enter the result here and on Form W-4, line 6, page 1. This is the additional amount to be withheld from each paycheck . . . .   **9** $ _____

Table 1: Two-Earner/Two-Job Worksheet

Married Filing Jointly				All Others			
If wages from **LOWEST** paying job are—	Enter on line 2 above	If wages from **LOWEST** paying job are—	Enter on line 2 above	If wages from **LOWEST** paying job are—	Enter on line 2 above	If wages from **LOWEST** paying job are—	Enter on line 2 above
$0 - $4,000	0	44,001 - 50,000	8	$0 - $6,000	0	75,001 - 95,000	8
4,001 - 9,000	1	50,001 - 55,000	9	6,001 - 11,000	1	95,001 - 110,000	9
9,001 - 15,000	2	55,001 - 65,000	10	11,001 - 17,000	2	110,001 and over	10
15,001 - 20,000	3	65,001 - 80,000	11	17,001 - 23,000	3		
20,001 - 25,000	4	80,001 - 95,000	12	23,001 - 28,000	4		
25,001 - 32,000	5	95,001 - 110,000	13	28,001 - 38,000	5		
32,001 - 38,000	6	110,001 - 125,000	14	38,001 - 55,000	6		
38,001 - 44,000	7	125,000 and over	15	55,001 - 75,000	7		

Table 2: Two-Earner/Two-Job Worksheet

Married Filing Jointly		All Others	
If wages from **HIGHEST** paying job are—	Enter on line 7 above	If wages from **HIGHEST** paying job are—	Enter on line 7 above
$0 - $50,000	$450	$0 - $30,000	$450
50,001 - 100,000	800	30,001 - 70,000	800
100,001 - 150,000	900	70,001 - 140,000	900
150,001 - 270,000	1,050	140,001 - 300,000	1,050
270,001 and over,	1,150	300,001 and over .	1,150

The second page of the form is a considerably more complex variation of the top portion of the first page, and is intended to assist employees who itemize their tax returns in determining the correct amount of their projected withholdings. The page is split into thirds. The top third is for the use of single filers; the middle third is intended for a household of two wage earners; and the bottom third is a wage table to be used by households of two wage earners.

If for some reason the payroll staff has not received a W-4 form from a new employee as of the date when payroll must be calculated, the IRS requires payroll to assume the person to be single, with no withholding allowances. This is the most conservative way to calculate someone's income taxes, resulting in the largest possible amount of taxes withheld.

 TIPS & TECHNIQUES

Employees who claim complete exemption from federal tax withholdings on their W-4 forms must file a new form each year, or else be liable for withholding that equates to a single marital status and zero allowances. Employees probably will not know about this refiling requirement, so the payroll department should send them periodic reminders. This can be time-consuming, since W-4 forms are usually buried in an employee's payroll file and are not reviewed regularly. One approach is to create a "tickler" file containing copies of only those W-4 forms that must be replaced regularly; and make a notation on the departmental activities calendar to review the tickler file on specific dates. Another solution is to set up a meeting date in an electronic planner (such as Microsoft Outlook) that will issue an alert on the user's computer to review this issue on specific dates. The meeting alert can even be sent automatically to those people who are required to complete new W-4 forms, though you must be sure they must have ready access to a computer to receive this warning.

A little-known rule is that the IRS requires an employer to send to it any W-4 forms for employees who may be taking an excessive number of allowances or who are claiming exemption from withholdings. This is the case when an existing employee claims more than 10 withholdings, or claims full exemption from withholding despite earning more than $200 per week. The W-4 form should be sent to the IRS only if the employees submitting the forms are still in employment at the end of the quarter. The forms should be sent to the same IRS office where the corporate Form 941 is filed, along with a cover letter that identifies the business and notes its Employer Identification Number (EIN).

Federal Income Taxes

An employer is required by law to deduct income taxes from employee pay. If it uses a payroll supplier, then the calculation of the appropriate income tax amounts is completely invisible to it, since the supplier handles this task. If the employer calculates income taxes using a software package, then the software supplier will issue new tax tables each year to accompany the software. In this case, too, there is little need for an employer to know how the tax tables function. However, if a business calculates its payroll internally and manually, then it needs the wage bracket tax tables published by the IRS. They are contained within Publications 15 and 15-A, which can be downloaded from the IRS web site at *www.irs.gov*. These tables are published for a variety of scenarios, such as for single or married employees; a variety of payroll periods; and for withholding allowances numbering from 0 to 10. An example is shown in Exhibit 7.2, which is taken from page 35 of the 2002 Publication 15-A. It lists the amount of income, Social Security, and Medicare taxes to be withheld for a single person. Note, however, the exhibit is incomplete; it shows only taxes due for wages in a small range, and for 0 through 5 withholding allowances.

EXHIBIT 7.2

Tax Table for a Single Filer on a Weekly Payroll Period

		Number of Withholding Allowances					
Pay of at least	But less than	0	1	2	3	4	5
$400	$410	$77.98	$69.98	$60.98	$51.98	$43.98	$37.98
410	420	80.75	71.75	63.75	54.75	45.75	39.75
420	430	82.51	74.51	65.51	56.51	48.51	41.51
430	440	85.28	76.28	68.28	59.28	50.28	43.28
440	450	87.04	79.04	70.04	61.04	53.04	45.04
450	460	89.81	80.81	72.81	63.81	54.81	46.81
460	470	91.57	83.57	74.57	65.57	57.57	48.57
470	480	94.34	85.34	77.34	68.34	59.34	51.34
480	490	96.10	88.10	79.10	70.10	62.10	53.10
490	500	98.87	89.87	81.87	72.87	63.87	55.87

Example. Ms. Storm Dunaway works in the Humble Pie Company's baking division, which pays its employees once a week. She earned $462 in the past week and has claimed three withholding allowances. Using the wage bracket table in Exhibit 7.2, it's easy to find the correct wage bracket that contains her pay range (of at least $460 but less than $470), and then shift horizontally across the table from that wage bracket to the column for three withholding allowances, which shows that her total taxes should be $65.57.

Two alternative calculations are shown in Exhibit 7.3, which show the underlying formulas that were used to derive the wage bracket tax table in Exhibit 7.2. Using Alternative 1 in Exhibit 7.3, subtract a dollar amount from an employee's base wage that corresponds to the number of withholding allowances taken, multiply by a base tax rate, and then reduce the tax rate by a fixed amount to arrive at the income tax. (Note that these tables *do not* include the Social Security or Medicare taxes, as was the case in Exhibit 7.2.) Using Alternative 2 in Exhibit 7.3, subtract a dollar amount from an employee's base wage that corresponds to the number of withholding allowances taken, reduce the taxable wage by a fixed amount, and then multiply by a base tax rate to arrive at the income tax. Either method results in an identical income tax.

Example. The Humble Pie Company's baking division is switching to an in-house computer-based payroll processing system and wants to ensure that both IRS formula tables contained within it are correctly calculating income tax withholdings. As a baseline, they use the $65.57 withholding that was calculated for Storm Dunaway in the previous example. By netting out the 6.2 percent Social Security and 1.45 percent Medicare taxes that were included in that figure, they arrive at a baseline income tax of $30.23.

Using the formulas listed under Alternative 1 for a weekly pay period for a single person in Exhibit 7.3, they first subtract $57.69 from Ms. Dunaway's gross pay for each withholding allowance claimed, which reduces her gross income for calculation purposes to $288.93. They next multiply this amount by 15 percent and then subtract $13.30 from it, as specified in the table. This results in a calculated income tax of $30.04, which is substantially the same figure found under the wage bracket method.

They then switch to the formulas listed under Alternative 2 for a weekly pay period for a single person in Exhibit 7.3, which requires the same deduction of $57.69 from Ms. Dunaway's gross pay for each withholding allowance claimed, once again resulting in gross pay of $288.93. Under this approach, they subtract $88.67 from the gross pay to arrive

EXHIBIT 7.3

Alternative Formulas for Calculating Income Taxes

(For Wages Paid in 2002)

Alternative 1.—Tables for Percentage Method Withholding Computations

Table A(1)—WEEKLY PAYROLL PERIOD (Amount for each allowance claimed is $57.69)

Single Person				Married Person			
If the wage in excess of allowance amount is:		The income tax to be withheld is:		If the wage in excess of allowance amount is:		The income tax to be withheld is:	
Over—	But not over—	Of such wage—	From product	Over—	But not over—	Of such wage—	From product
$0	—$51	0%	$0	$124	—$0	0%	$0
$51	—$164	10% less	$5.10	$124	—$355	10% less	$12.40
$164	—$570	15% less	$13.30	$355	—$991	15% less	$30.15
$570	—$1,247	27% less	$81.70	$991	—$2,110	27% less	$149.07
$1,247	—$2,749	30% less	$119.11	$2,110	—$3,400	30% less	$212.37
$2,749	—$5,938	35% less	$256.56	$3,400	—$5,998	35% less	$382.37
$5,938	—	38.6% less	$470.33	$5,998	—	38.6% less	$598.30

Table B(1)—BIWEEKLY PAYROLL PERIOD (Amount for each allowance claimed is $115.38)

Single Person				Married Person			
If the wage in excess of allowance amount is:		The income tax to be withheld is:		If the wage in excess of allowance amount is:		The income tax to be withheld is:	
Over—	But not over—	Of such wage—	From product	Over—	But not over—	Of such wage—	From product
$0	—$102	0%	$0	$0	—$248	0%	$0
$102	—$329	10% less	$10.20	$248	—$710	10% less	$24.80
$329	—$1,140	15% less	$26.65	$710	—$1,983	15% less	$60.30
$1,140	—$2,493	27% less	$163.45	$1,983	—$4,219	27% less	$298.26
$2,493	—$5,498	30% less	$238.24	$4,219	—$6,800	30% less	$424.83
$5,498	—$11,875	35% less	$513.14	$6,800	—$11,996	35% less	$764.83
$11,875	—	38.6% less	$940.64	$11,996	—	38.6% less	$1,196.69

Table C(1)—SEMIMONTHLY PAYROLL PERIOD (Amount for each allowance claimed is $125.00)

Single Person				Married Person			
If the wage in excess of allowance amount is:		The income tax to be withheld is:		If the wage in excess of allowance amount is:		The income tax to be withheld is:	
Over—	But not over—	Of such wage—	From product	Over—	But not over—	Of such wage—	From product
$0	—$110	0%	$0	$0	—$269	0%	$0
$110	—$356	10% less	$11.00	$269	—$769	10% less	$26.90
$356	—$1,235	15% less	$28.80	$769	—$2,148	15% less	$65.35
$1,235	—$2,701	27% less	$177.00	$2,148	—$4,571	27% less	$323.11
$2,701	—$5,956	30% less	$258.03	$4,571	—$7,367	30% less	$460.24
$5,956	—$12,865	35% less	$555.83	$7,367	—$12,996	35% less	$828.59
$12,865	—	38.6% less	1,018.97	$12,996	—	38.6% less	$1,296.45

Table D(1)—MONTHLY PAYROLL PERIOD (Amount for each allowance claimed is $250.00)

Single Person				Married Person			
If the wage in excess of allowance amount is:		The income tax to be withheld is:		If the wage in excess of allowance amount is:		The income tax to be withheld is:	
Over—	But not over—	Of such wage—	From product	Over—	But not over—	Of such wage—	From product
$0	—$221	0%	$0	$0	—$538	0%	$0
$221	—$713	10% less	$22.10	$538	—$1,538	10% less	$53.80
$713	—$2,471	15% less	$57.75	$1,538	—$4,296	15% less	$130.70
$2,471	—$5,402	27% less	$354.27	$4,296	—$9,142	27% less	$646.22
$5,402	—$11,913	30% less	$516.33	$9,142	—$14,733	30% less	$920.48
$11,913	—$25,729	35% less	1,111.98	$14,733	—$25,992	35% less	$1,657.13
$25,729	—	38.6% less	2,038.22	$25,992	—	38.6% less	$2,592.84

Table E(1)—DAILY OR MISCELLANEOUS PAYROLL PERIOD
(Amount for each allowance claimed per day for such period is $11.54)

Single Person				Married Person			
If the wage in excess of allowance amount divided by the number of days in the pay period is:		The income tax to be withheld multiplied by the number of days in such period is:		If the wage in excess of allowance amount divided by the number of days in the pay period is:		The income tax to be withheld multiplied by the number of days in such period is:	
Over—	But not over—	Of such wage—	From product	Over—	But not over—	Of such wage—	From product
$0.00	—$10.20	0%	$0	$0.00	—$24.80	0%	$0
$10.20	—$32.90	10% less	$1.02	$24.80	—$71.00	10% less	$2.48
$32.90	—$114.00	15% less	$2.67	$71.00	—$198.30	15% less	$6.03
$114.00	—$249.30	27% less	$16.34	$198.30	—$421.90	27% less	$29.82
$249.30	—$549.80	30% less	$23.82	$421.90	—$680.00	30% less	$42.48
$549.80	—$1,187.50	35% less	$51.31	$680.00	—$1,199.60	35% less	$76.48
$1,187.50	—	38.6% less	$94.06	$1,199.60	—	38.6% less	$119.67

Note.—The adjustment factors may be reduced by one-half cent (e.g., 7.50 to 7.495; 69.38 to 69.375) to eliminate separate half rounding operations.

The first two brackets of these tables may be combined, provided zero withholding is used to credit withholding amounts computed by the

combined bracket rates, e.g., $0 to $51 and $51 to $536 combined to read, Over $0, But not over $536.

The employee's excess wage (gross wage less amount for allowances claimed) is used with the applicable percentage rates and subtraction factors to calculate the amount of income tax withheld.

Page 23

178

EXHIBIT 7.3 (CONTINUED)

(For Wages Paid in 2002)
Alternative 2.—Tables for Percentage Method Withholding Computations

Table A(2)—WEEKLY PAYROLL PERIOD (Amount for each allowance claimed is $57.69)

Single Person					Married Person				
If the wage in excess of allowance amount is:		The income tax to be withheld is:			If the wage in excess of allowance amount is:		The income tax to be withheld is:		
Over—	But not over—	Such wage—		Times	Over—	But not over—	Such wage—		Times
$0	—$51	$0.00		0%	$0	—$124	$0.00		0%
$51	—$164	minus $51.00		10%	$124	—$355	minus $124.00		10%
$164	—$570	minus $88.67		15%	$355	—$991	minus $201.00		15%
$570	—$1,247	minus $302.59		27%	$991	—$2,110	minus $552.11		27%
$1,247	—$2,749	minus $397.03		30%	$2,110	—$3,400	minus $707.90		30%
$2,749	—$5,938	minus $733.03		35%	$3,400	—$5,998	minus $1,092.49		35%
$5,938	—	minus $1,218.47		38.6%	$5,998	—	minus $1,549.99		38.6%

Table B(2)—BIWEEKLY PAYROLL PERIOD (Amount for each allowance claimed is $115.38)

Single Person					Married Person				
If the wage in excess of allowance amount is:		The income tax to be withheld is:			If the wage in excess of allowance amount is:		The income tax to be withheld is:		
Over—	But not over—	Such wage—		Times	Over—	But not over—	Such wage—		Times
$0	—$102	$0.00		0%	$0	—$248	$0.00		0%
$102	—$329	minus $102.00		10%	$248	—$710	minus $248.00		10%
$329	—$1,140	minus $177.67		15%	$710	—$1,983	minus $402.00		15%
$1,140	—$2,493	minus $605.37		27%	$1,983	—$4,219	minus $1,104.67		27%
$2,493	—$5,498	minus $794.13		30%	$4,219	—$6,800	minus $1,416.10		30%
$5,498	—$11,875	minus $1,466.11		35%	$6,800	—$11,996	minus $2,185.23		35%
$11,875	—	minus $2,436.89		38.6%	$11,996	—	minus $3,100.22		38.6%

Table C(2)—SEMIMONTHLY PAYROLL PERIOD (Amount for each allowance claimed is $125.00)

Single Person					Married Person				
If the wage in excess of allowance amount is:		The income tax to be withheld is:			If the wage in excess of allowance amount is:		The income tax to be withheld is:		
Over—	But not over—	Such wage—		Times	Over—	But not over—	Such wage—		Times
$0	—$110	$0.00		0%	$0	—$269	$0.00		0%
$110	—$356	minus $110.00		10%	$269	—$769	minus $269.00		10%
$356	—$1,235	minus $192.00		15%	$769	—$2,148	minus $435.67		15%
$1,235	—$2,701	minus $655.56		27%	$2,148	—$4,571	minus $1,196.70		27%
$2,701	—$5,956	minus $860.10		30%	$4,571	—$7,367	minus $1,534.13		30%
$5,956	—$12,865	minus $1,588.09		35%	$7,367	—$12,996	minus $2,367.40		35%
$12,865	—	minus $2,639.82		38.6%	$12,996	—	minus $3,358.67		38.6%

Table D(2)—MONTHLY PAYROLL PERIOD (Amount for each allowance claimed is $250.00)

Single Person					Married Person				
If the wage in excess of allowance amount is:		The income tax to be withheld is:			If the wage in excess of allowance amount is:		The income tax to be withheld is:		
Over—	But not over—	Such wage—		Times	Over—	But not over—	Such wage—		Times
$0	—$221	$0.00		0%	$0	—$538	$0.00		0%
$221	—$713	minus $221.00		10%	$538	—$1,538	minus $538.00		10%
$713	—$2,471	minus $385.00		15%	$1,538	—$4,296	minus $871.33		15%
$2,471	—$5,402	minus $1,312.11		27%	$4,296	—$9,142	minus $2,393.41		27%
$5,402	—$11,913	minus $1,721.10		30%	$9,142	—$14,733	minus $3,068.27		30%
$11,913	—$25,729	minus $3,177.09		35%	$14,733	—$25,992	minus $4,734.66		35%
$25,729	—	minus $5,280.37		38.6%	$25,992	—	minus $6,717.21		38.6%

Table E(2)—DAILY OR MISCELLANEOUS PAYROLL PERIOD
(Amount for each allowance claimed per day for such period is $11.54)

Single Person					Married Person				
If the wage in excess of allowance amount divided by the number of days in the pay period is:		The income tax to be withheld multiplied by the number of days in such period is:			If the wage in excess of allowance amount divided by the number of days in the pay period is:		The income tax to be withheld multiplied by the number of days in such period is:		
Over—	But not over—	Such wage—		Times	Over—	But not over—	Such wage—		Times
$0.00	—$10.20	$0.00		0%	$0.00	—$24.80	$0.00		0%
$10.20	—$32.90	minus $10.20		10%	$24.80	—$71.00	minus $24.80		10%
$32.90	—$114.00	minus $17.77		15%	$71.00	—$198.30	minus $40.20		15%
$114.00	—$249.30	minus $60.52		27%	$198.30	—$421.90	minus $110.45		27%
$249.30	—$549.80	minus $79.40		30%	$421.90	—$680.00	minus $141.60		30%
$549.80	—$1,187.50	minus $146.60		35%	$680.00	—$1,199.60	minus $218.51		35%
$1,187.50	—	minus $243.67		38.6%	$1,199.60	—	minus $310.01		38.6%

Note.—The first two brackets of these tables may be combined, provided zero withholding is used to credit withholding amounts computed by the combined bracket rates, e.g., $0 to $51 and $51 to $536 combined to read, Over $0, But not over $536.

The employee's excess wage (gross wage less amount for allowances claimed) is used with the applicable percentage rates and subtraction factors to calculate the amount of income tax withheld.

at $200.26, and then multiply by 15 percent to arrive at the same income tax of $30.04.

Several other, less-used methods for calculating tax withholding amounts require the override of a computerized withholding calculation system with manual calculations. They are:

- *Basis is annualized wages.* Under this approach, calculate an employee's annual pay rate and then determine the annual withholding amount in the IRS Annual Payroll Period tax table. Divide this amount by the number of pay periods in the year to determine the deduction for an individual pay-check.

- *Basis is partial-year employment.* This method can be used only at an employee's written request, which must state the last day of work with any prior employer, that the employee uses the calendar year accounting method, and that the employee does not expect to work during the year for more than 245 days. The company then compiles all wages paid to the employee during his or her current term of employment, including the current pay period. The next step is to determine the number of pay periods from the date of the employee's last employment, through and including the current pay period, and divide this amount into the total wages figure, resulting in an average wage per pay period. Use the correct tax table to arrive at a withholding amount for the average wage, then multiply this amount by the total number of pay periods, as already calcu-lated. Finally, subtract the total amount of withholdings already made, resulting in the withholding to be made in the current pay period.

  This approach is requested by employees such as part-time students or seasonal workers who expect to be out of work so much during the calendar year that their full-year pay will drop them into a lower tax bracket, resulting in smaller income tax withholdings.

- *Basis is year-to-date cumulative wages.* This method can only be used at an employee's written request. To calculate it, compile all wages paid to the employee for the year-to-date through and including the current pay period, and divide the sum by the total number of year-to-date pay periods, including the current period. Then use the percentage method to calculate the withholding on this average wage. Multiply the withholding amount by the total number of year-to-date payroll periods, and subtract the actual amount of withholdings made year-to-date. The remainder is the amount to withhold from the employee's wages during the current pay period.

This complicated approach is requested by employees who may have had an excessive amount of taxes withheld from their pay earlier in the year, perhaps due to a large commission or bonus payment that bumped them into a higher income tax bracket. By using the cumulative wages calculation, these excessive withholdings may sometimes result in a one-time withholding on the payroll in which this calculation is requested that is much smaller than usual.

Supplemental Pay

Several of the alternative tax calculation methods just described are used because the amount withheld from employee pay for the year-to-date is higher than will be needed by the end of the calendar year. This may be caused by a large payment to an employee earlier in the year, perhaps a commission or bonus; when this happens, the extra payment is typically lumped into the person's regular pay, which bumps the person into a higher tax bracket on the assumption that he or she always receives this amount of money during every pay period. As a result, there will be an excessively large withholding at the end of the year, and the employee will receive a tax refund.

One approach for avoiding the excessive amount of tax withholdings is to separate the supplemental pay from the base pay and issue two separate payments to an employee. Under this approach, the percentage withheld will likely be smaller than if the pay had been combined into a single paycheck. Another approach that is acceptable to the IRS is to combine the payments and then withhold a flat 27 percent rate from it. For most computerized payroll systems, it is easier to implement the first approach.

Sick Pay

In general, sick pay made to employees requires all of the Social Security, Medicare, and income tax withholdings that are calculated for normal wages; however, there are a few exceptions. For example, if an employee dies and sick pay is made to his or her estate in the following calendar year, this amount is not subject to any of the usual payroll withholdings or taxes. The same rules apply if sick payments are made to an employee who has been absent from work for at least six months.

If employees contribute to a sick pay plan with after-tax dollars, then any payments made to them from that plan will not require any withholdings or payroll taxes, on the grounds that the employee already paid those taxes on the initial cash used to fund the plan. Alternatively, if the sick pay plan is funded with pretax dollars (as can occur through a cafeteria plan), then any pay from the sick pay plan will require income tax withholdings and all other normal payroll taxes, on the grounds that the employee would otherwise never pay taxes on the wages paid.

If employees are paid sick pay through a third party, such as an independent insurance company, the third party has no obligation to withhold income taxes, though it can do so if an employee submits to it a Form W-4S that states how much is to be withheld. The *minimum* amount that can be withheld in this manner is $20 per week.

Social Security Taxes

Employers are required to withhold 6.2 percent of each employee's pay, which is forwarded to the government Social Security fund. The employer must also match this amount, so the total remittance to the government is 12.4 percent. This withholding applies to the first $84,900 of employee pay in each calendar year, though this number increases regularly by act of Congress.

Example. The president of the Humble Pie Company is Elinor Plump. She earned $185,000 in calendar year 2001. She expects to be paid the same amount in 2002, and wants to know how much Social Security tax will be deducted from her pay in that year, so she can budget her cash flow. The calculation is as follows:

Total annual pay	$185,000
Total annual pay subject to the Social Security tax	$ 84,900
Tax rate	6.2%
Social Security taxes to be withheld	**$5,263.80**

If a company takes over another business, or purchases its assets, the buying entity can include the year-to-date wages paid to the acquiree's employees in determining the amount of Social Security taxes withheld. This reduces the amount of withholdings for those employees who earn more than $84,900 per year, and reduces the amount of matching taxes paid by the business.

Medicare Taxes

Employers are required to withhold 1.45 percent of each employee's pay, which is forwarded to the government Medicare fund. The employer must also match this amount, so the total remittance to the government is 2.9 percent. This withholding applies to all employee earnings during the year, with no upper limit.

Example. The Humble Pie Company's most productive salesperson is Elma Soders, whose annual base pay is $25,000. The total of her commissions and performance bonuses for the past year was $147,000, giving her a total compensation of $171,000. What will both Mrs. Soders and the company pay to the government for her Medicare taxes?

Total annual pay	$171,000
Total annual pay subject to the Medicare tax	$171,000
Tax rate	2.9%
Medicare taxes to be remitted	$ 4,959

State Income Taxes

All states require state income tax withholding, with the exceptions of Alaska, Connecticut, Florida, Nevada, New Hampshire, South Dakota, Tennessee, Texas, Washington, and Wyoming. Those states requiring a business to withhold state income taxes from its employees all have different methods and forms for doing so, which requires a detailed knowledge of the withholding and remittance requirements of each state. If an organization calculates its own payroll, then it will likely be sent this information on a regular basis through the mail by each state government with which it has registered. For most states, this information is also accessible via their official web sites. A much easier approach, however, is to outsource the payroll processing function, which makes the payroll supplier responsible for making the correct withholdings and remittances (if the employer chooses this service).

Unlike the federal government, which allows most payroll tax payments to be remitted with a single document, states may require employers to use a variety of forms, perhaps one for income taxes, another for unemployment insurance, and another for disability insurance (though this is required only by a small number of states). Given the amount of paperwork involved, a company that remits its own state taxes should construct a calendar of remittances, which the payroll manager can use to ensure that payments are always made, thereby avoiding late-payment penalties and interest charges.

If an employer has nonresident employees, and the state in which it does business has an income tax, the employer will usually withhold income for each employee's state of residence. Alternatively, an employer can withhold income on behalf of the state in which it does business and let the employee claim a credit on his or her state tax return to avoid double taxation. The ability to do this will vary by individual state law.

Payroll Taxes for Employees Working Abroad

Special withholding rules apply if an employee works in other countries. The first consideration is the duration: If an employee works abroad for only part of the year, in general normal withholdings must be made, with the employer matching Social Security and Medicare taxes in the normal percentages. However, an employer is not required to withhold Social Security or Medicare taxes if its employees work in any of the following countries:

Austria	Korea
Belgium	Luxembourg
Canada	The Netherlands
Finland	Norway
France	Portugal
Germany	Spain
Greece	Sweden
Ireland	Switzerland
Italy	United Kingdom

These countries all have *totalization* agreements with the United States, whereby an employee only has to pay Social Security taxes to the country in which he or she is working. This makes a person exempt from U.S. Social Security and Medicare taxes while working in the listed countries.

If another country requires the withholding of income taxes for income earned while working there, then a company does not have to also withhold U.S. taxes, since this would be regarded as double taxation.

If an employee qualifies for the foreign earned income exclusion, he or she can exclude the first $80,000 of foreign earned income from his or her gross income, but only if that employee's home during the tax year is considered to be abroad, or he or she is physically present in the foreign country for 330 full days out of a 12-month period (which does not have to correspond to a calendar year). The exclusion must be formally elected by filling out either Form 2555 or Form 2555-EZ.

Payroll Taxes for Aliens

An employer is required to withhold all types of taxes for resident aliens. Holders of the I-551 Permanent Resident Card ("Green Card") fall into this category. However, employers *do not* withhold Social Security or Medicare taxes if the alien is an agricultural worker or holds a variety of nonimmigrant visas, such as F-1 (students), H-1B (professionals and technical workers), or Q (cultural exchange visitors).

A nonresident alien is required to complete a W-4 form. When doing so, the person cannot claim exemption from withholding, must state his or her marital status as being single, and in most cases can only claim one allowance.

Registering with the Government for Tax Remittances

When a company sends payroll tax remittances to the federal government, the government needs to identify the company so it can give the company proper credit for the remittances. This is done with an Employer Identification Number (EIN). An employer applies for an EIN number using the Application for Employer Identification Number, Form SS-4, which is shown in Exhibit 7.4. Once this form is sent to the IRS, it takes four weeks to receive an EIN number in the mail.

If the first payroll deposit is due before the receipt of the EIN, the employer can call the IRS Tele-TIN or Fax-TIN number to obtain the number more quickly. The Tele-TIN number is 1-866-816-2065. If you choose to call, be sure to fill out Form SS-4 beforehand, since most of the information on it will be needed to complete the request. You will be given an EIN over the phone. To accelerate the processing of the regular Form SS-4, fax it to the regional Fax-TIN number, which will result in the fax-back of an EIN number in about four business days. (Note: One problem with this approach is that the IRS does not use a cover sheet when sending a response through a company's fax machine, so the transmitted document containing the new EIN number may be lost.) The Fax-TIN numbers for all regions are listed in Exhibit 7.5.

Instructions for filling out the Form SS-4 are as follows:

Line 1. Enter the legal name of the entity (not its doing-business-as name). If the business is a person or sole proprietorship, enter the person's first, middle, and last names.

Line 2. If there is a doing-business-as (dba or "trade" name), enter it on this line.

Line 3. If there is an executor or trustee of a trust, enter that person's first, middle, and last names here.

Lines 4–6. Enter the complete mailing address, including the county name. The EIN will be sent to this location.

Line 7. Enter the first, middle, and last names of the principal officer, general partner, or sole proprietor, depending on the type of business entity.

Line 8. Check the type of business entity under which the business is legally organized. If it is a sole proprietorship, also enter the

EXHIBIT 7.4

Application for Employer Identification Number

Form **SS-4**	**Application for Employer Identification Number**		EIN
(Rev. December 2001)	(For use by employers, corporations, partnerships, trusts, estates, churches, government agencies, Indian tribal entities, certain individuals, and others.)		
Department of the Treasury Internal Revenue Service	► See separate instructions for each line. ► Keep a copy for your records.		OMB No. 1545-0003

1 Legal name of entity (or individual) for whom the EIN is being requested

<table>
<tr><td colspan="2">Type or print clearly.</td></tr>
</table>

Type or print clearly.

2 Trade name of business (if different from name on line 1) | **3** Executor, trustee, "care of" name

4a Mailing address (room, apt., suite no. and street, or P.O. box) | **5a** Street address (if different) (Do not enter a P.O. box.)

4b City, state, and ZIP code | **5b** City, state, and ZIP code

6 County and state where principal business is located

7a Name of principal officer, general partner, grantor, owner, or trustor | **7b** SSN, ITIN, or EIN

8a Type of entity (check only one box)
- ☐ Sole proprietor (SSN) _____
- ☐ Partnership
- ☐ Corporation (enter form number to be filed) ► _____
- ☐ Personal service corp.
- ☐ Church or church-controlled organization
- ☐ Other nonprofit organization (specify) ► _____
- ☐ Other (specify) ►

- ☐ Estate (SSN of decedent) _____
- ☐ Plan administrator (SSN) _____
- ☐ Trust (SSN of grantor) _____
- ☐ National Guard ☐ State/local government
- ☐ Farmers' cooperative ☐ Federal government/military
- ☐ REMIC ☐ Indian tribal governments/enterprises
- Group Exemption Number (GEN) ► _____

8b If a corporation, name the state or foreign country (if applicable) where incorporated | State | Foreign country

9 Reason for applying (check only one box)
- ☐ Started new business (specify type) ► _____
- ☐ Hired employees (Check the box and see line 12.)
- ☐ Compliance with IRS withholding regulations
- ☐ Other (specify) ►

- ☐ Banking purpose (specify purpose) ► _____
- ☐ Changed type of organization (specify new type) ► _____
- ☐ Purchased going business
- ☐ Created a trust (specify type) ► _____
- ☐ Created a pension plan (specify type) ► _____

10 Date business started or acquired (month, day, year) | **11** Closing month of accounting year

12 First date wages or annuities were paid or will be paid (month, day, year). **Note:** If applicant is a withholding agent, enter date income will first be paid to nonresident alien. (month, day, year) . . . . ►

13 Highest number of employees expected in the next 12 months. **Note:** If the applicant does not expect to have any employees during the period, enter "-0-." . . . . ► | Agricultural | Household | Other

14 Check **one** box that best describes the principal activity of your business.
- ☐ Construction ☐ Rental & leasing ☐ Transportation & warehousing
- ☐ Real estate ☐ Manufacturing ☐ Finance & insurance
- ☐ Health care & social assistance ☐ Wholesale–agent/broker
- ☐ Accommodation & food service ☐ Wholesale–other ☐ Retail
- ☐ Other (specify)

15 Indicate principal line of merchandise sold; specific construction work done; products produced; or services provided.

16a Has the applicant ever applied for an employer identification number for this or any other business? . . . . ☐ Yes ☐ No
Note: If "Yes," please complete lines 16b and 16c.

16b If you checked "Yes" on line 16a, give applicant's legal name and trade name shown on prior application if different from line 1 or 2 above.
Legal name ► Trade name ►

16c Approximate date when, and city and state where, the application was filed. Enter previous employer identification number if known.
Approximate date when filed (mo., day, year) | City and state where filed | Previous EIN

Third Party Designee	Complete this section **only** if you want to authorize the named individual to receive the entity's EIN and answer questions about the completion of this form.	
	Designee's name	Designee's telephone number (include area code) ( )
	Address and ZIP code	Designee's fax number (include area code) ( )

Under penalties of perjury, I declare that I have examined this application, and to the best of my knowledge and belief, it is true, correct, and complete. | Applicant's telephone number (include area code) ( )

Name and title (type or print clearly) ► | Applicant's fax number (include area code) ( )

Signature ► Date ►

For Privacy Act and Paperwork Reduction Act Notice, see separate instructions. Cat. No. 16055N Form **SS-4** (Rev. 12-2001)

Social Security number. If it is a corporation, enter the state or foreign country in which it is organized.

Line 9. Check just one of the listed options as a reason for applying for the EIN. That is, you should not be applying for an EIN if you are simply hiring additional employees, since you should already have obtained an EIN for the existing entity. If you have created a pension plan, it must have a separate EIN from that of the business entity.

Line 10. If the business was just started, enter its start date. If you purchased an existing business, enter the purchase date.

Line 11. Enter the last month of the business's accounting year. For an individual, this is usually the calendar year-end, though it can vary for other types of business entities.

Line 12. Enter the date on which wages were first paid or are expected to be paid. If there is no prospective date, enter "N/A" in this space.

Line 13. Enter in each space provided the maximum number of employees expected to be on the payroll during the next 12 months. There are spaces for agricultural, household, and other employees.

Line 14. Check just one box next to the industry group that best describes your business's main area of operations. If none apply, check the "Other" box and briefly describe the principal activity.

Line 15. Describe the business entity's principal activities in somewhat more detail, noting specific types of products or services sold.

Line 16. Indicate whether the business has ever applied for an EIN before. If so, list the legal and trade names of the business used on the prior application, as well as the date and location where it was filed.

EXHIBIT 7.5

Fax–TIN Numbers by State

Fax-TIN Number	Applicable State
631-447-8960	Connecticut, Delaware, District of Columbia, Florida, Georgia, Maine, Maryland, Massachusetts, New Hampshire, New Jersey, New York, North Carolina, Ohio, Pennsylvania, Rhode Island, South Carolina, Vermont, Virginia, West Virginia
859-669-5760	Illinois, Indiana, Kentucky, Michigan
215-516-3990	Alabama, Alaska, Arizona, Arkansas, California, Colorado, Hawaii, Idaho, Iowa, Kansas, Louisiana, Minnesota, Mississippi, Missouri, Montana, Nebraska, Nevada, New Mexico, North Dakota, Oklahoma, Oregon, Puerto Rico, South Dakota, Tennessee, Texas, Utah, Washington, Wisconsin, Wyoming
215-516-3990	No legal residence or principal place of business

If you have no EIN number by the time a deposit is due to the government, send the payment in anyway, noting the business's legal name, address, type of tax, period covered, and the date on which you applied for the EIN. If the EIN has not yet been received by the time a return is due, write "Applied for" in the space on the form where the EIN would normally go, along with the date when you applied for the EIN.

Remitting Federal Taxes

Once Social Security, income tax, and Medicare taxes have been withheld from an employee's pay, they are essentially the property of the federal government; the company is merely holding them in escrow until the next required remittance date. Depending upon the size of the remittances, a company may periodically cut a check for the remittance amount and deliver it to a local bank or Federal Reserve Bank that is authorized to forward the funds to the IRS. However, companies with larger remittances are *required* to make electronic funds transfers directly to the IRS. If a company uses a payroll supplier, then this process is invisible to the company, since the supplier will handle remittances.

Assuming that a company processes its own payroll, it must then determine the frequency with which it remits tax deposits to the federal government. A business can make deposits in three ways:

- *On a monthly basis.* Under this approach, a business must deposit its payroll taxes no later than the fifteenth day of the month following the reporting month. This method can be used only if the total amount of deposits during the *lookback period* is less than $50,000. The lookback period is the four previous quarters during which deposits were reported on Form 941, beginning with July 1 and ending on June 30 of the next year. When making this determination, include all Social Security, federal income, and Medicare taxes withheld during the lookback period. A new employer will generally fall into this category, because the amount of the lookback period (which does not yet exist) is assumed to be zero.

- *On a semiweekly basis.* The government makes it mandatory to use the semiweekly deposit schedule if the dollar volume of taxes during the annual lookback period exceeded $50,000. If it did not, deposits can be made on a monthly basis. Semiweekly refers to two possible dates in each week by which deposits must be made if a payroll payment date falls within that week. If a payment date falls on a weekend, Monday, or Tuesday, then the deposit must be made by the following Friday. If the payment date falls on a Wednesday, Thursday, or Friday, then the deposit must be made by

Wednesday of the following week. One additional business day is added to this schedule if the day by which a deposit is required falls on a banking holiday.

- *Using electronic funds transfers.* The minimum threshold for this approach is $200,000 in deposits during the lookback period, or if the company was required to use it in the previous year. Once a company is required to use this method but fails to do so, it will be subject to a 10 percent penalty. Payments are made using the Electronic Federal Tax Payment System (EFTPS). Under this approach, a business notifies its bank of the amount to be deposited with the government; the bank then electronically shifts the funds from the business's account to the government's. This gives the government more immediate access to the funds. No deposit coupon is required if this system is used, since a coupon is required only to identify an accompanying check, and this method requires no check. The payment intervals are the same as those used for semiweekly depositors, except that any company accumulating $100,000 of taxes for any payroll must deposit it on the business day immediately following the payroll payment date. A business can enroll in the EFTPS by completing the EFTPS Business Enrollment Form (Form 9779).

There is one special case that overrides all of the preceding depositing scenarios. If a company accumulates a payroll tax liability of $100,000 or more as a result of a payroll, the amount must be deposited no later than the next business day, irrespective of the company's status as determined through the lookback method. This special case does not continue to apply if a company's subsequent payroll tax liabilities drop below $100,000; however, if a company had previously been a monthly depositor, this situation will result in the company immediately converting to a semiweekly deposit schedule.

Example. The Red Light Company, maker of lighting fixtures for traffic intersections, reported the following deposit totals:

First quarter 2002	$ 8,500
Second quarter 2002	$ 9,000
Third quarter 2002	$ 10,000
Fourth quarter 2002	$ 11,000
First quarter 2003	$ 15,000
Second quarter 2003	$ 16,000

The controller wants to know if the company will have to make semiweekly or monthly deposits for the calendar year 2004. Though the total deposits made during 2002 only totaled $38,500, the lookback period is for just the last two quarters of 2002 and the first two quarters of 2003, when tax deposits were somewhat higher. The official lookback period contains deposits of $52,000, which is higher than the government-mandated threshold of $50,000. Consequently, the company must deposit on a semiweekly basis.

Example. The Red Light Company's payroll manager wants to know when deposits must be made to the government, now that the company is required to remit deposits on a semiweekly basis. The company pays its employees on Tuesday of each week, based on hours worked during the preceding calendar week. Since the company always pays its employees on a Tuesday, it has until the following Friday to deposit its taxes.

If remittances are to be made to the local bank, then the check must be accompanied by a Form 8109, which is a standard remittance coupon used for a variety of tax remittances. To obtain a booklet of blank Form 8109s, you must file for an Employee Identification Number (EIN) (described earlier in the "Registering with the Government for Tax Remittances" section). The EIN is required because the IRS preprints an organization's EIN, name, and address on each form in the booklet. Filling out the form is simple enough: just enter the dollar amount being remitted and the company's contact phone number, then darken the ovals corresponding to the type of tax being remitted (in this case, always "941") and the applicable quarter to which the remittance applies. (Note: The information on this form is entered into the IRS database with an optical scanner, so write clearly to avoid scanning errors.)

Special handling of tax deposits is necessary if an employer is a semiweekly depositor and has multiple pay days within the same semi-weekly period, but which apply to different calendar quarters. If this situation arises, the employer must determine which portion of the semiweekly deposit applies to payroll occurring within each of the two calendar quarters, and make a separate deposit for each portion.

Example. The Red Light Company has a pay date on Saturday, September 28, 2002, and another on Tuesday, October 1, 2002. Deposits for the two pay dates are both due on the following Friday, October 4, but they must be deposited separately.

Federal Tax Deposit Penalties

The IRS imposes significant penalties if a business does not make its tax deposits on time, makes insufficient deposits, or does not use the EFTPS electronic filing system when it is required to do so. Its penalty structure is:

- 2 percent penalty if deposits are made from one to five days late
- 5 percent penalty if deposits are made 6 to 15 days late
- 10 percent penalty if deposits are made 16 or more days late
- 10 percent penalty if deposits are remitted to the wrong location
- 10 percent penalty if the EFTPS is not used when it is required
- 15 percent penalty if funds have not been remitted at least 10 days after the IRS sent a payment warning notification

Penalties can be avoided for very small payment shortfalls. There is no penalty if a deposit of up to $5,000 is short by no more than $100, or a larger deposit is short by no more than 2 percent of the total. If a shortfall of this size occurs, a semiweekly depositor must deposit the shortfall by the earlier of the next Form 941 due date or the first Wednesday or Friday following the fifteenth day of the next month. A monthly depositor must make the deposit with its next Form 941.

If an employer does not file its quarterly Form 941 in a timely manner, it will be penalized 5 percent for the amount of all net unpaid taxes shown on the return for each month during which the form is not filed. This penalty is capped at 25 percent, which essentially means that a business will be penalized for the first five months during which it does not file a Form 941.

TIPS & TECHNIQUES

A company that acquires another business should closely examine the acquiree's payroll remittances to ensure that all remittances have been made. By doing so, it can determine if a liability for unpaid withholdings lurks, one that might not crop up for several years, when federal or state auditors file claims that may include stiff penalties and interest charges. (Note: This is an issue only if the acquiring entity purchases the other business as a going concern, since it takes on all liabilities of the acquired entity. A purchase of business assets will not present this problem.)

A potential flag for remittance problems is that an acquiree does all of its own remittance filings, rather than using the services of a payroll provider. In this case, there is a greater risk that remittances were sporadically made or never made. Anyone conducting a due diligence review of such a company should establish that every remittance was made in sequence, that cashed checks verify the transfer of funds to the government, and that the amounts paid match the amounts calculated as due and payable in the payroll register.

Example. The Red Herring Fish Company's controller forgets to file a quarterly Form 941, which would have shown a net tax due of $2,200. Upon discovering the error 10 months later and filing the return, the IRS penalizes the firm for five percent of the $2,200 due, multiplied by five months, which is a 25 percent penalty, or $550.

It is possible to convince the IRS to mitigate or eliminate these penalties if reasonable cause is proven. However, given the size of the potential penalties, it is best to make the proper remittance of tax deposits a high priority by the payroll staff.

Employer's Quarterly Federal Tax Return

Form 941 must be filed by employers on a quarterly basis with the federal government. This form identifies the amount of all wages on which taxes were withheld, the amount of taxes withheld, and any adjustments to withheld taxes from previous reporting periods. If there is a shortfall between the amount of withheld taxes on this form and the amount of taxes actually withheld and deposited with the government during the quarter, then the difference must accompany this form when it is submitted. Taxes to be reported on this form include income taxes withheld from wages, including tips, supplementary unemployment compensation benefits, and third-party payments of sick pay, plus Social Security and Medicare taxes. An example of the form is shown in Exhibit 7.6.

Use the following steps to complete the form:

Line 1. Enter the number of employees on the payroll during the pay period that includes March 12. This figure should not include household employees or anyone who received no pay during the period.

Line 2. Enter the total amount of all wages paid, which includes tips and taxable fringe benefits, but not supplemental unemployment compensation benefits and contributions to employee pension plans that are not itemized as employee wages.

EXHIBIT 7.6

Form 941

Form **941**
(Rev. January 2002)
Department of the Treasury
Internal Revenue Service (99)

Employer's Quarterly Federal Tax Return
▶ See separate instructions revised January 2002 for information on completing this return.
Please type or print.

Enter state code for state in which deposits were made **only** if different from state in address to the right ▶ ⬚ (see page 2 of instructions).

Name (as distinguished from trade name)	Date quarter ended		OMB No. 1545-0029
Trade name, if any	Employer identification number		T
			FF
Address (number and street)	City, state, and ZIP code		FD
			FP
			I
			T

If address is different from prior return, check here ▶

IRS Use

1 1 1 1 1 1 1 1 1 1 2 3 3 3 3 3 3 3 3 4 4 4 5 5 5
6 7 8 8 8 8 8 8 8 8 9 9 9 9 9 10 10 10 10 10 10 10 10 10 10

If you do not have to file returns in the future, check here ▶ ⬚ and enter date final wages paid ▶
If you are a seasonal employer, see **Seasonal employers** on page 1 of the instructions and check here ▶ ⬚

1	Number of employees in the pay period that includes March 12th . ▶	**1**	
2	Total wages and tips, plus other compensation	**2**	
3	Total income tax withheld from wages, tips, and sick pay	**3**	
4	Adjustment of withheld income tax for preceding quarters of calendar year	**4**	
5	Adjusted total of income tax withheld (line 3 as adjusted by line 4—see instructions) . . .	**5**	
6	Taxable social security wages . . . . . **6a** | × 12.4% (.124) =	**6b**	
	Taxable social security tips . . . . . . **6c** | × 12.4% (.124) =	**6d**	
7	Taxable Medicare wages and tips . . . **7a** | × 2.9% (.029) =	**7b**	
8	Total social security and Medicare taxes (add lines 6b, 6d, and 7b). Check here if wages are not subject to social security and/or Medicare tax . . . . ▶ ⬚	**8**	
9	Adjustment of social security and Medicare taxes (see instructions for required explanation) Sick Pay \$_____ ± Fractions of Cents \$_____ ± Other \$_____ =	**9**	
10	Adjusted total of social security and Medicare taxes (line 8 as adjusted by line 9—see instructions)	**10**	
11	**Total taxes** (add lines 5 and 10)	**11**	
12	Advance earned income credit (EIC) payments made to employees	**12**	
13	Net taxes (subtract line 12 from line 11). **If \$2,500 or more, this must equal line 17, column (d) below (or line D of Schedule B (Form 941))**	**13**	
14	Total deposits for quarter, including overpayment applied from a prior quarter	**14**	
15	**Balance due** (subtract line 14 from line 13). See instructions . . . _____	**15**	
16	**Overpayment.** If line 14 is more than line 13, enter excess here ▶ \$ _____ and check if to be: ⬚ Applied to next return **or** ⬚ Refunded.		

- **All filers:** If line 13 is less than \$2,500, you need not complete line 17 or Schedule B (Form 941).
- **Semiweekly schedule depositors:** Complete Schedule B (Form 941) and check here . . . . ▶ ⬚
- **Monthly schedule depositors:** Complete line 17, columns (a) through (d), and check here . . . . ▶ ⬚

17	**Monthly Summary of Federal Tax Liability.** Do not complete if you were a semiweekly schedule depositor.		
	(a) First month liability	**(b)** Second month liability	**(c)** Third month liability	**(d)** Total liability for quarter

Third Party Designee

Do you want to allow another person to discuss this return with the IRS (see separate instructions)? ⬚ **Yes.** Complete the following. ⬚ **No**

| Designee's name ▶ | Phone no. ▶ ( ) | Personal identification number (PIN) ▶ ⬚⬚⬚⬚⬚ |

Sign Here

Under penalties of perjury, I declare that I have examined this return, including accompanying schedules and statements, and to the best of my knowledge and belief, it is true, correct, and complete.

Signature ▶ Print Your Name and Title ▶ Date ▶

For Privacy Act and Paperwork Reduction Act Notice, see back of Payment Voucher. Cat. No. 17001Z Form **941** (Rev. 1-2002)

Line 3. Enter the total amount of income taxes withheld on wages, tips, taxable fringe benefits, and supplemental unemployment compensation benefits.

Line 4. If there were errors in the reported amount of income taxes withheld from previous quarters of the same calendar year, enter the adjustments on this line. Adjustments to reported quarters in previous years are not allowed. The amount of any adjustment must also be included on line 17, and itemized separately on Form 941c, "Supporting Statement to Correct Information."

Line 5. Net line 4 against line 3, and enter the merged amount on this line.

Line 6. Enter the amount of all wages paid on line 6a, except tips that are subject to Social Security taxes. For the year 2002, this would be all wages up to $84,900. Multiply this figure by the Social Security tax rate of 12.4 percent, and enter the tax on line 6b. Enter the same information for tip wages on line 6c, and the tax due on line 6d.

Line 7. Enter the amount of all wages and tips subject to Medicare taxes; there is no upper wage limitation on the amount subject to this tax. Then multiply the result by the Medicare tax rate of 2.9 percent and enter the tax due on line 7b.

Line 8. Summarize all taxes due from lines 6 and 7.

Line 9. Enter any adjustments to the reported amounts of Social Security and Medicare taxes previously listed on lines 6 and 7. These adjustments can include the uncollected employee share of tip taxes, adjustments for the employee share of Social Security and Medicare taxes on group term life insurance premiums paid to former employees, and adjustments for the employee share of taxes withheld by an independent provider of sick pay. An accompanying statement should itemize these adjustments.

Line 10. Net lines 8 and 9 to arrive at the adjusted total of Social Security and Medicare taxes.

Line 11. Add lines 5 and 10 to arrive at the total amount of taxes withheld.

Line 12. Enter the total amount of any earned income credit payments made to employees. If the amount of these credit payments exceeds the total taxes listed on line 11, you can either claim a refund or let the credit forward into the next quarter.

Line 13. Subtract line 12 from line 11 and enter it here.

Line 14. Enter the total deposits made during the quarter, as well as any overpayment remaining from a preceding quarter.

Line 15. Subtract the deposit total on line 14 from the tax due on line 13 to arrive at the balance due.

Line 16. If there is a credit balance on line 15, enter it here and then check your choice of rolling it forward to the next quarterly return or receiving a refund.

Line 17. Enter the total tax liability for each month of the reporting quarter, as well as the total amount for the quarter.

The form should be signed by a business owner, corporate officer, partner, or fiduciary, depending on the type of business entity filing the report.

If a company operates only seasonally, it can avoid filling out the report for quarters when there is no activity by checking the "Seasonal Employers" box above line 1 on the form. And if a company is going out of business, be sure to check the "Final Return" box above line 1 of the form.

The form is due one month after each calendar quarter and must be filed at one of three IRS locations, depending on the location of the filing company. Exhibit 7.7 shows the correct filing location for each state of residence.

If an employer is making a payment with Form 941, it must use the Form 941-V Payment Voucher to accompany the payment. This form is used to identify the taxpayer, as well as the quarter to which the deposit is to be credited, and the amount of the payment. This form is available on the Internal Revenue Service's web site in Adobe Acrobat format. An example is shown in Exhibit 7.8.

EXHIBIT 7.7

Filing Address for Form 941

Filing Location if No Payment	Filing Location if Includes a Payment	For Employers Located In
Cincinnati, OH 45999-0005	P.O. Box 105703 Atlanta, GA 30348-5703	Connecticut, Delaware, District of Columbia, Illinois, Indiana, Kentucky, Maine, Maryland, Massachusetts, Michigan, New Hampshire, New Jersey, New York, North Carolina, Ohio, Pennsylvania, Rhode Island, South Carolina, Vermont, Virginia, West Virginia, Wisconsin
Ogden, UT 84201-0005	P.O. Box 660264 Dallas, TX 75266-0264	Alabama, Alaska, Arizona, Arkansas, California, Colorado, Florida, Georgia, Hawaii, Idaho, Iowa, Kansas, Louisiana, Minnesota, Mississippi, Missouri, Montana, Nebraska, Nevada, New Mexico, North Dakota, Oklahoma, Oregon, South Dakota, Tennessee, Texas, Utah, Washington, Wyoming
Philadelphia, PA 19255-0005	P.O. Box 80106 Cincinnati, OH 45280-0006	No legal residence or principal place of business

EXHIBIT 7.8

Form 941-V Payment Voucher

Form 941
Payment Voucher

Purpose of Form

Complete Form 941-V if you are making a payment with **Form 941**, Employer's Quarterly Federal Tax Return. We will use the completed voucher to credit your payment more promptly and accurately, and to improve our service to you.

If you have your return prepared by a third party and make a payment with that return, please provide this payment voucher to the return preparer.

Making Payments With Form 941

Make payments with Form 941 only if:

1. Your net taxes for the quarter (line 13 on Form 941) are less than $2,500 and you are paying in full with a timely filed return or

2. You are a monthly schedule depositor making a payment in accordance with the **accuracy of deposits** rule. (See section 11 of **Circular E**, Employer's Tax Guide, for details.) This amount may be $2,500 or more.

Otherwise, you must deposit the amount at an authorized financial institution or by electronic funds transfer. (See section 11 of Circular E for deposit instructions.) Do not use the Form 941-V payment voucher to make Federal tax deposits.

Caution: *If you pay amounts with Form 941 that should have been deposited, you may be subject to a penalty. See Circular E.*

Specific Instructions

Box 1- Employer identification number (EIN). If you do not have an EIN, apply for one on **Form SS-4**, Application for Employer Identification Number, and write "Applied for" and the date you applied in this entry space.

Box 2- Amount paid. Enter the amount paid with Form 941.

Box 3- Tax period. Darken the capsule identifying the quarter for which the payment is made. Darken only one capsule.

Box 4- Name and address. Enter your name and address as shown on Form 941.

● Make your check or money order payable to the United States Treasury. Be sure to enter your EIN, "Form 941," and the tax period on your check or money order. Do not send cash. Please do not staple this voucher or your payment to the return or to each other.

● Detach the completed voucher and send it with your payment and Form 941 to the address provided on the back of Form 941.

▼ Detach Here and Mail With Your Payment ▼   Form **941-V** (2002)

Form **941-V** Department of the Treasury Internal Revenue Service (99)	**Payment Voucher** ▶ Do not staple or attach this voucher to your payment.	OMB No. 1545-0029 2002

1 Enter your employer identification number	2 **Enter the amount of the payment**	Dollars	Cents

3 Tax period		4 Enter your business name (individual name if sole proprietor)
O 1st Quarter	*O* 3rd Quarter	Enter your address
O 2nd Quarter	*O* 4th Quarter	Enter your city, state, and ZIP code

IN THE REAL WORLD

The Case of the Missing States

A Colorado company purchased a Maryland-based consulting company that had conducted operations in a variety of states during the past decade. The acquiree had processed payroll using an internal software system and had manually remitted tax withholdings to many states. Shortly after the acquisition, the acquirer began to receive a number of unpaid withholding notices from various states, all claiming that taxes had not been paid for years, along with substantial penalties and interest charges. The underlying problem was that the acquiree had done business in so many states that its accounting staff had not kept up with making withholding filings with all required governments. The acquirer found itself in the unpleasant position of being liable for all of these payments. Furthermore, it did not know when the next notice to pay might arrive in the mail. Since the acquiree's tax remittance records were not complete, there was no way to research the extent of the problem.

Subsequently, the acquirer's finance team decided to include in its acquisition review documentation a warning flag that this problem could arise whenever a potential acquiree's payroll operations were not conducted through a payroll supplier (which would have made the filings on behalf of the company); the team also noted that future acquisition deals should make the owner of an acquiree liable for any unpaid payroll tax liabilities for several years following the closure of the acquisition transaction.

Summary

Much of the information contained in this chapter is a summary of a number of Internal Revenue Service's publications. In particular, you may want to download from *www.irs.gov* the following publications, which contain additional information about payroll taxes and remittances:

- *Publication 509, Tax Calendars.* As the name implies, this publication lists the dates on which a variety of taxes are due throughout the year. Of particular use for semiweekly depositors is a table listing the due dates for deposit of taxes under the semiweekly rule for all weeks of the current year.

- *Publication 15, Employer's Tax Guide.* This manual itemizes how to obtain an Employer Identification Number; defines employees; and discusses wages, payroll periods, withholding and depositing taxes, and a variety of other tax-related subjects.

- *Publication 15-A, Employer's Supplemental Tax Guide.* This manual discusses the legal definition of an employee, special types of wage compensation, sick pay reporting, pensions and annuities, and alternative methods for calculating withholding.

- *Publication 15-B, Employer's Tax Guide to Fringe Benefits.* This publication covers a wide range of fringe benefit exclusion rules, ranging from accident and health benefits to working condition benefits. It also addresses fringe benefit valuation rules, as well as rules for withholding, depositing, and reporting taxes.

CHAPTER 8

Payroll Deductions

After reading this chapter you will be able to

- Create asset purchase rules that restrict an employer's risk of not being paid back by employees for purchases made

- Understand which contributions require a confirming receipt from a charity, as well as the types of information that can substitute for this receipt

- Create rules both for restricting the size of employee advances and for controlling the speed and size of advance paybacks to reduce the risk of nonpayment by employees

- Calculate the amount of a tax levy to which an employee is subject

There is a wide array of possible payroll deductions, most of which are at the behest of employees, but some required by court order. This chapter covers several possible payroll deductions; it gives an overview of each item, discusses the problems associated with each, and offers an example of how several might be administered. (For more information on deductions related to employee benefits, refer back to Chapter 6.)

Asset Purchases

An employer may allow its employees to either purchase assets from the company or through it. In the first case, the company may be liquidating assets and so offers to sell them to its employees. In the latter case, employees are allowed to use the company's bulk-purchase discounts to obtain items at reduced prices from other suppliers. The company may also sell its own products at reduced prices to employees through a company store.

Perhaps because of the discount prices, some employees make such large asset purchases that they are unable to pay back the company immediately for the full amount. Therefore, the company allows them to make payments through a series of payroll deductions. In such a case, an employee should sign an agreement with the company, acknowledging responsibility for paying back the company and agreeing to a specific payment schedule. Though not common, the company can also charge the employee an interest rate, which may encourage the person to pay back the company sooner to avoid an excessive interest expense.

For long repayment schedules, it may be useful to keep employees apprised of the remaining amount of each loan, therefore the payroll staff should consider either maintaining a separate schedule of payments or creating a loan goal through its payroll software that tracks the amount of the debt that has not yet been paid.

Charitable Contributions

Many employers encourage their employees to give regular contributions to local or national charities, of which the United Way is the most common example. Employers typically have employees sign a pledge card that authorizes certain amounts to be deducted from their pay. After payrolls are completed, the accounting staff then creates a single lump-sum check representing the contributions of all employees, matches the

Some employees can get into the habit of purchasing a large num-ber of items through the company, which can cause two problems. First, the payroll staff may find itself tracking multiple repayment schedules for each employee, which is quite time-consuming. Second, if an employee leaves the company, the amount of the out-standing loans to the company for unreimbursed asset purchases may exceed the person's final paycheck by a significant amount, making it difficult for the company to collect on the outstanding loans. Following two simple rules can prevent these problems. First, do not allow an employee to purchase something from or through the company until the last purchase has been fully paid off. Second, make it company policy that the full amount of such a purchase can-not exceed the amount of an employee's net pay for one month, or perhaps just a single paycheck. These rules reduce the number of purchase reimbursements to track and lowers the risk of loss to the company if an employee quits before paying his or her loans.

amounts withheld if this is part of the deal offered to employees, and forwards the payment to the designated charity. Some employees prefer to make a single lump-sum payment to the charity, in which case the company usually forwards its check directly to the charity without gen-erating a deduction through the payroll system.

Employees can renege on a pledge and ask the payroll department to stop making further deductions from their pay, though this request (as is the case for all deductions) should be made in writing and kept in each employee's personnel or payroll file for future reference. Also, the remittance advice that accompanies each employee's paycheck should itemize both the amount of each deduction and the year-to-date total deduction that has gone to the charity. If there are multiple charities for which deductions are being made, the remittance advice should list each one separately. The employee needs this information when filing his or her income tax return at year-end in order to prove the amount of contributions itemized on the tax return.

The Internal Revenue Code (IRC) requires employees to have written substantiation from a charity if the amount of a contribution exceeds $250. However, this requirement is for *individual* contributions of $250 or more, which is unlikely to be the case for a single payroll deduction (each of which is considered an individual contribution). Furthermore, charities are unlikely to have enough information to issue a written substantiation because they receive a lump-sum payment from the employer and usually have no means for tracking individual contributions. Consequently, employees who make such large contributions should use the year-end remittance advice attached to their paychecks as proof of the year-to-date amount of the contributions made; they should also retain their original pledge cards as proof of the commitment made.

Example. David Anderson and Charles Weymouth both make contributions to the United Way. Mr. Anderson has authorized the company to make regular deductions of $80 from each of his weekly paychecks, which the company will match and forward to the charity. Because each contribution is less than $250, there is no need to obtain a written substantiation from the United Way.

Charles Weymouth has authorized the company to make exactly the same-size annual contribution, but he wants it to be taken from his month-end paycheck, which increases the individual deduction to $320 ($80 x 4 weekly paychecks). Because the individual deduction exceeds $250, Mr. Weymouth must obtain a written substantiation of the contribution from the United Way or obtain some similar form of evidence for the IRS.

Child Support Payments

The payroll manager will almost certainly see court-ordered child support withholding orders at some point during his or her career. Tightly enforced federal laws help to track down parents who are not making support payments; these laws also require employers to withhold various amounts from the pay of parents in arrears to meet mandated child support payments.

The maximum amount of an employee's disposable earnings subject to child support withholding is 60 percent of his or her pay, or 50 percent if the employee is already making payments to support other children or spouses. Both of these percentages increase by 5 percent if an employee is 12 or more weeks in arrears in making support payments.

To calculate disposable earnings, subtract all legally mandated deductions from an employee's gross pay, such as federal and state income taxes, Social Security and Medicare taxes, and any locally mandated disability or unemployment taxes. Voluntary deductions, such as pension and medical insurance deductions, are not used to calculate disposable earnings.

Example. The Dim Bulb I.Q. Testing Company receives a court order to withhold child support payments from the pay of its employee Ernest Evans, in the amount of $390 per weekly paycheck. The payroll manager needs to determine how much can actually be withheld from Mr. Evans's pay, who earns $850 per week and does not make support payments to another child or spouse. His typical paycheck remittance advice is:

Gross pay	$850
Federal income tax	125
State income tax	35
Social Security tax	53
Medicare tax	12
Medical insurance	62
401(k) plan deduction	80
Net pay	**$483**

Of the amounts listed on the remittance advice, the medical insurance and 401(k) deductions are voluntary and so cannot be included in the calculation of disposable earnings. This increases Mr. Evans's disposable earnings to $625. The payroll manager then multiplies this amount by 60 percent, which is the maximum amount of disposable earnings that can be remitted for child support. The result is $375, which is $15 less than the $390 listed on the court order. The payroll manager begins deducting and remitting $375 per week.

When a child support court order is received, it takes precedence over all other types of garnishment orders, with the exception of tax levies that were received prior to the date of the court order. An employer must begin withholding the maximum allowable amount from an employee's pay no later than the first pay period beginning 14 working days after the posted date of the court order, and must continue to withhold funds until the order is rescinded by the court.

A common point of confusion is where to send child support payments. Contrary to any demands by the parent who is designated to receive the payments, they typically go to a court-designated person, who then disburses the funds to the recipient parent—payments never go straight to that parent. Instructions for remitting funds will be listed on the court order; the employer should follow these instructions to the letter.

An employer can charge an employee an administrative fee for withholding child support from his or her paycheck. The amount is mandated by state law, and is itemized in Exhibit 8.1. The fee can only be taken from an employee's remaining wages after the support payment amount has already been withheld.

If an employee leaves the company before the obligations of a court order are discharged, the employer is obliged to notify the issuing enforcement agency of the employee's last known address, as well as the

EXHIBIT 8.1

Administrative Fees for
Child Support Withholding, by State

Allowable Fee	Applicable States
None	Connecticut, Delaware, Michigan, New York, South Dakota
$1/payment	California, Kentucky, Massachusetts, Minnesota, New Hampshire, New Jersey, New Mexico, Washington, West Virginia
$2/month	Alabama
$2/payment	District of Columbia, Florida, Hawaii, Indiana, Iowa, Maine, Maryland, Mississippi, North Carolina, Ohio, Rhode Island
$2.50/month	Nebraska
$2.50/pay period	Arkansas
$3/month	North Dakota
$3/payment	Georgia, Nevada, South Carolina, Wisconsin
$4/month	Arizona
$5/month	Colorado, Illinois, Oregon, Tennessee, Vermont
$5/payment	Alaska, Idaho, Montana, Oklahoma, Virginia, Wyoming
$5/pay period	Kansas, Louisiana
$6/payment	Missouri
$10/month	Texas, Utah
Other: 2% of payment	Pennsylvania

location of a new employer (if known). The agency needs this information to track the employee and continue to enforce the court order.

If an employer chooses to ignore a court order, it will be liable for the total amount that should have been withheld. This means that an employer must act promptly to begin withholding by the date specified in the court order, and must withhold the full required amount, taking into account the rules noted earlier in this section.

Deduction of Prior Pay Advances

Employees who require more cash than they earn on their normal paychecks sometimes ask their employers for an advance on their pay. The need may be nonbusiness-related, such as a sudden medical crisis or to purchase a home; or it may be to buy something on behalf of the company. The most common example of the latter case is to receive funds for a company trip, for which the employee will be reimbursed once an expense report is submitted. In this case, it is most common to reimburse employees through the accounts payable system if there is a shortfall between the amount of expenses incurred and the original advance. However, if an employee neglects to turn in an expense report, then he or she is liable to the company for the amount of the advance that was

TIPS & TECHNIQUES

Keep a calendar that itemizes the amount of each garnishment, the declining balance on each debt, and the date on which the last deduction and related payment to a third party is due. Also, because there may be some dispute regarding the start date of the deductions, which are frequently tied to the date of receipt of a withholding order, mark and initial the date of receipt, as well as the postmark date, on the withholding order.

issued. This is also the case when an employee has obtained an advance prior to his or her normal paycheck.

In all cases, the payroll staff must track the amount of outstanding advances and make deductions from employee paychecks to recover the amounts outstanding. Deductions frequently are made in smaller increments over multiple paychecks, so that employees have enough left for their personal needs. Managing this process properly calls for interaction with the accounts payable staff (who would have paid out the initial advances) and the employees (to determine the appropriate amount of deductions for each paycheck). Standard policies should also be in place that regulate the amount of advances handed out, and the speed with which they must be paid back. Such policies serve to ensure that a company does not become a personal bank for its employees and to minimize the risk of it losing outstanding advances if employees quit work before paying them back.

Example. Andrew Wodehouse, a warehouse worker, has requested an advance of $400 on his next paycheck. Company policy states that advances cannot exceed the net amount of an employee's prior paycheck, which limits the amount to $360. Mr. Wodehouse also requested that the advance be taken out of his pay over the next six paychecks, which would be $60 per paycheck. However, company policy requires all advances to be paid back within no more than four paychecks, so the amount deducted from his paychecks is increased to $90. After three paychecks, a garnishment order is sent to the company for a loan repayment that Mr. Wodehouse owes another creditor. He promptly quits work and disappears. But thanks to the company's strict rules for employee advances, only $90 is left on the advance that will not be paid back to the company.

Employee Portion of Insurance Expenses

Most businesses offer some form of medical and related insurance to their employees. This can include medical, dental, vision, short-term disability, long-term disability, life, and supplemental life insurance coverage. An employer may pay for all of this expense, a portion of it, or merely make it available to employees, who must foot the entire bill. It is rare for an employer to pay for all of this expense, since insurance is very expensive; consequently, there will usually be a deduction from employee's pay to cover some portion of the cost.

The type of deduction calculation used is typically employer reimbursement of a relatively high percentage of the medical insurance for an employee and a lesser percentage for that person's portion of the insurance that covers his or her family members. For example, the employer might pay for 80 percent of an employee's medical insurance and 50 percent of the portion of additional coverage that applies to the employee's family. Additional types of insurance, such as vision or life insurance, are less commonly paid by employers; more commonly, employees are given the option to purchase and fully pay for them.

When the payroll department sets up deductions for the various types of insurance, it is better to itemize each one separately on the employee paycheck remittance advice, so there is no question about the amount of each deduction being withheld for each type of insurance. This approach makes it easier for employees to judge whether they want to continue to pay for various types of insurance; it also makes it easier for the payroll staff to calculate and track deduction levels.

The insurance companies that provide the various types of insurance may enter into a contract with a company to freeze expense levels for up to a year, which makes this calculation a simple once-a-year event to determine the amount of employee insurance deductions. Other insurance providers may alter rates on a more frequent basis, necessitating more frequent reviews and recalculations of employee deduction levels. In this case, employees should be warned of upcoming changes to the rates they are paying.

Example. The Doughboy Donut Company pays for 90 percent of its employees' medical insurance, 25 percent of the additional medical insurance for the families of employees, and 90 percent of employee life insurance. It also makes short- and long-term disability and dental insurance available to its employees, who must pay in full for these benefits. Emily Swankart is a single parent who has subscribed to all of these types of insurance. Here's how the total amount of deductions for her would be calculated:

Type of Insurance	Total Cost	Deduction %	Deduction $
Medical insurance	$225	90%	$23
Medical insurance, dependent	200	25%	150
Life insurance	35	90%	32
Short-term disability insurance	42	0%	42
Long-term disability insurance	15	0%	15
Dental insurance	28	0%	28
		Total	**$290**

As is commonly the case under this type of deduction plan, note that the largest portion of the expense to be paid by the employee is the medical insurance for the dependent.

Garnishments for Unpaid Taxes

If an employee does not pay his or her federal or local income taxes, the employer may receive a notification from the IRS to garnish that person's wages in order to repay the taxes. The garnishment will cover not only the original amount of unpaid taxes, but also any penalties and interest expenses added by the government.

TIPS & TECHNIQUES

When an employer has multiple pay periods in a month, it can choose to make payroll deductions all in one pay period or spread them equally throughout the month. The preferred approach is to spread them throughout the month. By doing so, employees do not suffer a significant decline in their take-home pay for one of their paychecks. Also, by setting up deductions to occur in the same amounts in all pay periods, the payroll staff does not have to constantly delete deductions from the payroll system and then reenter them for one payroll per month. Instead, the deductions stay in the payroll database as active deductions for all pay periods; this requires much less maintenance.

A garnishment for unpaid taxes takes priority over all other types of garnishments, except for child support orders that were received prior to the date of the tax garnishment. If a business receives orders from multiple taxing authorities to garnish an employee's wages and there are not enough wages to pay everyone, then the orders are implemented in the order in which they were received.

The "Notice of Levy on Wages, Salary, and Other Income," Form 668-W, is the standard form used for notifying a company to garnish an employee's wages. It has the following six parts:

Part 1. This is for the employer. It states the employer's obligation to withhold and remit the unpaid tax, and states the amount of the unpaid tax.

Part 2. This is the employee's copy of the notification.

Parts 3–4. The employee must complete these pages and return them to the employer within three business days. The employer completes the back side of part 3, returns it to the IRS, and retains part 4.

Part 5. The employee keeps this page, which includes tax status and exemption information.

Part 6. The IRS keeps this page for its records.

If an employee fails to remit parts 3 and 4 of Form 668-W to the employer, the employer is required to calculate the employee's exempt amount of wages under the assumption that the person is married, filing separately, with one exemption. These assumptions result in the smallest possible amount of exempt wages, so employees should be strongly encouraged to turn in parts 3 and 4 in order to avoid having the maximum amount withheld from their pay.

When a Form 668-W order is received to garnish an employee's wages, the payroll staff must first determine if any wages are *not* subject to the order. Only 15 percent of the following types of wages are subject to a tax payment order issued by the IRS, and they are completely exempt from an unpaid tax order issued by a *state* government:

- Armed forces disability benefits
- Pension and annuity payments as specified under the Railroad Retirement Act
- Unemployment compensation benefits
- Welfare and supplemental Social Security payments
- Workers' compensation benefits

Once these types of wages have been accounted for, the payroll staff must determine which deductions can be made from an affected employee's pay before determining the amount of the tax levy. Allowable deductions include:

- Federal and state income taxes
- Social Security and Medicare taxes
- Increases in deductions over which an employee has no control, such as a medical insurance increase imposed by a health care provider
- Deductions required in order to be employed by the company

- Deductions in effect *prior* to the tax garnishment notice, which can include deductions for medical, life and disability insurance, as well as cafeteria plan deductions

Once the applicable deductions have been used to reduce an employee's wages to the amount to which the tax levy will be applied, the payroll staff should use an IRS-supplied table to determine the amount of net wages that are exempt from the tax levy. This table is shown in Exhibit 8.2.

Example. Molly Gammon has not been paying her federal income taxes, so her employer, the Red Herring Fish Company, receives a notice from the IRS, informing it that she owes the government $10,000 in back taxes. The company is obligated to withhold this amount and remit it to the IRS. The payroll manager must calculate the amount of the tax levy to withhold from each paycheck. He obtains the following information from her pay records:

Weekly salary	$1,000
Federal and state income taxes	192
Social Security and Medicare taxes	77
Medical insurance deductions	40
Stock purchase plan deductions	50
Net Pay	$ **641**

To calculate the amount of her net pay that is exempt from the tax levy, the payroll manager turns to the table for figuring exemptions, shown in Exhibit 8.2. Molly is an unmarried head of household with four exemptions. For a weekly pay period, this gives her an exemption of $363.46 from the tax levy. This means that $277.54 is subject to the tax levy, which is calculated as her net pay of $641, less the exemption of $363.46.

If Molly subsequently asks to have her stock purchase plan deductions increased, the net change will not reduce her tax levy, since this

EXHIBIT 8.2

Table for Figuring the Amount Exempt from Levy on Wages, Salary, and Other Income

I. Table for Figuring Amount Exempt from Levy on Wages, Salary, and Other Income—Forms 668-W(c) and 668-W(c)(DO)
(NOTE: Amounts are for each pay period.)

2002

Filing Status: Single

Pay Period	Number of Exemptions Claimed on Statement						More than 6
	1	2	3	4	5	6	
Daily	29.62	41.15	52.69	64.23	75.77	87.31	18.08 plus 11.54 for each exemption
Weekly	148.08	205.77	263.46	321.15	378.85	436.54	90.38 plus 57.69 for each exemption
Biweekly	296.15	411.54	526.92	642.31	757.69	873.08	180.77 plus 115.38 for each exemption
Semimonthly	320.83	445.83	570.83	695.83	820.83	945.83	195.83 plus 125.00 for each exemption
Monthly	641.67	891.67	1141.67	1391.67	1641.67	1891.67	391.66 plus 250.00 for each exemption

Filing Status: Married Filing Joint Return (and Qualifying Widow(er)s)

Pay Period	Number of Exemptions Claimed on Statement						More than 6
	1	2	3	4	5	6	
Daily	41.73	53.27	64.81	76.35	87.88	99.42	30.19 plus 11.54 for each exemption
Weekly	208.65	266.35	324.04	381.73	439.42	497.12	150.96 plus 57.69 for each exemption
Biweekly	417.31	532.69	648.08	763.46	878.85	994.23	301.92 plus 115.38 for each exemption
Semimonthly	452.08	577.08	702.08	827.08	952.08	1077.08	327.08 plus 125.00 for each exemption
Monthly	904.17	1154.17	1404.17	1654.17	1904.17	2154.17	654.17 plus 250.00 for each exemption

Filing Status: Unmarried Head of Household

Pay Period	Number of Exemptions Claimed on Statement						More than 6
	1	2	3	4	5	6	
Daily	38.08	49.62	61.15	72.69	84.23	95.77	26.54 plus 11.54 for each exemption
Weekly	190.38	248.08	305.77	363.46	421.15	478.85	132.69 plus 57.69 for each exemption
Biweekly	380.77	496.15	611.54	726.92	842.31	957.69	265.38 plus 115.38 for each exemption
Semimonthly	412.50	537.50	662.50	787.50	912.50	1037.50	287.50 plus 125.00 for each exemption
Monthly	825.00	1075.00	1325.00	1575.00	1825.00	2075.00	575.00 plus 250.00 for each exemption

Filing Status: Married Filing Separate Return

Pay Period	Number of Exemptions Claimed on Statement						More than 6
	1	2	3	4	5	6	
Daily	26.63	38.17	49.71	61.25	72.79	84.33	15.10 plus 11.54 for each exemption
Weekly	133.17	190.87	248.56	306.25	363.94	421.63	75.48 plus 57.69 for each exemption
Biweekly	266.35	381.73	497.12	612.50	727.88	843.27	150.96 plus 115.38 for each exemption
Semimonthly	288.54	413.54	538.54	663.54	788.54	913.54	163.54 plus 125.00 for each exemption
Monthly	577.08	827.08	1077.08	1327.08	1577.08	1827.08	327.08 plus 250.00 for each exemption

II. Table for Figuring Additional Exempt Amount for Taxpayers at Least 65 Years Old and / or Blind

Filing Status	*	Additional Exempt Amount				
		Daily	Weekly	Biweekly	Semimonthly	Monthly
Single or Head of Household	1	4.42	22.12	44.23	47.92	95.83
	2	8.85	44.23	88.46	95.83	191.67
Any other Filing Status	1	3.46	17.31	34.62	37.50	75.00
	2	6.92	34.62	69.23	75.00	150.00
	3	10.38	51.92	103.85	112.50	225.00
	4	13.85	69.23	138.46	150.00	300.00

* ADDITIONAL STANDARD DEDUCTION claimed on Parts 3, 4, and 5 of levy

Examples

These tables show the amount exempt from a levy on wages, salary, and other income. For example:

1. A single taxpayer who is paid weekly and claims three exemptions *(including one for the taxpayer)* has $263.46 exempt from levy.

2. *If the taxpayer in number 1 is over 65 and writes 1 in the ADDITIONAL STANDARD DEDUCTION space on Parts 3, 4, and 5 of the levy, $285.58 is exempt from this levy ($263.46 plus $22.12).*

3. A taxpayer who is married, files jointly, is paid biweekly, and claims two exemptions *(including one for the taxpayer)* has $532.69 exempt from levy.

4. *If the taxpayer in number 3 is over 65 and has a spouse who is blind, this taxpayer should write 2 in the ADDITIONAL STANDARD DEDUCTION space on Parts 3, 4, and 5 of the levy. Then, $601.92 is exempt from this levy ($532.69 plus $69.23).*

Publication 1494 (Rev. 1-2002)   www.irs.gov   Catalog Number 11439T   Department of the Treasury - Internal Revenue Service change occurred *after* receipt of the tax levy notice. However, if the company becomes unionized subsequent to the tax levy date, and Molly is required to pay union dues as a condition of her employment, then the tax levy will be reduced by the amount of her dues. Finally, if her medical insurance deduction increases, the tax levy will also be reduced by this amount.

Once a Form 668-W is received, the company is obligated to begin withholding the mandated amount of taxes from an employee's next paycheck, even if the applicable wages were earned prior to receipt of the form. The company should forward the withheld amount to the IRS, with the employee's name and Social Security number noted on the check.

If the employee leaves the company while this tax levy is still being deducted, the employer must notify the IRS of this event, and if possible forward the name and address of the new employer to the IRS. If the employee continues to work for the company, the IRS will inform the company when to stop making these deductions on a Form 668-D.

If an employer for any reason does not withhold and forward to the IRS the periodic garnishments required by Form 668-W, the company will be held liable for the amounts that it should have withheld, in addition to incurring a stiff penalty.

Loan Repayments

Employees may either have loans payable to the company, or the company may have obtained loans on their behalf. For example, a corporate officer may have been extended a loan in order to move to a different company location and purchase a larger house. Alternatively, a company may have a computer purchasing arrangement with a local bank, whereby employees buy computers for their personal use and the company both guarantees payment to the bank and collects periodic payments from

TIPS & TECHNIQUES

The calculation of a government-imposed tax levy is complex and can change whenever an employee's circumstances are altered; for example, as a result of a change in employee pay, changes in medical insurance deductions, or the addition of union dues as a new deduction. If an employer does not adjust for these changes, it can be subject to penalties imposed by the IRS for the amount of any tax levies that should have been withheld from the employee's pay. To avoid this problem, the payroll staff should maintain a "tickler list" for all employees who are subject to tax levies. This list should be incorporated into the processing procedure for every payroll, to remind the payroll staff to verify any changes to the targeted employees' pay and to alter the amount of their tax levies as necessary.

employees and remits them to the bank. In either case, the payroll staff must create a loan payback schedule for all affected employees and use it to set up deductions from their paychecks. If the loan is through a local bank, then the bank will likely provide a payback schedule to the payroll department. If the loan is internal, then the payroll staff must create a payback schedule in accordance with the terms of the loan agreement.

If a standard loan program for asset purchases with the company guarantees payment of the loans, then it behooves the company to require relatively short payback intervals, such as one to three years, to minimize its risk of having to pay back loans for employees who leave the company. The agreement with employees should include—in writing—a statement that if they leave the company prior to paying off the loan, as much as is legally allowable will be deducted from their final paychecks in order to pay down the remainder of any outstanding loans.

Pensions and Other Savings Plans

An employer may offer several types of savings plans to its employees. In its simplest form, a business may arrange to make regular deductions from employee paychecks and deposit these funds in any number of pension plans. A slightly more complex arrangement is for the company to match some portion of the contributed funds and deposit them together with the employee funds. These contributions may vest immediately or at some point in the future; vesting gives ownership in the company-contributed amount to the employee. The company may also retain the contributed funds and pay back employees with company stock.

If funds are being matched by the company, there will be an upper limit on the amount of matching, as well as a matching percentage. For example, a company may contribute 50 percent of the amounts contributed by its employees, up to a maximum of 6 percent of an employee's total pay.

This topic was covered in considerable detail in the section titled "Pension Plan Benefits," in Chapter 6, "Benefits."

Student Loans

The government can mandate the garnishment of an employee's wages in order to pay back the overdue portion of an outstanding student loan. Garnishment orders can be issued either by the Department of Education or a state guarantee agency, depending on which is guaranteeing the loan. Upon receipt of the order, the employer must give an employee 30 days notice prior to making deductions from his or her wages. An employee cannot be fired from work because of the garnishment order; an employer that does so is liable for the employee's lost wages. Also, if an employer neglects to withhold the authorized garnishment amount, it is liable for the amount that was not withheld.

Union Dues

If an employer has entered into a collective bargaining agreement with a union, it is generally required to deduct union dues from employee wages, per the terms of the agreement, and forward them to the union. It can stop doing this as of the date when the collective bargaining agreement terminates. The requirement to make this deduction will vary by agreement; and in some cases it may not be required at all, with the union instead obtaining dues directly from its members.

Summary

A key item to remember for all the voluntary deductions discussed in this chapter is that an employee's written approval must be obtained for all of them, to prevent employees claiming that they never authorized a deduction, possibly resulting in the company not being compensated for an expenditure (such as medical insurance) that it has already made on behalf of the employee. For this reason, a company should not automatically sign up employees for various benefits, and have them only decline the benefit in writing, as then employees can state that they were never properly informed of the nature of the benefit.

CHAPTER 9

Payments to Employees

After reading this chapter you will be able to

- Determine the number of allowed days before employees must be paid

- Learn the mechanics of paying employees with cash, checks, direct deposit, and payments into their credit card accounts

- Know how soon voluntarily and involuntarily terminated employees must be given their final paychecks

- Know how long to retain unclaimed pay before forwarding it to the presiding state government

This chapter covers the ostensibly simple topic of physically paying employees for their work. Just cut a check, right? Not exactly. There are a multitude of considerations, such as the allowable and practical frequency of payment, the type of payment to be made (whether in cash, by check or direct deposit, or even directly into an employee's credit card account). There are also a number of state laws governing the allowable time period that can elapse before a terminated employee must be paid— and these vary based on a voluntary or involuntary termination. Finally, there are state-specific laws concerning what to do with unclaimed payments to employees. All of these topics are covered in this chapter.

Frequency of Payment

The frequency of payment to employees covers two areas: the number of days over which pay is accumulated before being paid out and the number of days subsequent to this period before payment is physically made.

Organizations with a large proportion of employees who are relatively transient or who are at very low pay levels usually pay once a week, since their staffs do not have sufficient funds to make it until the next pay period. If these businesses attempt to lengthen the pay period, they usually find that they become a bank to their employees, constantly issuing advances. Consequently, the effort required to issue and track advances offsets the labor savings from calculating and issuing fewer payrolls per month.

The most common pay periods are either biweekly (once every two weeks) or semimonthly (twice a month). The semimonthly approach requires 24 payrolls per year, as opposed to the 26 that must be calculated for biweekly payrolls, so there is not much labor difference between the two time periods. However, it is much easier from an accounting perspective to use the semimonthly approach, because the information recorded over two payrolls exactly corresponds to the monthly reporting period, so there are fewer accruals to calculate. Offsetting this advantage is the slight difference between the number of days covered by a semimonthly reporting period and the standard one-week time sheet reporting system. For example, a semimonthly payroll period covers 15 days, whereas the standard seven-day time cards used by employees mean that only 14 days of time card information is available to include in the payroll. The usual result is that employees are paid for two weeks of work in each semimonthly payroll, except for one payroll every three months, in which a third week is also paid that catches up the timing difference between the time card system and the payroll system.

A monthly pay period is the least common, since it is difficult for low-pay workers to wait so long to be paid. However, it can be useful in cases where employees are highly compensated and can tolerate the long wait. Because there are only 12 payrolls per year, this is highly efficient from the accounting perspective. One downside is that any error in a payroll must usually be rectified with a manual payment, since it is such a long wait before the adjustment can be made to the next regular payroll.

The general provision for payroll periods under state law is that hourly employees be paid no less frequently than biweekly or semimonthly, while exempt employees can generally be paid once a month. Those states having no special provisions at all or generally requiring pay periods of one month or more are Alabama, Colorado, Florida, Idaho, Iowa, Kansas, Minnesota, Montana, Nebraska, North Dakota, Oregon, Pennsylvania, South Carolina, South Dakota, Washington, and Wisconsin. But these rules vary considerably by state, so it is best to consult with the local state government to be certain you have accurate information.

The other pay frequency issue is how long a company can wait after a pay period is completed before it can issue pay to its employees. A delay of several days is usually necessary to compile time cards, verify totals, correct errors, calculate withholdings, and generate checks. If a company outsources its payroll, there may be additional delays built into the process, due to the payroll input dates mandated by the supplier. A typical time frame during which a pay delay occurs is three days to a week. The duration of this interval is frequently mandated by state law; it is summarized in Exhibit 9.1.

The days of delay listed in the exhibit are subject to slight changes under certain situations, so be sure to check applicable state laws to be certain of their exact provisions. Also, be aware that any states not included in the table have no legal provisions for the maximum time period before which payroll payments must be made.

EXHIBIT 9.1

Allowable Days of
Payment Delay by State

Allowable Days of Delay	State
5	Arizona
6	Massachusetts, Vermont
7	Delaware, Hawaii, New York, Washington
8	Connecticut, Maine, New Hampshire
9	Rhode Island
10	California, Colorado, District of Columbia, Indiana, Louisiana, Mississippi, Montana, New Jersey, New Mexico, Utah
11	Oklahoma
12	Iowa
15	Idaho, Kansas, Michigan, Minnesota, Nevada, Ohio, Pennsylvania, Wyoming
16	Missouri
18	Kentucky
20	Tennessee
31	Wisconsin
Special Provisions	Illinois (varies by length of pay period)

Cash Payments

Though cash payments are still used, this practice tends to be limited to day laborers who work for short periods. It is not a recommended payment approach, as it requires a considerable amount of labor to calculate and distribute cash; it also presents a high risk that the large quantities of cash on hand for payroll may be stolen. To make cash payments, follow these steps:

1. Calculate the amount of gross pay, deductions, and net pay due to each employee. This can be calculated manually or through the use of payroll software.

2. Write a check to the local bank for the total amount of the payroll that will be paid in cash. This check will be converted into cash.

3. Determine the exact amount of bills and coins required to pay each employee; the form used in Exhibit 9.2 can assist in this process. To use the form, list the net pay due to each person in the second column, then work across the form from left to right, listing the number of the largest denominations allowable that will pay each person. For example, to determine the exact number of bills and coins required to pay the first person in the form, John Anderson, determine the maximum number of $20 bills that can be used, which is six. His net pay is $129.12, so six $20 bills will reduce the remainder to $9.12. The next largest useable denomination is the $5 bill, of which one can be used, followed by four $1 bills. This leaves coinage, of which one dime and two pennies are required to complete the payment. Then cross-foot the form to ensure that the bills and coinage for all employees add up to the total amount of the check that will be cashed at the bank.

4. Highlight the totals row on the form. Take the completed form to the bank, along with the check, and requisition the correct amount of each type of currency.

5. Obtain a set of pay envelopes, which can be simple mailing envelopes with a stamped, fill-in-the-blanks form on the outside. An example of this stamp is shown in Exhibit 9.3. This stamp

EXHIBIT 9.2

Payroll Bill and Coin Requirements Form

| Payroll Bill and Coin Requirements Form | | | | | | Payroll Period Ended _____May 15____ | | | |
Employee Name	Net Pay	$20	$10	$5	$1	$0.25	$0.10	$0.05	$0.01
Anderson, John	$129.12	6		1	4		1		2
Brickmeyer, Charles	207.03	10		1	2				3
Caldwell, Dorian	119.82	5	1	1	4	3		1	2
Devon, Ernest	173.14	8	1		3		1		4
Franklin, Gregory	215.19	10	1	1			1	1	4
Hartwell, Alan	198.37	9	1	1	3	1	1		2
Inglenook, Mary	248.43	12		1	3	1	1	1	3
	$1,291.10	60	4	6	19	5	5	3	20

separately lists the regular and overtime hours worked, and then combines this information into a single total earnings amount from which standard deductions are made, with the net pay figure noted at the bottom. If there are other deductions, such as for employee purchases, 401k deductions, and so on, the stamp can be altered to include these items. Write the total earnings, deductions, and net pay in the spaces provided (see the exhibit). This gives each employee a complete breakdown of how his or her pay was calculated.

6. When an employee takes receipt of his or her pay envelope, there must be some evidence that the money has shifted into that person's possession, to prevent later claims of not having been paid. This issue is readily solved by creating a pay receipt, an example

EXHIBIT 9.3

Stamp for Pay Envelope

Employee Name   Wilbur Smythe

Pay Period Beginning Date   May 8

Pay Period Ending Date   May 15

Hours Worked   Regular: 40   Overtime: 5

Hourly Rate   Regular: $ 10   Overtime: $ 15

Earnings   Regular: $ 400   Overtime: $ 75

Total Earnings $ 475

Pay Deductions

  Social Security Tax $ 29

  Federal Income Tax $ 100

  Medicare Tax $ 12

  State Income Tax $ 47

Total Deductions $ 188

Net Pay $ 287

of which is shown in Exhibit 9.4. This receipt allows you to manually list the name of each employee and the amount of money paid. Each employee must sign this document at the time of cash receipt. It is also useful to have them enter the date on which they received the cash, as evidence against claims that monies were paid out later than the state-mandated date.

The main problem with the form shown in Exhibit 9.4 is that each employee signing the receipt can see the net amount paid to every other employee on the list, which breaches the confidentiality of

EXHIBIT 9.4

Pay Receipt

For Pay Period Ended _____ May 15, 2003 _____

Employee Name	Cash Paid	Date Received	Employee Signature
Barclay, David	$231.14	May 19, 2003	David Barclay
Fairchild, Enoch	$402.19	May 19, 2003	Enoch Fairchild
Harley, Jeff	$300.78	May 19, 2003	Jeff Harley
Jimenez, Sandra	$220.82	May 19, 2003	Sandra Jimenez
Nindle, Allison	$275.03	May 19, 2003	Allison Nindle

employee pay rates. If this is a problem, use a separate pay receipt page for each employee.

Check Payments

A far more common method for paying employees is to create a check payment for each one. It is increasingly rare to see a company manually calculate and create payroll checks, since very inexpensive software can be purchased to tackle these chores. Also available are the services of numerous payroll suppliers.

That said, to prepare checks manually, carefully copy the information from the payroll register onto the check, using ink so the results cannot be easily altered. Also, to prevent fraudulent modifications to the check, be sure to draw a line through all blank spots on the check, and begin writing as far to the left in each space provided as possible. Once all checks are complete, conduct a final comparison of each one against the payroll register, possibly including an independent recalculation of the payment to each person.

The much more common method for issuing checks is to integrate this task into the workings of a standard payroll software package. Under this approach, the software generates a payroll register report, which the payroll manager reviews and approves. If it is acceptable, blank checks are loaded into the local printer and the software quickly churns out completed checks. Checks are then taken to an authorized signer for a final review and signature (note, however, even this step can be avoided by adding a signature image to the checks before they are printed). If the cashed checks are not returned by the bank, retrieve them either by contacting the bank to request check images be mailed to the company, or access the images online and print them out.

If a payroll supplier is used, it will print checks and send them to the company for distribution to employees. Additional supplier services include incorporating a signature image on the stamps, stuffing the checks into envelopes, and sending them directly to multiple company locations.

Direct Deposit Payments

Direct deposit is the most prevalent method for paying employees. It involves the direct transfer of funds from the company payroll account

 TIPS & TECHNIQUES

When a company has a sufficient number of employees to warrant issuing a large number of payroll checks, it usually opens a separate bank account from which to issue them. This makes it much easier to reconcile the account at month-end. However, if payroll is outsourced, the checks are run through the supplier's bank account, with only two deductions being made from the company's account—a total deduction for all payroll taxes and a total deduction for all net pay amounts. With only two entries being made per payroll, there is no longer a need for a separate payroll account at the bank.

to the personal savings or checking accounts of its employees. By doing so, employees avoid taking paychecks anywhere for cashing, which saves time and possibly a check-cashing fee. This method also lowers the risk of employees losing a paycheck. It is particularly useful for people who are either on the road or on vacation on payday, since the deposit will be made in their absence.

Direct deposit works most simply if a company uses a payroll supplier, since this third party will have an automated direct deposit linkage. If payroll is processed in-house, then a company must send an electronic file containing information about where money is to be transferred, as well as the accounts into which they will be deposited, to a financial institution that is equipped to process direct deposit transactions. This file is processed through the Automated Clearing House (ACH) network, which transfers the funds. The employer then issues a payment advice to employees, either on paper or electronically, that details their gross pay, taxes and other deductions, and net pay.

Employers can require employees to accept direct deposit, though this requirement is frequently overridden by state laws that require employee concurrence. Consequently, it is best to obtain written permission from employees prior to setting them up for direct deposit payments. This permission should include the routing number of the bank to which payments are to be sent, the account number within that bank, and the amount of funds to be deposited in each account. Typically, funds may be deposited in multiple accounts, such as $100 in a savings account and the remainder in a checking account. When asking for written permission from employees, it is best to also obtain a voided check for the account to which the funds are to be sent, in order to verify the routing and account numbers. Using a deposit slip to verify this information is not recommended, since the identification numbers on the slip may not match those of the bank.

When an employee signs up for direct deposit, he or she should be informed that the next paycheck will still be issued as a check, since the direct deposit transaction must first be verified with a prenotification transaction to verify that a regular paycheck will arrive properly in the employee's account. A prenotification transaction, in which a zero-dollar payment is sent to the employee, is quite useful for verifying that a standard direct deposit transaction will process properly. Consequently, though it is not required, a company should always insist on a prenotification transaction when first setting up an employee on direct deposit.

If a company has locations in multiple states and processes its payroll from a single central location, then the checks sent to outlying locations will take longer to clear (since they are drawn on an out-of-state bank). This issue should be brought to the attention of employees in the outlying locations, which may convince them to switch over to direct deposit payments, which require no timing delay in making payments.

Payments to Employee Credit Cards

Some companies employ people who, for whatever reason, either are unable to set up personal bank accounts or choose not to do so. In these cases, they must take their paychecks to a check-cashing service, which will charge them a high fee to convert the check into cash. Not only is it expensive, but the check-cashing service can have a long approval process. Also, employees will be carrying large amounts of cash just after cashing their checks, which increases their risk of theft. They also run the risk of losing their paychecks prior to cashing them. Thus, the lack of a bank account poses serious problems for a company's employees.

A good solution to this problem is to set up a Visa debit card, called the Visa Paycard, for any employees requesting one, and then shift payroll funds directly into the card. This allows employees to take any amount of cash they need from an ATM, rather than the entire amount at one time from a check-cashing service. The card can also be used as a credit card, so employees have little need to make purchases with cash. Further, the fee to convert to cash at an ATM is much lower than the fee charged by a check-cashing service. There is also less risk of theft through the card, since it is protected by a personal identification number (PIN). Employees will also receive a monthly statement showing their account activity, which they can use to get a better idea of their spending habits.

Termination Payments

A variety of state laws govern how soon employees are to be paid after their employment is terminated. The key factor in these laws is whether an employee leaves a company under his or her own volition or if the termination was forced by the company. Exhibit 9.5 lists the time periods by state by which termination pay must be given to those employees

EXHIBIT 9.5

Required Pay Interval for Voluntary Terminations

Maximum Payment Delay	Applicable States
4 Days	California
5 Days	Oregon, Wyoming
7 Days	District of Columbia, Nevada
10 Days	Idaho
14 Days	Kentucky, Maine, Nebraska
15 Days	Louisiana, Montana
20 Days	Minnesota
21 Days	Tennessee

EXHIBIT 9.6

Required Pay Interval
for Involuntary Terminations

Maximum Payment Delay	Applicable States
Immediately	Colorado, Hawaii, Illinois, Massachusetts, Michigan, Minnesota, Missouri, Montana, Nevada
1 Day	Connecticut, District of Columbia, Oregon, Utah
2 Days	South Carolina
3 Days	Alaska, Arizona, Louisiana
4 Days	California, New Hampshire, Vermont, West Virginia
5 Days	New Mexico, Wyoming
6 Days	Texas
7 Days	Arkansas
10 Days	Idaho
14 Days	Kentucky, Nebraska
15 Days	North Dakota
21 Days	Tennessee

who have voluntarily left employment. In all cases, the intervals listed are for the *earlier* of the next regularly scheduled pay date or the number of days listed in the first column. If a state is not listed in the table, assume that the termination payment is required at the time of the next regularly scheduled pay date.

Exhibit 9.6 lists the time periods by state by which termination pay must be given to those employees who have involuntarily left employment. In all cases, the intervals listed are for the *earlier* of the

TIPS & TECHNIQUES

If the human resources department is coordinating an employee lay-off, it is best to notify the payroll supervisor at least a day in advance, so this person can coordinate the proper calculation, printing, and signing of termination payments before the layoffs are begun. By doing so, an employer can hand out final paychecks at the time of termination and not have to worry about state laws that sometimes mandate immediate payments to employees. Also, by calculating these payments in advance, there is less chance of incorporating a calculation error, which is likelier to occur when under the pressure of having a terminated employee waiting for his or her final payment.

next regularly scheduled pay date or the number of days listed in the first column. If a state is not listed in the table, assume that the termination payment is required at the time of the next regularly scheduled pay date. Also, note that many more states have adopted early-payment laws for involuntary terminations, indicating a much greater degree of interest in paying off employees who fall into this category.

Unclaimed Pay

Sometimes, when an employee is terminated or becomes aware of a garnishment order that is about to be implemented against him or her, he or she will disappear without taking receipt of a final paycheck. These paychecks should not be cancelled and the funds retained by the company; instead, individual state laws typically mandate some effort to contact an employee; after a designated waiting period, the state takes ownership of the pay. The length of the waiting period, by state, is as shown in Exhibit 9.7.

Most states also require that these unclaimed pay amounts be listed on an annual report that is filed with the state.

EXHIBIT 9.7

Years Required to Hold Unclaimed Pay, by State

Number of Years to Hold	Applicable States
1	Alabama, Alaska, Arizona, Arkansas, Colorado, District of Columbia, Florida, Georgia, Montana, Nebraska, Nevada, New Hampshire, New Jersey, New Mexico, Ohio, Oklahoma, Hawaii, Idaho, Indiana, Kansas, Louisiana, Maine, Michigan, Minnesota, Rhode Island, South Carolina, South Dakota, Tennessee, Utah, Virginia, Washington, West Virginia, Wisconsin, Wyoming
2	North Carolina, North Dakota, Vermont
3	California, Connecticut, New York, Iowa, Massachusetts, Texas
5	Delaware, Illinois, Maryland, Mississippi, Missouri, Oregon
7	Kentucky, Pennsylvania

Summary

The state-imposed limitations noted in the "Frequency of Payment" section are generally not a problem, since all states allow at least a one-week delay between the termination of a reporting period and required payments to employees. It is much more likely to run afoul of state laws in the area of termination payments, as many states require payments either immediately or within one day to employees who are involuntarily terminated. Making sure that these payments are made in a timely manner requires tight coordination between the payroll and human resources departments. State laws regarding the remittance of unclaimed

The Proper Use
of Payroll Advances

The newly hired controller of a small manufacturing business was looking to improve efficiencies within the accounting department and noticed that payrolls were being calculated and distributed once a week. In an effort to reduce the payroll staff's workload, she decided to shift these tasks to once every two weeks. However, many of the people in the production department were clearly living from paycheck to paycheck, and would have great difficulty waiting an extra week to be paid during the initial changeover. To alleviate this problem, she offered to extend pay advances to everyone for the first two months, in gradually declining amounts, so they could slowly build up enough cash to tolerate the new payroll cycle. After the two months, she gave everyone the address of a local finance company to give them further assistance, in order to keep the company from becoming an occasional no-interest lender of advances to its employees.

wages are usually easy to follow, because this is a rare circumstance. Of the options presented for paying employees, cash payments are the least recommended, since this option requires additional controls over increased levels of cash on hand and is more labor-intensive to process than other payment methods.

CHAPTER 10

Unemployment Insurance

After reading this chapter you will be able to

- Understand the structure of the federal unemployment tax system
- Know which labor categories are exempt from federal unemployment taxes
- Know how to deposit federal unemployment taxes
- Know how to fill out annual federal unemployment tax returns

Federal and state unemployment taxes were initiated in order to create unemployment funds, which give former employees some money to tide them over until they can find work again. The laws supporting these actions were the Social Security Act and the Federal Unemployment Tax Act.

Benefits are paid by the state-sponsored programs, which require a short waiting period (usually a week, plus the vacation, holiday, and severance pay portion of any final payment) before payments can be made to unemployed persons. The amount paid is a percentage of a person's former pay, up to a low maximum level. If an employee looks for work and proves it by reporting back to the state agency, then payments can continue for up to half a year. The amount of benefits, their calculation, and the terms of payment vary by state program.

This chapter reviews several components of the unemployment tax program, including the calculation of both federal and state unemployment taxes, the calculation of the contribution rate, the reason for filing voluntary unemployment tax contributions, and how to fill out the 940 and 940-EZ forms.

Federal Unemployment Tax

The Federal Unemployment Tax (FUTA) is paid by employers only. It is currently set at 6.2 percent of the first $7,000 of a person's wages earned in a year. However, the actual amount paid to the federal government is substantially lower, since employers take a credit based on the amount of funds paid into their state unemployment programs (not including any FUTA payments deducted from employee pay, additional penalties paid as part of the state-assigned percentage, and any voluntary contributions to the state unemployment fund). Employers with a history of minimal layoffs can receive an extra credit above amounts paid into their state funds that brings their total credit against the federal tax to 5.4 percent. When the maximum credit amount is applied to the federal tax rate, the effective rate paid drops to 0.8 percent. This maximum credit is based on 90 percent of the total federal rate.

If a state experiences a large amount of unemployment claims and uses up its funds, it can borrow money from the federal fund, which must be paid back by the end of the next calendar year. If not, then the amount of the FUTA credit is reduced for employers within that state, which brings in enough additional funds to eventually pay back the loan.

According to government instructions accompanying Form 940 (discussed later in the chapter), FUTA taxes are *not* payable in the following situations:

- When a household employer pays cash wages of less than $1,000 for all household employees in any calendar quarter for household work in a private home, local college club, or local chapter of a college fraternity or sorority.

- When an agricultural employer pays cash wages of less than $20,000 to farm workers in any calendar quarter, or employs fewer than 10 farm workers during at least some part of a day during any 20 or more different weeks during the year.

- When wages are paid to an H-2(A) visa worker.

- When services are rendered to a federally recognized Native American tribal government.

- When the employer is a religious, educational, or charitable organization that qualifies as a 501(c)(3) entity under the federal tax laws.

- The employer is a state or local government.

Furthermore, wages are not subject to the tax if they are noncash payments, expense reimbursements, or various disability payments; and there is no FUTA requirement for full-commission insurance agents, working inmates, work within a family, work by nonemployees (such as consultants), and several other limited situations.

An employer must calculate the amount of FUTA tax owed at the end of each calendar quarter, after which they must be deposited (see next section). If there are no new hires during the year, this usually results in nearly all FUTA taxes being paid in the first quarter, with the remainder falling into the second quarter.

If payroll is outsourced, the supplier makes money by withholding the FUTA tax in every pay period and retaining the funds in an interest-bearing account until they are due for payment to the government at the end of the quarter.

Depositing FUTA Taxes

When a company applies for an Employer Identification Number (EIN), the IRS will send a Federal Tax Deposit Coupon book containing a number of Form 8109s, which are used as an attachment that identifies each type of deposit made to the IRS. When making a deposit, black out the "940" box on the form. Make deposits at a local bank that is authorized to accept federal tax deposits; do not mail deposits to the IRS. It is also useful to list the business's EIN, form number, and period for which the payment is being made on the accompanying check, in case the IRS loses the Tax Deposit Coupon. The check should be made out to the United States Treasury.

FUTA deposits are made once a quarter, and must be completed within 30 days of the end of the preceding calendar quarter. However, if the thirtieth day of the filing period falls on a weekend or federal holiday, then it may be filed on the following business day. The deposit schedule for a typical year is shown in Exhibit 10.1.

If the total amount of FUTA due in any quarter is less than $100, then the deposit can be skipped for that quarter. Instead, roll the outstanding amount into the next quarter. If the sub-$100 amount continues

EXHIBIT 10.1

FUTA Deposit Schedule

For the first quarter,	January thru March,	Must pay by	April 30
For the second quarter,	April thru June,	Must pay by	July 31
For the third quarter,	July thru September,	Must pay by	October 31
For the fourth quarter,	October thru December	Must pay by	January 31

for multiple quarters, it must still be paid following the year-end quarter, when Form 940 is filed.

If FUTA deposits are filed late, a penalty will be assessed by the IRS. The amount is 2 percent of the amount of the late deposit if it is no more than five days late; 5 percent if between 6 and 15 days late; 10 percent if more than 15 days late; or 15 percent if not paid within 10 days from the date of the company's receipt of a delinquency notice from the IRS. This penalty may be waived for small businesses or those that have just started filing payments.

Filing 940 and 940-EZ Forms

The FUTA tax return is used to calculate how much was paid out in wages during the preceding year, how much of this amount was subject to the FUTA tax, the amount of the tax, and any prior quarterly deposits made to reduce the payable tax, resulting in a net payment due to the government. The form must be filed no later than January 31 of the year following the reporting year, or by February 10 if all quarterly deposits for the calendar year were made in a timely manner. The form can be filed at an even later date if the company requests an extension from the IRS, but this is only for submission of the form—all quarterly payments must still be filed by the required dates.

A company can file Form 940-EZ instead of Form 940 if it paid unemployment contributions to only one state, paid all state unemployment taxes by January 31, and all wages that were taxable for the FUTA tax were also taxable for its state unemployment tax. An IRS chart showing the logic steps for this decision is shown in Exhibit 10.2.

EXHIBIT 10.2

Decision Steps for Use of 940-EZ Form

Form 940-EZ (2001)   Page **2**

Who May Use Form 940-EZ

The following chart will lead you to the right form to use-

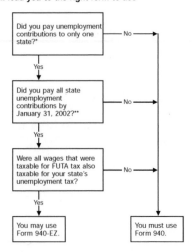

* Do not file Form 940-EZ if-
● You owe FUTA tax only for household work in a private home. See Schedule H (Form 1040).
● You are a successor employer claiming a credit for state unemployment contributions paid by a prior employer. File Form 940.

**If you deposited all FUTA tax when due, you may answer "Yes" if you paid all state unemployment contributions by February 11, 2002.

The Form 940 is shown in Exhibit 10.3. To fill out the form, follow these steps:

1. *Identification section.* If the form is not preaddressed, fill in the business address and Employer Identification Number (EIN). If there is no EIN, apply for one with Form SS-4. If no EIN has been received from the government by the time the form is due to be filed, print "Applied for" and the date of application in this area.

2. *Questions A–C.* If the answers to all three questions posed in this section are yes, then you may file the simpler Form 940-EZ instead. Any no answers require completion of Form 940. The questions match the logic steps given earlier in Exhibit 10.2.

3. *Amended or final return.* There are two check-off boxes immediately above the Part I section. Check the first box if there will be no future FUTA filings; check the second one if this is an amended return. Otherwise, continue to Part I.

4. *Total payments (Part I, Line 1).* Enter the total gross wages paid during the calendar year to employees, including wages not eligible for the FUTA tax. Total gross wages should include commissions, bonuses, 401k plan contributions, the fair value of goods paid, and vacation and sick pay.

5. *Exempt payments (Part 1, Line 2).* Include all wages that are exempt from the FUTA tax. Many of these exemptions were noted earlier in the "Federal Unemployment Tax" section. Do not include on this line any wages exceeding the statutory $7,000 annual wage limitation on the FUTA tax, since this is addressed by the next line item.

6. *Wages exceeding $7,000 (Part I, Line 3).* Enter the total amount of wages paid that exceed the $7,000 annual wage limitation on the FUTA tax.

7. *Total taxable wages (Part I, Line 5).* Subtract the total exempt payments and total payments exceeding $7,000 from the total payments to arrive at this figure.

8. *Gross FUTA tax (Part I, Line 2).* Multiply the total taxable wages noted in the last line by 6.2 percent to arrive at the maximum possible FUTA tax liability.

9. *Maximum credit (Part II, Line 2).* Multiply the total taxable wages calculated on line 7 by 5.4 percent to arrive at the maximum possible FUTA tax credit.

10. *Computation of credit (Part II, Line 3).* This is a table requiring entries in a number of columns. The information to be entered in these columns is:

- *Name of state.* Enter the two-letter abbreviation representing the state in which wages were paid.

- *State reporting number.* Enter the State Identification Number assigned to the company by the state referenced in the first column.

- *Taxable payroll.* Enter the total wages paid within the identified state that the state has defined as being subject to unemployment taxes.

- *State experience rate period.* Enter the beginning and ending dates covered by the state experience rate that is listed in the following column. If an experience rate is granted partway through a year, then enter one line for the period of the calendar year covered by the first experience rate and a second line for the period covered by the succeeding experience rate.

- *State experience rate.* Enter the experience rate percentage. This is the percentage assigned to a company by each state in which it does business. It is based on the amount of unemployment tax paid, as well as the amount of unemployment compensation paid to former employees. The latest experience rate is usually mailed to an employer once a year, but you may also call the state unemployment office to obtain it.

- *Contributions if rate had been 5.4 percent.* Multiply the taxable payroll from the third column by 5.4 percent.

- *Contributions payable at experience rate.* Multiply the taxable payroll from the third column by the state experience rate.

- *Additional credit.* Subtract the total contributions payable at the experience rate from the total contributions if the rate had been 5.4 percent. If the result is zero or less, enter a zero in this field; otherwise, enter the difference.

- *Contributions paid to state by 940 due date.* Enter the total amount of all payments actually paid to the state by the due date for this tax. Any amounts not paid are excluded from this calculation, which essentially imposes a significant penalty on any FUTA late payers.

11. *Total tentative credit (Part II, Line 3b).* Combine the totals from the additional credit and state contributions columns. The result is the minimum total amount of the credit that can potentially be applied against the FUTA tax.

12. *Credit (Part II, Line 6).* This is the actual amount of credit used to offset the FUTA tax. It is the *lesser* of the total tentative credit (which is based on actual payments to state governments) or the theoretical maximum credit of 5.4 percent of applicable wages.

13. *Total FUTA tax (Part II, Line 7).* Subtract the preceding credit from the total amount of the gross FUTA tax listed on line 2 of Part II. If the amount of this tax exceeds $100, be sure to complete Part III of the form as well.

14. *Total FUTA tax deposited (Part II, Line 8).* Summarize all FUTA payments already made, as well as any overpayment carried forward from the previous year.

15. *Balance due (Part II, Line 9).* Subtract the total amount of FUTA taxes already deposited from the total amount of the tax to arrive at the net liability. If the amount due is less than $1, do not pay it.

16. *Record of quarterly FUTA liability (Part III).* This section should only be completed if a company's total annual FUTA tax exceeds $100. If so, enter the amount of the liability for each quarter of the year, as well as the grand total.

Form 940-EZ is significantly easier to complete, but it applies only to a restricted number of situations, as outlined in Exhibit 10.2. Form 940-EZ is shown in Exhibit 10.4. To fill out the form, follow these steps:

1. *Identification section.* If the form is not preaddressed, fill in the business address and Employer Identification Number (EIN). If there is no EIN, apply for one with Form SS-4. If no EIN has been received from the government by the time the form is due to be filed, print "Applied for" and the date of application in this area.

2. *Amount of contributions paid.* List the total amount of contributions made to the unemployment fund of the state in which the company does business.

3. *State and identification number.* Enter the name of the state where the company does business, as well as the identification number assigned to the company by the state.

4. *Total payments (Part I, Line 1).* Enter the total gross wages paid during the calendar year to employees, including wages not eligible for the FUTA tax. Total gross wages should include commissions, bonuses, 401k plan contributions, the fair value of goods paid, and vacation and sick pay.

5. *Exempt payments (Part I, Line 2).* Include all wages that are exempt from the FUTA tax. Many of these exemptions were noted earlier

EXHIBIT 10.3

Form 940

Form **940**	**Employer's Annual Federal Unemployment (FUTA) Tax Return**	OMB No. 1545-0028

Department of the Treasury
Internal Revenue Service (99)

► **See separate Instructions for Form 940 for information on completing this form.**

2001

	T	
	FF	
	FD	
	FP	
	I	
	T	

You must complete this section. ▶

⌐ Name (as distinguished from trade name)   Calendar year ⌐

Trade name, if any

Address and ZIP code   Employer identification number

⌐_____⌐

A Are you required to pay unemployment contributions to only one state? (If "No," skip questions B and C.) . ☐ Yes ☐ No

B Did you pay all state unemployment contributions by January 31, 2002? ((1) If you deposited your total FUTA tax when due, check "Yes" if you paid all state unemployment contributions by February 11, 2002. (2) If a 0% experience rate is granted, check "Yes." (3) If "No," skip question C.) . . . . ☐ Yes ☐ No

C Were all wages that were taxable for FUTA tax also taxable for your state's unemployment tax? . . . . . ☐ Yes ☐ No

If you answered "No" to any of these questions, you must file Form 940. If you answered "Yes" to all the questions, you may file Form 940-EZ, which is a simplified version of Form 940. (Successor employers see **Special credit for successor employers** on page 3 of the instructions.) You can get Form 940-EZ by calling 1-800-TAX-FORM (1-800-829-3676) or from the IRS Web Site at **www.irs.gov.**

If you will not have to file returns in the future, check here (see **Who Must File** in separate instructions), **and complete and sign the return** . . . . ▶ ☐

If this is an Amended Return, check here. . . . . ▶ ☐

Part I   Computation of Taxable Wages

1 Total payments (including payments shown on lines 2 and 3) during the calendar year for services of employees **1**

2 Exempt payments. (Explain all exempt payments, attaching additional sheets if necessary.) ▶ **2**

3 Payments of more than $7,000 for services. Enter only amounts over the first $7,000 paid to each employee. (See separate instructions.) Do not include any exempt payments from line 2. The $7,000 amount is the Federal wage base. Your state wage base may be different. **Do not use your state wage limitation.** **3**

4 Add lines 2 and 3 . . . . **4**

5 **Total taxable wages** (subtract line 4 from line 1) . . . . ▶ **5**

Be sure to complete both sides of this form, and sign in the space provided on the back.

For Privacy Act and Paperwork Reduction Act Notice, see separate instructions.   ▼ **DETACH HERE** ▼   Cat. No. 11234O   Form **940** (2001)

Form **940-V**	**Form 940 Payment Voucher**	OMB No. 1545-0028

Department of the Treasury
Internal Revenue Service

Use this voucher only when making a payment with your return.

2001

Complete boxes 1, 2, and 3. Do not send cash, and do not staple your payment to this voucher. Make your check or money order payable to the **"United States Treasury."** Be sure to enter your employer identification number, "Form 940," and "2001" on your payment.

1 Enter your employer identification number.

2 **Enter the amount of your payment.** ▶ | Dollars | Cents |

3 Enter your business name (individual name for sole proprietors).

Enter your address.

Enter your city, state, and ZIP code.

EXHIBIT 10.3 (CONTINUED)

Form 940 (2001)   Page **2**

Part II	Tax Due or Refund

1	Gross FUTA tax. Multiply the wages from Part I, line 5, by .062	**1**
2	Maximum credit. Multiply the wages from Part I, line 5, by .054 . . | **2** |	
3	Computation of tentative credit (**Note:** *All taxpayers must complete the applicable columns.*)	

(a) Name of state	(b) State reporting number(s) as shown on employer's state contribution returns	(c) Taxable payroll (as defined in state act)	(d) State experience rate period From	(d) State experience rate period To	(e) State experience rate	(f) Contributions if rate had been 5.4% (col. (c) x .054)	(g) Contributions payable at experience rate (col. (c) x col. (e))	(h) Additional credit (col. (f) minus col.(g)) If 0 or less, enter -0-	(i) Contributions paid to state by 940 due date

3a	Totals . . . ▶		
3b	**Total tentative credit** (add line 3a, columns (h) and (i) only—for late payments, also see the instructions for Part II, line 6) . . . . ▶	**3b**	
4			
5			
6	**Credit:** Enter the smaller of the amount from Part II, line 2 or line 3b; or the amount from the worksheet in the Part II, line 6 instructions	**6**	
7	**Total FUTA tax** (subtract line 6 from line 1). If the result is over $100, also complete Part III . .	**7**	
8	Total FUTA tax deposited for the year, including any overpayment applied from a prior year . .	**8**	
9	**Balance due** (subtract line 8 from line 7). Pay to the **"United States Treasury."** If you owe more than $100, see **Depositing FUTA Tax** on page 3 of the separate instructions . . . . . . ▶	**9**	
10	**Overpayment** (subtract line 7 from line 8). Check if it is to be: ☐ **Applied to next return** or ☐ **Refunded** . . . . ▶	**10**	

Part III	**Record of Quarterly Federal Unemployment Tax Liability** (Do not include state liability.) **Complete only if line 7 is over $100.** See page 6 of the separate instructions.

Quarter	First (Jan. 1–Mar. 31)	Second (Apr. 1–June 30)	Third (July 1–Sept. 30)	Fourth (Oct. 1–Dec. 31)	Total for year
Liability for quarter					

Third Party Designee	Do you want to allow another person to discuss this return with the IRS (see instructions page 4)? ☐ **Yes.** Complete the following. ☐ **No**		
	Designee's name ▶	Phone no. ▶ ( )	Personal identification number (PIN) ▶ ☐☐☐☐☐

Under penalties of perjury, I declare that I have examined this return, including accompanying schedules and statements, and, to the best of my knowledge and belief, it is true, correct, and complete, and that no part of any payment made to a state unemployment fund claimed as a credit was, or is to be, deducted from the payments to employees.

Signature ▶   Title (Owner, etc.) ▶   Date ▶

✪   Form **940** (2001)

in the "Federal Unemployment Tax" section. Do not include on this line any wages exceeding the statutory $7,000 annual wage limitation on the FUTA tax, since this is addressed by the next line item.

6. *Wages exceeding $7,000 (Part I, Line 3).* Enter the total amount of wages paid that exceed the $7,000 annual wage limitation on the FUTA tax.

7. *Total taxable wages (Part I, Line 5).* Subtract the total exempt payments and total payments exceeding $7,000 from the total payments to arrive at this figure.

EXHIBIT 10.4

Form 940-EZ

Form **940-EZ**	**Employer's Annual Federal Unemployment (FUTA) Tax Return**	OMB No. 1545-1110
Department of the Treasury Internal Revenue Service (99)	▶ **See separate Instructions for Form 940-EZ for information on completing this form.**	**2001**

			T
	Name (as distinguished from trade name)	Calendar year	FF
You must complete this section. ▶			FD
	Trade name, if any		FP
			I
	Address and ZIP code	Employer identification number	T

*Answer the questions under **Who May Use Form 940-EZ** on page 2. If you cannot use Form 940-EZ, you must use Form 940.*

A Enter the amount of contributions paid to your state unemployment fund. (see separate instructions) . . . ▶ $ ....

B (1) Enter the name of the state where you have to pay contributions . . . . ▶ ....
   (2) Enter your state reporting number as shown on your state unemployment tax return ▶

If you will not have to file returns in the future, check here (see **Who Must File** in separate instructions), **and complete and sign the return.** ▶ ☐

If this is an Amended Return, check here . . . . ▶ ☐

Part I   **Taxable Wages and FUTA Tax**

1	Total payments (including payments shown on lines 2 and 3) during the calendar year for services of employees	**1**	
2	Exempt payments. (Explain all exempt payments, attaching additional sheets if necessary.) ▶	**2**	
3	Payments of more than $7,000 for services. Enter only amounts over the first $7,000 paid to each employee. **(see separate instructions)**	**3**	
4	Add lines 2 and 3	**4**	
5	**Total taxable wages** (subtract line 4 from line 1) . . . . ▶	**5**	
6	FUTA tax. Multiply the wages on line 5 by .008 and enter here. **(If the result is over $100, also complete Part II.)**	**6**	
7	Total FUTA tax deposited for the year, including any overpayment applied from a prior year	**7**	
8	**Balance due** (subtract line 7 from line 6). Pay to the "United States Treasury." . . . . ▶	**8**	
	If you owe more than $100, see **Depositing FUTA tax** in separate instructions.		
9	**Overpayment** (subtract line 6 from line 7). Check if it is to be: ☐ Applied to next return or ☐ Refunded ▶	**9**	

Part II   **Record of Quarterly Federal Unemployment Tax Liability** (Do not include state liability.) Complete only if line 6 is over $100.

Quarter	First (Jan. 1 – Mar. 31)	Second (Apr. 1 – June 30)	Third (July 1 – Sept. 30)	Fourth (Oct. 1 – Dec. 31)	Total for year
Liability for quarter					

Third Party Designee   Do you want to allow another person to discuss this return with the IRS (see instructions page 4)? ☐ **Yes.** Complete the following.   ☐ **No**

Designee's name ▶	Phone no. ▶ ( )	Personal identification number (PIN) ▶

Under penalties of perjury, I declare that I have examined this return, including accompanying schedules and statements, and, to the best of my knowledge and belief, it is true, correct, and complete, and that no part of any payment made to a state unemployment fund claimed as a credit was, or is to be, deducted from the payments to employees.

Signature ▶   Title (Owner, etc.) ▶   Date ▶

For Privacy Act and Paperwork Reduction Act Notice, see separate instructions.   ▼ **DETACH HERE** ▼   Cat. No. 10983G   Form **940-EZ** (2001)

Form **940-EZ(V)**	**Form 940-EZ Payment Voucher**	OMB No. 1545-1110
Department of the Treasury Internal Revenue Service	**Use this voucher only when making a payment with your return.**	**2001**

Complete boxes 1, 2, and 3. Do not send cash, and do not staple your payment to this voucher. Make your check or money order payable to the **"United States Treasury."** Be sure to enter your employer identification number, "Form 940-EZ," and "2001" on your payment.

1 Enter your employer identification number.	**2** **Enter the amount of your payment.** ▶	Dollars	Cents
	3 Enter your business name (individual name for sole proprietors).		
	Enter your address.		
	Enter your city, state, and ZIP code.		

253

8. *Gross FUTA tax (Part I, Line 6).* Multiply the total taxable wages noted on the last line by 6.2 percent to arrive at the maximum possible FUTA tax liability.

9. *Total FUTA tax deposited (Part I, Line 7).* Summarize all FUTA payments already made, as well as any overpayment carried forward from the previous year.

10. *Balance due (Part I, Line 8).* Subtract the total amount of FUTA taxes already deposited from the total amount of the tax to arrive at the net liability. If the amount due is less than $1, do not pay it.

11. *Record of quarterly FUTA liability (Part II).* This section should only be completed if a company's total annual FUTA tax exceeds $100. If so, enter the amount of the liability for each quarter of the year, as well as the grand total.

For both Form 940 and Form 940-EZ, if a fourth quarter payment of less than $100 is due, fill out the payment voucher located at the bottom of either form, listing the amount of the payment, the business name and address, and its EIN number. It is also useful to list the EIN, form number, and payment period covered on the accompanying check, in case the IRS loses the voucher.

State Unemployment Tax

Tax rates imposed by states can be quite low, but can also range up to 5.4 percent (the amount of the credit allowed against the federal unemployment tax), and some states even exceed this amount. The rate charged is based on a company's history of layoffs, which is called an *experience rating*. If it has a history of laying off a large proportion of its employees, then this action will likely drain a significant amount from the state's unemployment funds through the payment of unemployment benefits. Thus, a layoff in one year will likely be followed by a notice of increase in the state unemployment tax (or "contribution") rate.

The taxable wage base used by states is required by federal law to be at least as much as the federal level, which is currently set at $7,000. Exhibit 10.5 shows the employer tax rates, employee tax rates (where applicable), taxable wage limits, and coverages for all 50 states, plus the District of Columbia and Puerto Rico. There is also a column listing the *new* employer tax rate, which is the default tax rate given to any company that does not yet have an experience rating. This default rate can change in some cases (see Note 1 to Exhibit 10.5), depending on the industry in which a new organization is based; industries with historically high employee turnover rates deplete the state unemployment funds more rapidly, so companies operating in those industries are assigned a higher contribution rate.

When a person's employment is terminated, he or she goes to the local state unemployment office and applies for unemployment benefits. The state agency then sends a form to the company, asking it to verify basic information about the former employee, such as the amount of hourly pay at the time of termination and the amount and composition of the severance payment. After verification, the state sends the employer another form, notifying it of the maximum amount of unemployment benefits that can be paid to the employee (which can be greatly reduced if the employee finds work soon). A key issue in this process is whether an employee was terminated for cause (such as theft), was laid off, or voluntarily resigned. Unemployment benefits are not paid when a person quits or is terminated for cause, so be sure to contest employee benefit claims if either was the cause for termination. Proper documentation of the termination is crucial to this determination, which is made by an employee of the state division of employment. If determination is made in favor of the former employee, then any benefits paid will be

EXHIBIT 10.5

State Wage Bases Used for State Unemployment Tax Calculations

State	Employer Tax Rate	New Employer Tax Rate	Employee Withholding Rate	Taxable Wage Limit	Coverage
Alabama	2.7%–6.8%	2.7%	None	$8,000	Same as federal
Alaska	5.4%	(1)	0.5%–1.0%	$25,500	Any company paying 1+ employees for at least a day in the year
Arizona	5.4% Std	2.7%	None	$7,000	Same as federal
Arkansas	0.5%–8.4%	3.3%	None	$9,000	Any company paying 1+ employees for at least 10 days in the current or preceding year
California	0.7%-5.4%	3.4%	None	$7,000	Any company paying 1+ employees in the current or preceding year
Colorado	2.7% Std	2.7%	None	$10,000	Any company paying 1+ employees for at least a day in the year
Connecticut	0.5%–5.4%	2.4%	None	$15,000	Same as federal
Delaware	5.4% Std	1.8%	None	$8,500	Same as federal
District of Columbia	2.7% Std	2.7%	None	$9,000	Any company paying 1+ employees in the current year
Florida	0.1%–5.4%	2.7%	None	$7,000	Same as federal
Georgia	5.4% Std	2.62%	None	$8,500	Same as federal
Hawaii	0%–5.4%	2.4%	None	$29,300	Any company paying 1+ employees in the current year
Idaho	1.5% Std	—	None	$25,700	Any company with 1+ employees in 20 weeks of the current or preceding year

EXHIBIT 10.5 (CONTINUED)

State	Employer Tax Rate	New Employer Tax Rate	Employee Withholding Rate	Taxable Wage Limit	Coverage
Illinois	0.6%–6.8%	3.1%	None	$9,000	Same as federal
Indiana	5.4% Std	2.7%	None	$7,000	Same as federal
Iowa	0%–7.5%	—	None	$18,600	Same as federal
Kansas	5.4% Std	2%	None	$8,000	Same as federal
Kentucky	0%–10%	2.7%	None	$8,000	Same as federal
Louisiana	0.15%–6.2%	(1)	None	$7,000	Same as federal
Maine	5.4% Std	1.83%	None	$12,000	Same as federal
Maryland	0.3%–7.5%	2%	None	$8,500	Any company paying 1+ employees in the current year
Massachusetts	1.325%–7.225%	2.2%	None	$10,800	Any company with 1+ employees in 13 weeks of the current or preceding year
Michigan	0.1%–8.1%	2.7%	None	$9,500	Any company with 1+ employees in 20 weeks of the current or preceding year or that is subject to FUTA
Minnesota	0.17%–9.07%	1.29%	None	$21,000	Same as federal
Mississippi	5.4% Std	2.7%	None	$7,000	Same as federal
Missouri	0%–6%	2.97%	None	$7,000	Same as federal
Montana	6.5% Max	(1)	None	$18,900	Any company with payroll of $1,000+ in current or preceding year
Nebraska	0.05%–5.4%	3.5%	None	$7,000	Same as federal
Nevada	0.25%–5.4%	2.95%	None	$20,900	Any company paying 1+ employees in the current year
New Hampshire	0.05%–6.5%	2.7%	None	$8,000	Same as federal

EXHIBIT 10.5 (CONTINUED)

State	Employer Tax Rate	New Employer Tax Rate	Employee Withholding Rate	Taxable Wage Limit	Coverage
New Jersey	0.3%–5.4%	2.6825%	None	$23,500	Any company paying wages of $1,000+ in current or preceding year
New Mexico	0.05%–5.4%	2.7%	None	$15,900	Any company with 1+ employees in 20 weeks of the current or preceding year
New York	0.7%–9.1%	4.0%	None	$8,500	Any company paying $300+ in wages in any calendar quarter
North Carolina	0%–5.7%	1.2%	None	$14,700	Same as federal
North Dakota	0.49%–10.09%	2.08%	None	$17,400	Same as federal
Ohio	0.1%–6.5%	2.7%	None	$9,000	Same as federal
Oklahoma	0.1%–5.5%	1.0%	None	$10,500	Same as federal
Oregon	0.9%–5.4%	3.0%	None	$25,000	Any company with 1+ employees in 18 weeks of the year
Pennsylvania	1.479%–9.0712%	3.5%	None	$8,000	Any company with 1+ employees in the calendar year
Puerto Rico	1.2%–5.4%	2.9%	None	$7,000	Any company with 1+ employees in the current or preceding calendar year
Rhode Island	1.66%–9.76%	1.79%	None	$12,000	Any company with 1+ employees in the year
South Carolina	0.54%–5.4%	2.7%	None	$7,000	Same as federal
South Dakota	0%–7.0%	1.9%	None	$7,000	Same as federal
Tennessee	0%–10%	2.7%	None	$7,000	Same as federal
Texas	0%–6.24%	2.7%	None	$9,000	Same as federal

EXHIBIT 10.5 (CONTINUED)

State	Employer Tax Rate	New Employer Tax Rate	Employee Withholding Rate	Taxable Wage Limit	Coverage
Utah	0.1%–8.1%	(1)	None	$21,400	Any company paying $140+ in wages during any quarter of current or preceding year or that is subject to FUTA
Vermont	0.4%–8.4%	(1)	None	$8,000	Same as federal
Virginia	0%–6.2%	2.5%	None	$8,000	Same as federal
Washington	0.47%–5.6%	(1)	Optional	$28,500	Any company with 1+ employees during the year
West Virginia	1.5%–8.5%	2.7%	None	$8,000	Same as federal
Wisconsin	0%–9.75%	3.05%	None	$10,500	Same as federal
Wyoming	0.15%–8.71%	(1)	None	$14,700	Any company with 1+ employees during the year

Note 1: Industry-based rate is applied for a new employer.

charged against the company, which will impact its experience rating and therefore increase the amount of its contribution rate in the following year.

States have a preference for defining contractors as employees, since an employer can then be required to pay unemployment taxes based on the pay of these individuals. To determine the status of an employee under a state unemployment insurance program, use some portion or all of the so-called ABC test, which defines a person as a contractor only if:

- There is an *absence* of control by the company.
- *Business* conducted by the employee is substantially different from that of the company, or is conducted away from its premises.

- The person *customarily* works independently from the company as a separate business.

Twenty-six states use all three elements of this test to determine the status of an employee or contractor, while eight use just the first and third.

An important issue is to retain the notice of contribution rate change that the state unemployment division will mail to every company at least once a year. The new rate listed in the notice must be used in the calculation of the state unemployment tax payable, as of the date given on the notice. If a company outsources its payroll, this notice should be forwarded to the supplier, which incorporates it into its payroll tax calculations.

Calculating the Unemployment Tax Contribution Rate

The contribution rate is the percentage tax charged by a state to an employer to cover its share of the state unemployment insurance fund. The contribution rate is based on the experience rating, which is essen-

TIPS & TECHNIQUES

A business that is buying another company may have the opportunity to do so because the acquiree has fallen on hard times, and so can be purchased for a minimal price. However, if the acquiree has been laying off staff in the year leading up to the acquisition (quite likely, if there have been cash shortfalls), the acquirer may find itself saddled with a very high state unemployment contribution rate in the upcoming year. The acquirer can avoid this problem by purchasing the assets of the acquiree, rather than the entire business entity, thereby eliminating the acquiree's poor experience rating as tracked by the state unemployment agency.

tially the proportion of unemployment claims made against a company by former employees it has laid off, divided by its total payroll. In essence, those organizations with lower levels of employee turnover will have a better experience rating, which results in a smaller contribution rate.

States can choose the method by which they calculate the contribution rate charged to employers. The four methods currently in use are:

1. *Benefit ratio method.* This is the proportion of unemployment benefits paid to a company's former employees during the measurement period, divided by the total payroll during the period. A high ratio implies that a large proportion of employees are being laid off and are therefore using up unemployment funds, so the assessed contribution rate will be high. This calculation method is used by Alabama, Connecticut, Florida, Illinois, Iowa, Maryland, Michigan, Minnesota, Mississippi, Oregon, Texas, Utah, Vermont, Virginia, Washington, and Wyoming.

2. *Benefit wage ratio method.* This is similar to the benefit ratio method, but uses in the numerator the total taxable wages for laid-off employees, rather than the benefits actually paid. A high ratio has the same implications as for the benefit ratio method—the contribution rate assessed will be high. This method is used by Delaware and Oklahoma.

3. *Payroll stabilization.* This method links the contribution rate to fluctuations in a company's total payroll over time, with higher rates being assessed to those with shrinking payrolls, on the grounds that these entities are terminating an inordinate proportion of their employees. This method is used only by Alaska.

4. *Reserve ratio.* This is the most common method, being used by 32 states (all those not listed for the preceding three methods).

Under this approach, the ongoing balance of a firm's unclaimed contributions from previous years is reduced by unemployment claims for the past year and then divided by the average annual payroll, resulting in a reserve ratio. Each state then applies a tax rate to this ratio in inverse proportion to the amount (i.e., a low reserve ratio indicates that nearly all contributed funds are being used, so a high tax will be assessed).

Making Voluntary Unemployment Tax Contributions

If a state uses the reserve ratio method described in the previous section to arrive at the contribution rate charged to a business, then the business may have the option to contribute additional funds into its account. By doing so, it can improve its experience rating and thereby reduce the contribution rate charged by the state. In most cases, a company must

TIPS & TECHNIQUES

Changes in the state contribution rate are based on four possible formulas (see the "Calculating the Unemployment Tax Contribution Rate" section); however, the key issue for all formulas (excepting Alaska's) is the amount of unemployment benefit claims by former employees of a company, so obviously the smallest number of employee terminations will result in the smallest contribution rate. Keeping this in mind, if a possible layoff is coming up, it may be worthwhile to verify the exact time period over which the next contribution rate calculation will be made (usually the calendar year), and then time the layoff for a period immediately thereafter, so that the contribution rate for the next year will not be affected. By taking this action, the contribution rate in the *following* year will increase as a result of the layoff, thereby pushing the added expense further into the future.

make the decision to contribute additional funds within 30 days of the date when a state mails its notice of contribution rates to the company. The decision to pay additional funds to the state should be based on a cost-benefit analysis of the amount of funding required to reduce the contribution rate versus the reduced amount of required contributions that will be gained in the next calendar year by doing so.

State Disability Tax

A few states maintain disability insurance funds, from which payments are made to employees who are unable to work due to illness or injury. This tax is sometimes a joint payment by both employees and employers; in other cases it is borne solely by employees. Exhibit 10.6 shows the range of employer tax rates, employee withholding rates, taxable wage limits, and employee coverages for each state where a disability fund is used.

EXHIBIT 10.6

Specifics of State Disability Funds

State	Employer Tax Rate	Employee Withholding Rate	Taxable Wage Limit	Coverage
California	(1)	0.9%	$46,327	Any company with 1+ employees in the current or immediately preceding year and that paid $100+ in wages in any quarter
Hawaii	(2)	(3)	$33,316	Any company with 1+ employees in current year
New Jersey	0.1%–0.75%	0.5%	$22,100	Any company paying at least $1,000 wages in the current or immediately preceding year

EXHIBIT 10.6 (CONTINUED)

State	Employer Tax Rate	Employee Withholding Rate	Taxable Wage Limit	Coverage
New York	(4)	0.5% (5)	None	Any company employing someone in at least 30 days of the past calendar year
Puerto Rico	0.3%	0.3%	$9,000	Any company employing someone at any time in the current or immediately preceding year, for any interval
Rhode Island	None	1.4%	$42,000	Any company employing someone during the calendar year, for any interval

Note 1: None, though the employer can elect coverage up to 1.66 percent.

Note 2: None, though specific benefits must be paid.

Note 3: Half of benefits paid, up to a maximum of 0.5 percent.

Note 4: Employers cover the cost of the specified disability benefits, less amounts collected from employees.

Note 5: Not to exceed $0.60 per week for each employee.

IN THE REAL WORLD

What to Do with a Rate Change Notice

A company that outsourced its payroll function received a notice from the state, informing it of a change in its contribution rate for the upcoming year. An accounting clerk filed the notice, rather than informing the payroll supplier of the change. Due to this error, the company's state unemployment contributions were improperly low for the year, resulting in fines and penalties by the state government. Therefore, always forward notices of contribution rate changes to your payroll supplier!

Summary

Unemployment insurance may appear to be a "nuisance" tax that a company is forced by federal and state laws to pay out at regular intervals. Fortunately, as explained in this chapter, there are ways to manage the calculation of these taxes so they can be reduced to some extent. A knowledge of the authorizing laws and underlying calculations used to create federal and state employment taxes is key to these potential reductions.

Index